WINGED COMBAT

The Courage of the Early Morning
Courage in the Air
Courage on the Battlefield
Courage at Sea
The Splendid Hundred
Our Bravest and Best: Stories of Canada's Victoria Cross Winners
Canada's Glory: Battles that Forged a Nation
Salute! Canada's Great Military Leaders from Brock to Dextraze
Destruction at Dawn
Unsung Courage

Arthur Bishop

WINGED COMBAT

My Story as a Spitfire Pilot in World War II

HarperCollins*PublishersLtd*

Winged Combat: My Story as a Spitfire Pilot in WWII
Text copyright © 2002 by Arthur Bishop.
All rights reserved. No part of this book may be
used or reproduced in any manner whatsoever
without prior written permission except in the case
of brief quotations embodied in reviews.
For information address:
HarperCollins Publishers Ltd.,
2 Bloor Street East, 20th Floor
Toronto, Ontario, Canada M4W 1A8

www.harpercanada.com

HarperCollins books may be purchased for educa-
tional, business, or sales promotional use.
For information please write:
Special Markets Department,
HarperCollins Canada,
2 Bloor Street East, 20th Floor
Toronto, Ontario, Canada M4W 1A8

First edition

National Library of Canada Cataloguing
in Publication

Bishop, William Arthur, 1923–
Winged Combat : my story as a Spitfire pilot in
WWII / Arthur Bishop.

ISBN 0-00-200651-0

1. Bishop, William Arthur, 1923– 2. World War,
1939–1945 – Personal narratives, Canadian.
3. Fighter pilots – Canada – Biography. I. Title.

D811.B58 2002   940.54'4971'092
C2002-902443-9

HC 9 8 7 6 5 4 3 2 1

Printed and bound in the United States
Set in FF Scala and Scala Sans

To Cilla

1925–2001

Contents

My Standard

Being born of fame is not like earning it. You have to create your own worth in other coin; you have to escape history's shadow and get, as they say, a life.

JOHN UPDIKE

"A Hero to Me"

I never knew my grandfather, Billy Bishop. I was, after all, only three when he died in 1956 at the age of 62. But as youngsters, my brother and I thought it was pretty neat to have someone so famous in the family, and marvelled at how he ruled over us, larger than life, even in death. Once in a while, as a treat, my father let us play with his father's war medals, which, believe it or not, before they were donated to the Canadian War Museum, he kept for some time in his underwear drawer. One day I even carted them off to school in a brown paper bag.

No doubt it gave my teacher quite a start when I pulled out Billy Bishop's breastplate of military honours, which included the Distinguished Service Order and Bar, the Military Cross, the Distinguished Flying Cross, the Croix de Guerre, the Legion of Honour, and, of course, the most coveted of all, the Victoria Cross.

Still, I didn't know much about my grandfather the war hero, and his outstanding war record didn't mean a lot to me.

The grandfather I wanted to know about was the one my father talked about, the exciting and elegant man in the family photographs wearing the latest tailored suit from Savile Row in London, playing polo, and visiting at 10 Downing Street with Winston Churchill.

My father had lots of tales about how much fun his father was, what a good host he was, and how he liked to be different. I love the story about the time Billy served a whole dinner in reverse to his guests, starting with dessert and finishing with cocktails. Just for added effect he placed two of his beloved Chinese chows—fluffy dogs that look like lions—as the centrepiece of the table. I always wondered how he got them to sit there!

Of course, my grandfather wasn't around to answer those questions, but my father was, and it was he who became my window into the life and times of Billy Bishop. With such an interesting subject, it's no wonder Dad became a first-rate storyteller, sharing his talent not only with me, but with all Canadians who read his book *The Courage of the Early Morning.*

Still, it never occurred to me, until I got older, what it must have been like to grow up in the shadow of such a man, an icon in Canada's military and aviation history, not to mention a folk hero of sorts. No one epitomized better the romantic image of the First World War pilot in his biplane, looking dashing in his goggles and white scarf as he fought the first air battles.

They were so often compared, father and son, and for obvious reasons. They shared a striking resemblance, a devilish sense of humour, a strength of character.

Of course, there were other comparisons. My father followed in his father's footsteps as a fighter pilot, right into another war. It couldn't have been easy, and I often wondered whether he constantly had to seek his father's approval, and whether he was always trying to measure up.

My father glossed over these things, reluctant to share his thoughts. But I suspected that he channelled his feelings about the war into telling other people's war stories, both victories and tragedies. He now has ten books to his credit that carve out Canada's military heritage and bring to life the inspiring stories of Canadians who fought from the Plains of Abraham through to two world wars and Korea.

He is often asked whether he considers himself a war hero, a question that seems always to embarrass him, but for which he has a ready answer. "Not a war hero," he says, "a survivor." And I know he is thinking, "like so many other Canadian men and women who fought for their country and lived to tell the tale." Finally, here is my father's story. Not the story of a war hero perhaps, but a hero of sorts, and definitely a hero to me.

DIANA BISHOP

Introduction

June 23, 1943

It was a total bollix from the word go. A complete screw-up. Hardly a worthy start for the budding career of a fighter pilot whose father was called "the man without fear." If this initial baptism of fire was a foretaste, no such designation would ever be applied to his offspring.

A thick morning mist blanketed the English Channel, stretching from our forward base at Martlesham Heath on England's southeast coast all the way to Rotterdam, the Mitchell medium bombers' target. Visibility was so badly restricted that our top-cover high-altitude Spitfire IXs failed to rendezvous with us. That left our low-altitude (15,000 feet maximum) clipped-wing Spitfire Vs as sole protection for the bombers. Dicey—a bad omen.

As the Netherlands shoreline came hazily into view, the wing leader had doubts about continuing. His voice came over the radio transmitter (R/T) loud and clear: "Do you think we should turn back?" It was directed at the commanders of each of our two squadrons, but it was already too late for that.

Our CO answered back, "They're waiting for us. Straight ahead, above. The sun's glinting on their hoods." He sounded excited. But my throat went dry with fear. This was my first exposure to the enemy—dozens of deadly Focke-Wulf 190s poised to attack us.

One of them flipped neatly on its back and dived head-on at one of the bombers. The Mitchell's nose-gunner blew it to pieces. Spectacular, all right, but frightening, too. This was the real thing. War, for Chrissakes.

I tucked in close behind my flight leader, who already had a Hun singled out and was climbing toward him at full throttle. He had him cold. I figured I could get in a shot too, perhaps. But I don't mind admitting I was trembling at the prospect. Trembling, period. Then, all of a sudden, just as the flight commander was about to open fire, another Spitfire cut straight across in front of him. He pulled up sharply, too quickly for me to follow. And suddenly there I was—all on my lonesome. But only figuratively.

In fact, there seemed to be planes racing about all over the place, most of them Germans. There was no cohesive pattern—at least I couldn't make one out. I had not yet acquired what the American World War I ace Eddie Rickenbacker called "the feeling of the air"—being able to create order out of the confusion of aerial combat—that comes only with experience. Mix confusion with terror and you've got me pegged right down to a tee. Tracers were flying all around me. I decided to get the hell out of there. I did exactly what the experienced pilots in our outfit had told me to do in such a situation. I rolled over on my back and dived to the deck (zero feet), spiralling all the way down to make it difficult for anyone to take proper aim at me.

When I flattened out, I could faintly make out the rest of the wing in the distance over the Channel at an altitude that I gauged to be about 2000 feet, and I could hear a lot of R/T chatter indicating that they were being engaged. Then I saw two aircraft dive away. It happened so fast I was taken completely by surprise. I made them out to be two 190s, heading in my direction. The next thing I knew, they had flown right by me, only a few feet away on either side. I could even see the pilots' helmets. What struck me most was that, unlike our camouflaged aircraft, theirs were painted white, with vivid red lightning flashes along the fuselage. The pilots must have been just as surprised as I was. I doubt they were as scared, though. It was something I held an exclusive on that morning.

I set course back to Martlesham, feeling lucky to be alive, but harbouring a lot of self-doubt. Was I scared? Frightened out of my wits would be putting it mildly. I made no apology for it then, and I make none now. Fear is a normal reaction to combat, especially one's first experience of it. Fear is nothing to be ashamed of. It is a strange phenomenon, and like a sword, it has two edges. On one edge, it leads to cowardice. Such cases did not last long on fighter squadron. Cowardice jeopardizes the safety of others. On the other edge, fear heightens our senses as we go into battle. And while most of us didn't want anyone to know how goddamn scared we were—me in particular—I take pride, if I may, in our ability to overcome it.

In truth, let it be known, I had been scared even by my very first look at an airplane—a friendly one at that—which took place at Elstree, north of London, England, 16 years earlier almost to the day. The memory of that incident flashed before my eyes as I winged my way along the deck over the Channel's unfriendly watery waste.

Chapter 1

My Yearling Years

The Fortune, Elstree, England—June 13, 1927

> "Thank you, sir!"
> —Author to headmaster after a caning.

I had just turned four.

The sudden sight of that giant Avro biplane swooping down from over the ridge toward our Tudor-style house, combined with the roar of the piston-driven Wolseley Viper engine, frightened the hell out of me.

I scampered to the comfort and safety of my mother's skirts and clung to them frantically. Then I saw that it was my father, "the man without fear," who had landed the airplane in the field behind the house. He climbed down from the cockpit, all smiles.

Elstree was close to the Royal Air Force aerodrome at Hendon. My parents attended the annual RAF airshow there, which was at the time one of the world's foremost such events. In June 1928, despite my initial trepidation about the airplane, I accompanied them to the airshow. But it was to be another five years before I took my first ride in an airplane, and even then I felt a strange sensation that made me wonder if I would ever be able to fly. But first, let's go back to the very beginning.

At birth I had been given royal status. Born at home on June 13, 1923, at 34 Chester Terrace, near Regent's Park in London, I was christened Arthur Christian William Avery Bishop after my godfather, Arthur, Duke of Connaught, a former Governor General of

1

Canada. My godmother was Princess Louise, cousin to Queen Mary. I have often thought since (facetiously) that I would rather have had the money. Toronto, Ontario, was the home of my maternal grandparents, Charles and Margaret (née Eaton) Burden, and where my father and mother lived after the Great War of 1914–18. Had I been born there, I am sure I would have been baptized under far more plebeian auspices and been given a far less unwieldy nomenclature. ("Will the real Arthur Christian William Avery Bishop please stand up?") But my parents were snobbish enough to consider it fitting and merited. In England they were very much into the London scene, and royalty played a large part in their lives. Spending part of the winters at Cannes and Le Touquet, they joined the "Roaring Twenties" set, hobnobbing with the likes of Ernest Hemingway and the Scott Fitzgeralds.

In Canada after the war, my father had attempted an unsuccessful venture into commercial aviation with the Canadian air ace Billy Barker, VC, and had experienced differences and difficulties with his in-laws. Two years before I came into the world, he decided to seek his fortune in London, where, as the top Allied ace of the Great War, he had already developed significant business and social connections.

One of the enterprises in which he engaged was selling foreign rights for a new method of producing iron pipe by spinning it centrifugally, which had been developed by a French inventor, Dmitri de Lavaud, in Paris. My father's experience in that field led to his also representing Frank Pickett, an Englishman who dealt in surplus scrap metal. Part of my father's arrangement with him was to exercise and train—as well as buy and sell—polo ponies that Pickett kept at Elstree. (Because of his background as a cavalry officer, my father had become an accomplished polo player. He was a four-goal-handicap man and captain of his own team; among his teammates was Winston Churchill.) Fortuitously, "The Fortune," a Tudor-style residence, was available for rent at Elstree.

To my young eyes, that house, which stood by itself facing a slope to the west and to the east—the polo training field where my father landed the Avro that day—seemed like a mansion. Many years later, when I visited the town (which had become a motion picture colony) while researching my father's biography in 1960, I had no trouble finding it. Arriving in a chauffeur-driven limousine, courtesy of the Resident Senior RCAF Officer for Britain, I was greeted by the lady of the house. Yes, she assured me, I had the right place. This was where the Canadian VC Colonel Bishop had lived. The brown-and-white Tudor house stood out, wedged as it was between drab, faceless, narrow brick suburban dwellings crammed together on either side. But I was struck by how small it now seemed. Did we all—my mother, my father, my sister (born three years after me), our nanny, and the cook, maid, valet, and chauffeur—as well as Gin-Gin the chow—really live in this house? And where did they keep my Shetland pony? The dwelling must have shrunk since we lived there.

During the time we lived at the Fortune, my father began amassing a fortune, but his investments, like so many other people's in those days, were on margin—it was an irresponsible heyday that simply couldn't last. On "Black Thursday," October 24, 1929, the New York stock market crashed, with reverberations worldwide. My father was wiped out. Apart from a few thousand dollars in cash, he had lost nearly a million dollars in assets. By nature he never allowed a reversal, no matter how serious, to upset his equilibrium or shake his irrepressible sense of humour. A week earlier he had ordered one of the new radiophonographic player consoles—*très de rigueur*—from Harrods. It was delivered on the morning the market caved in. That evening when he arrived home, as my mother remembered it, "He walked over to it, kissed it, and said, 'Goodbye—it was nice knowing you.'" He never again bought on margin, a lesson he passed along to me that on one occasion— only one—I ignored.

The following summer, in 1930, we moved to Canada, where my father had been appointed vice-president of the McColl-Frontenac

Oil Company in Montreal, Quebec. He sublet an apartment in the Gleneagles, an imposing high-rise building in its day, while waiting for completion of the roof-garden penthouse in the Trafalgar apartments next door, where Côte des Neiges Road meets Westmount Boulevard, facing Mount Royal. Percy Lethbridge—"Leth" to me— the family chauffeur from London, accompanied him.

Meanwhile, my sister—whom I called "Babes"—and I, along with our mother, were to spend the summer at my grandparents' place, Ravenscrag, on Muskoka's Lake Rosseau across from the Windermere House Hotel. In September we moved into their town residence on Avenue Road in Toronto. I was by now seven years old and was sent to Hill School, just around the corner on the south side of St. Clair Avenue. The school's matriarchal headmistress, one Miss Winroberts, took delight in scolding her wards for infractions. I vividly recall the time she made my cousin Eddy Eaton stand in the corner for throwing a chocolate bar wrapper on the floor and noisily munching the candy in class. She even presided outside the school, roundly scolding me one afternoon on the north side of St. Clair because my shoelaces were untied.

In 1931, after summering in Muskoka, my mother, sister, and I and Nanny moved into the Trafalgar in Montreal, where I attended Selwyn House, a private preparatory boys' day school, on Redpath Street. During my first term at Selwyn House I came first in my class of 25 boys. The report card singled out four subjects for which I appeared to have had a special affinity: reading ("excellent"), writing ("good"), and history and geography ("shows interest" and "works well"). This had little to do with diligence. Concentration, perhaps. But at this stage schoolwork seemed to come easily to me—a phenomenon slated to be short-lived.

One morning I woke up with a stomach ache, a god-given excuse to play hookey. But I exaggerated it so much that my mother sent for the doctor. He too was taken in, and I was hustled off to Montreal General Hospital and operated on for appendicitis. One week in hospital and another two weeks at home recuperating—three blessed weeks away from school. AWOL, you might call it.

One day during that recuperative period, in which I was mostly confined to bed, I got bored. With nothing better to do, my sister and I began throwing my collection of books out the seventh-storey window of the apartment. The doorman phoned up and said, "It's raining books down here." When my father opened the door to the bedroom, my sister and I thought we were in for a scolding. But when he saw the fun we were having, he grinned. "Alright, just one more each—and I get the first throw."

At Selwyn House, I developed a lifelong friendship with Alfred Dobell, whose father was president of Ogilvie Flour Mills. Alf lived on Redpath Crescent, a snowball's throw from the school. Alfred recalls our first meeting: "When I first encountered Bishop, shortly after enrolling at Selwyn House, he was called Arthur, as in Arthur, Duke of Connaught, his godfather. Early on, one of the masters, Major Cyril Jackson, saw no reason why young Bishop should be referred to as anything other than Billy Bishop (like Dad), ducal godparents notwithstanding. So, Bishop became 'Bill' to his school chums, remaining Arthur at home.

"Even in those days he was quite a character. He had an infectious sense of the ridiculous, and our friendship was punctuated by roars of laughter."

It was at Selwyn House that I had my first brushes with disciplinary action. Serious infractions were dealt with by a caning from the headmaster, Geoffrey Wanstall. My father had anticipated that I might come in for my fair share and had instructed me that following a caning it was proper to straighten up and say, "Thank you, sir." (This was probably a carry-over from his days as a Royal Military College cadet.) My first experience with that type of punishment stemmed from being late for school four times in a row. I was shivering with fright as I dutifully bent over to accept my punishment. So how do you say "Thank you, sir" right after you've wet your pants?

•   •   •

At "Chicken House," so-called because Selwyn House's school colours were yellow and black, I became seriously conscious of what it meant to be the son of Billy Bishop. I had never thought of it as an advantage. In fact, a lot of my schoolmates were far better off than we were—or so it seemed to me. I do not mean to imply that I downgraded my heritage. It just never occurred to me to give it much priority. I was too interested in my own situation pro and con—sports, fights, hobbies (high on the list: building model airplanes), and other pursuits that occupied me. But one instance does stand out in my mind.

It happened on Armistice Day, as November 11 was then called. Canadian military history meant a lot back in those days, when there was still a strong sense of patriotism. That particular morning was devoted to remembrance of those who had lost their lives in the Great War of 1914–18, and we observed a minute of silence at 11 o'clock. I recall that the teacher delivered a lesson on Canada's part in the conflict. She then asked me to sit beside her at her desk while she recounted my father's deeds as the top Allied air ace. I was somewhat embarrassed but also felt very proud. I had not really pictured my father in that context before or in those terms. To me he was a good guy, a lot of fun, and someone who showed an interest in whatever I was doing or not doing, but beyond that, I really hadn't given it much thought.

Back in those Selwyn House days, I was given a chilling insight into quite another aspect of what being the son of Billy Bishop meant. In 1932 the Lindbergh baby kidnapping was very much in the news, and I overheard the maid and the cook talking about how my sister and I had been under police surveillance. The Montreal police had been tipped off by an informer that two local prison inmates, who were due for parole, had been heard discussing the possibility of kidnapping either one or both of us. When I asked Leth about it, he was pretty sore at the cook and the maid. But he assured me that it had been only a temporary measure. The danger, if there ever had really been one, had passed. The conspirators had been denied parole and moved to a maximum security prison. Shortly thereafter I took my first flight. One of my schoolmates was Peter Holt, grandson of Sir Herbert Holt, president of the Royal Bank of Canada (as in Holt Renfrew, too). Peter's parents, Bob and Babbie Holt, were close friends of my mother and father. They owned a twin-engine cabin seaplane christened the *Peter and Pam* after their children. During the summer of 1933, when Peter was staying with us at Ravenscrag, his parents visited us in the *Peter and Pam*. I experienced the wonderful sensation of flying for the first time. And what an experience seeing that panorama of the scenic Muskoka Lakes from the air. I was fascinated by it. I felt quite at home in the air, absolutely thrilled by it all—until we came in to land. I had a weird feeling that the plane was not going down but rather the lake was coming up to meet us. I was relieved when the floats struck the water.

Next came my first experience at shooting. That Christmas my father gave me an air rifle. Perhaps he wanted to impart to me his own universally recognized skill with the gun. Relating his combat experiences in *Winged Warfare*, he wrote: "The most important thing in fighting is the shooting." His own record of 72 enemy aircraft destroyed certainly bore that out. He demonstrated that ability to me in the evenings at a secluded spot on Mount Royal. He would pin paper targets to a tree so that I could practise my marksmanship. His own shooting was so accurate it was uncanny. He was a good teacher, too. He instructed me on how to hold the rifle; how to take aim—by shutting one eye; how to squeeze—not jerk—the trigger to fire. In no time at all I became quite adept. I was ready to put my new skill to use.

During the Easter holidays of 1934, Bob Savage, a classmate, and I were guests of John Irwin, president of McColl-Frontenac Oil and my father's boss, and his wife at their estate at St. Andrew's, on the north shore of the Ottawa River west of Montreal. I took the air rifle with me, and every afternoon Bob and I roamed the premises in search of targets. Irene Irwin put any birds off limits, including sitting ducks. However, in the woods we noticed that tin pails had been strapped to the trees. What wonderful targets they made, with that satisfying *ping* as the BB pellets pierced them.

I was never invited back to the Irwins'. Small wonder. Those tin pails were to catch the sap from the maple trees. The syrup yield that year had been pitiful—the sap just ran out the holes our BB pellets had made.

My father was a great sports fan, which led to several memorable moments for me. As sponsor of the Montreal Maroons hockey club, McColl-Frontenac had a box seat at centre ice. I accompanied my parents to many of the games. The highlight came one night when I was taken to the team dressing room between periods, and the great Lionel Conacher, one of my sports idols, presented me with a hockey stick autographed by all the players. Not to take anything away from Wayne Gretzky, my vote for Canadian athlete of the twentieth century would have to go to the "Big Train," who was an outstanding athlete not only on the ice, but also at football, lacrosse, boxing, wrestling, and track and field. One Saturday in the 1930s he played football in the afternoon, scoring a touchdown or two and kicking several field goals, and that night was the outstanding player on the ice. I confess that I could not resist playing with that hockey stick—showing off, I suppose you'd call it—with the inevitable result that I broke it beyond repair and it was thrown away.

On another occasion my father took me to the Outremont Arena to see a wrestling match featuring the "Flying Tackler," Gus Sonnenberg. But the highlight for me came when my father lifted me up to the ring in between bouts to shake hands with the world boxing champion, Jack Dempsey, who was refereeing the matches.

Dempsey was known as the "Manassa Mauler," not without good reason. In the ring he exhibited the rough-and-tumble style of a street brawler—wade in fast regardless and hit the other guy before he has a chance to defend himself. It was about this time that I also met his opponent of two famous bouts in 1926 and 1927, Gene

Tunney, with whom my father had been associated in some mining ventures in northern Ontario. My father, who followed boxing
keenly and closely, filled me in on the details. The World War I
"Fighting Marine," who toppled Dempsey in their first fight, had
developed a style that was the antithesis of his hard-hitting opponent's. No less formidable a heavyweight than Dempsey, he would
stay out of reach of his adversary until he spotted an opening. But it
didn't always work.

In the seventh round of their return match, Dempsey landed six
straight blows to Tunney's head, which all but knocked him uncon-
scious. The referee wasted precious time instructing Dempsey to
go to his corner before beginning what became famous as the
"long count." In the interim, Tunney recovered his composure
sufficiently to go on, successfully defending his title.

I can still picture the fire in my father's eyes as he related the
incident. Every inch a scrapper himself (he had been a good ama-
teur boxer in his youth), though short, he was sturdy, with a massive chest and large fists, and would fight at the drop of a hat. "Hit
him in the balls" was his pugilistic philosophy. While he was
telling the Dempsey–Tunney story, his jaw jutted out and he kept
clenching and unclenching his fists. It was as if he were in the ring
with them.

In 1934, my father, who never lost his interest in aviation (he was
an honorary group captain of the RCAF at the time), took a
refresher course at the St. Hubert Flying School across the St.
Lawrence River from Montreal. His instructor was Tom Rawthall,
a veteran wartime pilot. The trainer was a twin-cockpit Fleet Finch.

The following year, when the school moved to Cartierville, north
of the city, I took my first flying lessons from Tom on my twelfth
birthday. So that I could see over the front cockpit, he had to put a
cushion on top of the parachute in the bucket seat. I was afraid that
I might again experience that sensation of the ground coming up

to meet me on landing, as I had in the Holts' seaplane. But my fear was unfounded, so the lessons were really exciting.

One evening after I had landed, I waited to drive home with my father, who was practising landings. Each time he alighted he would immediately put on full throttle and race straight for the hangar at the end of the field. As he did so, he would lean over the side of the cockpit and wave his left hand at me. Mere yards from the hangar, it seemed, he would pull up in a zooming climb and then repeat the performance all over again. When he finally landed for the last time, taxied in, and climbed out, he asked me, "Why didn't you open the hangar doors like I was trying to tell you to?"

I often accompanied my father on his flights. One that took place in late June 1935 is still fresh in my memory. I flew in the front cockpit, giving me a vantage but not the slightest inkling of what I was about to witness. My father had set an agenda without revealing his plans to me. We took off from Cartierville and flew due north of Montreal Island to Laval Golf Course. We circled around until my father spotted four friends of his putting out on one of the greens. He tapped me on the back of the head and pointed downward. Then he dived the Fleet straight down toward the golfers, sending them running in all directions. I turned around to see my father grinning from ear to ear. We swept over the green at no higher than five feet, then he pulled up and we were off to the west. Compared to what happened next, that episode was mere child's play.

We now flew west to Vaudreuil, on the Ottawa River, where a friend of my father's, Colonel Gus Rainville, had a summer place. Once again my father tapped me on the back of the head, this time pointing to a raft anchored offshore on which Rainville's guests were sunning themselves. Down we went again. As we neared them, the sunbathers plunged into the river and swam desperately for shore. It was just as well. That time my father bounced the aircraft's wheels on the raft.

I have said it many times before in relating this story: All through those capers I had utter confidence in my father. I was beginning to think of him as many others did—as invincible.

But that would be the last of my flying experiences for a while. That September of 1935, I was sent to Bishop's (no kin) College School in Lennoxville, Quebec, 90 miles east of Montreal.

Chapter 2

Boarding School Years

1935–1941

> "He's got skinny legs."
> —Cilla after seeing
> the author in a bathing suit.

My six years at Bishop's College School were punctuated by a series of high and low points, each one leading to others. There was a time I came close to death. Sometime later I had my first introduction to the RCAF. Next, a low point: I faced expulsion from school for drinking. Then came two key events that were to have a lasting bearing on my life. During the summer of 1938 I accompanied my father on a cross-country tour of air force bases. Two years later, I met the girl I would one day marry. On the downside, during that same period I flunked my junior matriculation exams.

My indoctrination period as a boarder was spent in the senior class of the BCS preparatory (prep) school, after which I would enter the junior class of the upper school. My roommates were Alf Dobell and his cousin Tony Mactier. At the end of the final term at prep school, we left with some trepidation about facing the next school year as new boys in the "upper." The graduating class ahead of us gave us some inkling of what that initiation might be like. None of it sounded particularly pleasant.

As Alfred Dobell recalls, "BCS was run roughly along the lines of a British Public School. Life for a New Boy in the Upper School provided some obstacles to peace and tranquility, what with fag-ging [each new boy was assigned as a sort of manservant to a pre-fect or headboy], onerous 'new kid rules' [no use of centre stairs, no hands in the pockets, address all seniors by their surnames], and caning for the unwary. Bishop was the sort of fellow who tended to treat a lot of this as a sort of comic opera. On one occasion, he and I decided to defy the rules by marching smartly down the centre stairs with our hands in our pockets and addressing one of the headboys by his first name. It earned us a caning. But the sense of satisfaction we got out of it was worth it. It kept us laughing for some time."

Halfway through my second term as a new boy, in the winter of 1937, I came close to succumbing to a near-fatal sinus infection that had started in the school infirmary with a bout of measles. I was taken by ambulance to Sherbrooke Hospital in a semi-coma-tose state. Meanwhile the headmaster, Crawford Grier, had tele-phoned my parents, who were on holiday in Palm Beach, Florida, to notify them. They sent for the family doctor, Ned London of Montreal—fortuitously a leading ear, nose, and throat specialist—who shepherded me to Montreal General Hospital. During the two-hour train ride I kept losing consciousness. Fortunately Ned was able to revive me each time. My mother and father flew to New York and then on to Montreal, and were at my bedside later the fol-lowing morning.

It was touch and go for a while, but under Dr. London's supervi-sion and expert care, I gradually recovered, and after a month was finally pronounced well enough to be discharged from the hospital. During all that time, what worried me most was that in one of my suits was a package of Sweet Caporal cigarettes—smoking at age 14 was strictly forbidden, at home as well as at school, where it was pun-ishable by caning (10 strokes for the first offence, 15 for second, and 20 as well as expulsion for a third). I knew that the suits were being sent home and I was terrified that the school might discover the cigarettes or, if they got past that possibility, that my parents would find them. I was lucky; the Sweet Caps got by both undetected.

Following the election of the Mackenzie King Liberal government in 1935 (my first year at BCS), my father was appointed Honorary Air Vice-Marshal of the RCAF by the new minister of defence, Ian Mackenzie. He was charged with assisting the government in appropriating more funds for air force expansion by wooing public support. A year earlier, as a member of the Opposition, Mackenzie had told the House of Commons, "If it is necessary to carry out a real defence policy for Canada in the future, I think that the air force will play a most prominent part in that policy."

My father wasted no time getting into gear. On February 13, 1936, he made a speech to the Empire Club in Toronto entitled "What Aviation Means to Canada," in which he deplored the general state of military affairs. He declared that "the air proportion is ludicrous," and vowed, "It will be my earnest endeavour, and I feel it incumbent upon me in view of my new rank, to do the utmost to further aviation in Canada."

The wind was soon blowing in the right direction. In May, Mackenzie was able to announce that appropriations for the RCAF had been increased by a million dollars to a sum of $4.13 million. My father's fresh prominence had a stimulating effect on me. I began to appreciate his eminence much more and took a profound interest in the air force. Two years later, my father arranged for me and a school chum of my choosing to spend a week of our Easter holidays at Trenton, Ontario, at the Royal Canadian Air Force (RCAF) Central Flying Training School, as guests of the commanding officer, Wing Commander Clifford "Black Mike" McEwen, MC, DFC and Bar, Légion d'honneur. During World War II, McEwen was to command No. 6 Group, RCAF Bomber Command.

•   •   •

At Bishop's the military spirit was impressed upon us through the cadet corps, which was affiliated with the famous Black Watch (the Royal Highland Regiment of Canada). It was compulsory for all students to participate, as was customary at most private schools. This was more a part of school discipline than recruitment for the military. BCS was not a military academy by any means, but we all took pride in the corps. And it had a strong influence on a few individuals, some of whom aspired to go on to the Royal Military College in Kingston, Ontario, after graduation. (An axiom of those days: the Perfect Shit—a Selwyn House, BCS, and RMC graduate.) Others joined one of the three services after graduation. While my interest in the air force and flying grew during my teenage years, I never gave much serious thought to a military career. I presumed that I would probably do what most Bishop's graduates did— attend McGill University.

I chose as my companion for the Trenton holiday my old Selwyn House classmate Alf Dobell. We had enrolled in Bishop's together a year earlier. But if I was interested in the air force, Alf's ambition was to one day join the navy, which indeed he did—the *Royal Navy*.

Before we left we familiarized ourselves with the various air force ranks: Aircraftsman Second Class (AC2), Leading Aircraftsman (LAC), Flight Sergeant (F/S), Flying Officer (F/O), Squadron Leader (S/L), and so on. On arrival at the railway station we were greeted by the commanding officer (CO), who drove us to the officers' mess, where we would take all our meals. After dinner he drove us to the control tower, where we watched the night flying exercises. We were off to an exciting start.

At the time, pilot officer trainees were taking their flying instruction on Fleet Finches. Among the trainees were Leonard Birchall and Keith Hodson. Birchell would become famous as the "Saviour of Ceylon" as well as for his brave efforts on behalf of his fellow prisoners of war of the Japanese. In 1961 Hodson was on his way to becoming chief of air staff. However, while serving as deputy chief of staff of the North American Air Defense Command (NORAD), he was killed as he bailed out of a trainer. During the war Hodson was my airfield commander in both Great Britain and France.

A training curriculum of a sort had been devised for Alf and me. We spent the mornings in ground school instruction. Among the subjects the instructors taught to us (in terms we could easily understand) were aerodynamics, aerial photography (a new, more sensitive type of film had recently been introduced that doubled the hours available for photographing), instruments, navigation, parachutes (how to pack them and the procedure for bailing out), and wireless communication.

I was fascinated by these lectures, in contrast to school lessons, which for the most part (except for English and history) I found tedious and boring—a chore. Shortly after I joined the air force I discussed this contradiction with the BCS head, Crawford Grier. A former artillery major in the Great War, he jokingly remarked, "Sometimes I wish I could rename our school subjects 'armament' or 'navigation' and such. There'd be a lot more interest and better concentration."

During the afternoons we studied—and were captivated by— flight familiarization. We flew as passengers in most of the types of aircraft on the station. One of the newest was the British-built Airspeed Oxford, a twin-engine bomber trainer. With an airspeed of 200 miles an hour, it was one of the fastest aircraft then in service with the RCAF. On our exercise flight, Alf occupied the copilot's seat while I manned the unarmed gun turret on the upper side of the fuselage.

The gun and its seat could be rotated a full 360 degrees in either direction, by a remote-control button. Once we were airborne I decided to try it out. I managed to get it rotating to the left (in correct air force terminology, to port), but I couldn't stop it from spinning around—and at so dizzying a speed I was afraid I was going to lose my lunch. Imagine how that would have gone down: "Our Air Vice-Marshal's Son Gets Airsick!"

Somehow, by fiddling with the control button, I stopped the gun from spinning around. I climbed down a bit shakily from the gun turret and spent the rest of the flight behind the pilots' seats. I knew one thing for certain: If I was ever going to join the air force, it wasn't going to be as an air gunner.

Trenton, in addition to being a flying training school, was also a seaplane base. It was in that milieu that Alf and I experienced one of the bigger thrills of our visit. Squadron Leader Fred Mawdesley, a veteran aerial distance pioneer and rescue pilot, introduced us to the double-wing, open-twin-cockpit Vickers Vedette seaplane. The first aircraft produced entirely by Canadian Vickers' own design team, it was introduced in 1925 and was taken on in strength by the RCAF for forestry work, photography, and light transportation. At the time it was described by the *Report on Civil Aviation* as "a remarkably efficient little boat . . . the equal, and for Canadian conditions, the superior of any flying boat in the world today."

By the time Alf and I were taken aboard (separately), as far as I was concerned, in the deft hands of S/L Mawdesley that definition still applied 13 years later. "Old Mawsey" really put the feisty little machine through its paces. He did everything but make it talk—takeoffs and landings on the lake, stall turns, spins—he even barrel-rolled it.

I was struck by the efficiency of the station. Everything seemed spick and span, bearing out that old air force adage: "If it moves, salute it. If it doesn't move, pick it up. And if you can't pick it up, paint it white."

Everywhere—on the parade ground: the daily rituals of raising the flag in the morning and lowering it in the evening; in the officers' mess: coming to attention at the doorway before entering the anteroom; around the aircraft: the mechanics plying their trade, the pilots coming and going—I had a tingling sensation of being witness to something exciting in which I might one day take part. Officers and men went about their business with a wilful, knowledgeable sense of dedication and pride—even a lone airman marching smartly from one building to another. An aura of discipline permeated every inch of the establishment. This was not surprising, since Black Mike McEwen was a stickler for discipline. In fact, he was the only RCAF officer at the time who was qualified to carry the swagger stick of a trained and graduated disciplinarian.

I remember very clearly an occasion on which Alf and I accompanied McEwen to the armament section. As we reached the building, a sergeant stepped from the door, saluted, and started to walk past us. He didn't get far. "Sergeant," Black Mike barked, stopping him in his tracks, "when an officer comes to the door at the same time you do, you make way for him first. You understand?"

"Yes, sir!" came the smart reply.

"Dismissed," Black Mike ended the exchange quietly but firmly. The errant airman saluted again and was off.

My father looked upon Alf's and my experience as a kind of experiment in air cadet training for boys. This resulted in my being labelled "Canada's first air cadet." This was not really true, and eminently unfair for the young men who really were Canada's first air cadets. In 1936, the first Canadian Air Cadet Corps was established at Trinity College School in Port Hope, Ontario. Among those freshman cadets was Dal Russel of Toronto, who first distinguished himself as a Battle of Britain pilot with No. 1 (later 401) Squadron RCAF. Subsequently he commanded Spitfire fighter wings on three different occasions, amassing an astounding 286 operational sorties. I served under Dal on two different occasions. Another distinguished pilot among that group was Pat Hingston of Montreal, who flew with 426 Transport Squadron RCAF in Burma, flying men and supplies over "the Hump," for which he was awarded the Distinguished Flying Cross.

In the summer of 1938, my father was promoted to the rank of Honorary Air Marshal of the RCAF, an occasion (if you could call it that) at which I was present. The events began in June at Ravenscrag, our place in Muskoka, where he and I were picked up in a Norduyn Norseman seaplane, piloted by Squadron Leader Dave Harding from Camp Borden, to fly to Ottawa. Known as "Dirty Dave" Harding when he played football at Queen's University (without a helmet), he was one of the RCAF's top pilots, having been a member of the Siskin Flight, the forerunner of the Golden Hawks and Snowbirds aerobatic teams. At one time, when he was temporarily attached to the Royal Air Force, Harding had also been Lawrence of Arabia's personal pilot.

In the Canadian capital, my father and I occupied the Quebec suite in the Château Laurier Hotel. We were greeted there by the defence minister, Ian Mackenzie. On deck also was Group Captain George Croil, senior officer for the RCAF. Then, one by one, members of the press and radio reporters arrived. This was my first exposure to the press conference—an apprenticeship, you might say. Next day the announcement of my father's promotion was front-page news: "Bishop Is Air Marshal For Canada."

At a luncheon following the conference the drinks flowed freely, but I was not included or invited. I spent the afternoon taking in many Ottawa sights. When I returned to the suite, I found my father asleep. The telephone rang. It was my mother calling from Muskoka.

"Dad's asleep," I told her.

"Well, wake him up!" was the response.

It took quite a few tugs to shake him out of his slumber. Then, still groggy from the lunchtime festivities, he mumbled less than coherently, "Where are we? In Ottawa?" It became a standard family joke. But *my* initial experience with drinking was treated far less jocularly.

Along with another student, whose family was staying at the Magog Hotel in Sherbrooke, I was caught drinking beer in the hotel bar by one of the school masters. We were threatened with expulsion but the sentence was reduced to temporary loss of seniority—an embarrassment among our peers.

●   ●   ●

During the last term of the very next year (1938–39), my father was guest speaker at the Cadet Corps mess dinner in May, following the annual inspection. I was a little embarrassed about it all, but the old man cut a commanding figure in his RCAF mess kit, his famous row of miniature medals pinned to his chest. He was a fine orator, and his speech, mostly about his war experiences, was exciting and went over well. In fact, at the end of it, when he asked the headmaster to grant the school a holiday on his behalf, Crawford Grier, well primed with after-dinner port, replied, "Alright, Air Marshal Bishop, provided you tell us another of your fighting stories." We got the holiday the next day.

Only a few weeks later came the royal visit of King George VI and Queen Elizabeth to the Eastern Townships, in June 1939, when we cadets formed part of the guard lining the route. This was pageantry of the highest order, the like of which we had never seen before. As the royal limousine crawled past us, we presented arms. For me it was spine-tingling—official ceremonies always have and always will affect me that way. I was struck by the graciousness of the royals as they waved to the cheering crowds, particularly the lovely Queen in her pale blue dress.

The purpose of this visit was to cement relations with Canada, as part of the Commonwealth, and with the United States before hostilities broke out in Europe. War was coming, and you could feel it. My father, together with Ian Mackenzie, began a last-minute campaign to enlist public support in favour of air force expansion. That summer they flew to RCAF stations from coast to coast in a twin-engine VIP Grumman Goose amphibian cabin monoplane based at Rockcliffe. It was captained by Flight Lieutenant Larry Wray, who, as a bomber field CO in World War II, would become the most senior RCAF officer (a group captain) to fall into enemy hands as a prisoner of war.

On the western half of the tour, my mother—as a Red Cross representative—and I accompanied them. It was my first look at western Canada and my introduction to a number of people with whom

I would later become friends in business. At one of our stops I sat in, with our pilot, Larry Wray, at a luncheon during which my father was speaking. Afterwards Larry struck up a conversation with one of the guests, asking him how he had liked the talk. He hadn't. "He's doing more to start a war—spouting off with that kind of stuff about needing a strong air force—than preventing it," he sneered. Larry grinned and replied, "By the way, I'd like you to meet the Air Marshal's son."

Our itinerary consisted of visits to Winnipeg, Calgary, Vancouver, and Victoria. At Winnipeg my father was greeted by a guard of honour. But for me, Calgary was the real highlight of the trip. The RCAF station there was the home of No. 1 Fighter Squadron, the outfit in which I would later serve (by then it would be renumbered 401), and which became the only Canadian squadron to fight in the Battle of Britain. Prior to our visit, on June 3, 1939, the squadron had been re-equipped with Hawker Hurricanes, the first of the new modern British fighters. At the time of our visit, the pilots were still in the process of converting from their obsolete Siskin biplanes to the new monoplane fighters.

The CO, Squadron Leader Elmer Fullerton, a highly experienced pilot and the first to fly the Hurricane in Canada, put on a special demonstration for us. (In February the first 10 aircraft purchased from the United Kingdom had arrived at Sea Island Airport in Vancouver, where they were uncrated and assembled. As soon as they were ready, Fullerton air-tested them.) He went through a series of aerobatics at speeds unheard of in Canada in those days—between 325 and 342 miles an hour, flat and level. It was an unforgettable performance.

World War II began shortly afterwards, when Germany invaded Poland on September 1, 1939. Britain and France declared war two days later, but it took another week before the Mackenzie King government of Canada finally drew the sword. However, the majority of Canadian male youth, as well as many Great War vets, refused to wait for official word. They immediately began flocking to the colours by the thousands.

Before returning to school, I made my annual three-day pilgrimage to the Canadian National Exhibition—the midway, the rides, the exhibits, the big bands. Returning from the "Ex" along King Street, I passed a lineup in front of an army recruiting centre. Someone turned to me and asked, "Going to join up?"

"Not old enough," I replied. "And anyway, when my turn comes, I'm joining the air force."

"Oh," was the response. "Going to be another Billy Bishop, eh?"

That evening, September 3, an incident occurred that brought the war home to Canadians with a jolt. Over the radio we learned that at 9:00 p.m. Greenwich time, the 13,500-ton passenger liner *Athenia*, en route to New York, had been sunk by the German submarine U-30. One hundred and twelve lives were lost. Fortunately, 12 Canadians aboard were rescued, among them Joan Patch, sister of Colin Patch, a schoolmate of mine from Selwyn House days. When I learned of this, I realized just how personal war could be.

The war had a profound effect on the BCS student body, particularly among those of us in the senior classes. A sense of change manifested itself. Though our lives were in no way altered at this stage, I, for one, realized that one day, no matter how far off, we students—and many of the faculty—would be putting on the uniform. Indeed, many in the graduating class looked forward to that prospect.

We read the newspapers and we listened to the radio, but although Canada was mobilizing in a hurry—the first contingent of the First Canadian Division set sail from Halifax on September 18, 1939—very little occurred that fall and winter to get excited about. The Western Front was wallowing in a stalemated *Sitzkrieg*. But there were two notable exceptions, both of which took place at sea.

At 1:30 on the morning of October 14, a German submarine, U-47, in the skilled hands of Kapitanleutnant Hans Prien of the

Kriegsmarine, penetrated the Royal Naval Fleet base at Scapa Flow in northern Scotland. There it torpedoed the *Royal Oak* as she lay at anchor, sending the British battleship to the bottom with all hands aboard.

Churchill, then First Lord of the Admiralty, recognized this episode for what it was—"a feat of arms." In Germany the daring U-boat commander was hailed as a conquering hero, driven through the streets of Berlin to the cheers of the crowds, and awarded the Knight's Cross with diamonds by Hitler himself. It was a bitter blow to the Allies that the home defences could so easily be breached, but to those of us eager for action, it represented an act of war at last.

The second event that year was more than just an incident. It involved a decisive battle at sea that electrified the world, bolstering the prestige of British naval power to heights not seen since the Battle of Jutland in May 1916. At the same time, it dealt a mortal blow to the German navy, and to Nazi might.

The battle was also an historic moment to which anyone who had access to a radio could be instantly privy. In this early stage of the war, in addition to the U-boat peril, Allied merchant shipping was at the mercy of fast new German pocket-battleships. Heavily armed and capable of a speed of 26 knots, no cruiser could catch them. The *Admiral Graf Spee* had been assigned to harass shipping in the South Atlantic. Off South America, a squadron of three cruisers under the command of Commodore Harold Harwood was guarding the River Plate and the Montevideo area of Uruguay.

On December 14, we read and heard news of a naval engagement between the British cruisers and the pocket-battleship on the previous day. The cruisers *Ajax* and *Exeter* had suffered severe damage and the *Achilles* to a lesser extent. The *Graf Spee*, however, was so badly hit that it was forced to break off, under a smoke screen, and seek sanctuary in the neutral port of Montevideo. Glued to the radio between classes, we avidly awaited the outcome. This marked the first live, on-the-spot coverage of a major wartime encounter—or what now had become a confrontation. And, so to speak, we *were there.*

As the drama unfolded, our schoolboy interest and excitement intensified. We were kept aware that just outside the three-mile international limit offshore, the British squadron was sending for reinforcements to seal the fate of the battleship should the Germans try make a run for it. It was all very exciting. Meanwhile, Kapitan Hans Langsdorff set about making repairs to his ship, took in supplies, and moved his wounded to a hospital.

The climax came on the afternoon of December 17, when the 72 hours of sanctuary allowed under international law expired. We heard that the *Graf Spee* crew of more than 700 men had begun transferring to a German merchant ship in the harbour. The radio reporter regaled us with a description of the thousands of anxious onlookers lining the docks and taking up other vantage points in eager anticipation of the forthcoming clash of naval might—none more anxious than this eager radio listener.

At 6:15 p.m. the merchantman weighed anchor and steamed slowly toward the battleship. The radio commentator gave a detailed description of the battle three days earlier and the odds of the *Graf Spee* breaking through the British screen, which had been reinforced by the heavy cruiser *Cumberland,* in full fighting trim. The battleships *Ark Royal* and *Renown* were reported to be in the vicinity, steering toward the scene. In the opinion of the announcer, the *Graf Spee* was doomed. But, he was quick to point out, it would be uncharacteristic of the German navy not to put up a stiff fight. However, he was wrong—dead wrong.

A few minutes later, he reported that the merchant ship had pulled away from the *Graf Spee,* from which smoke had begun to billow. Then suddenly the announcer exclaimed, "She's blown herself up!" The vaunted pocket-battleship, which had accounted for the sinking of some 50,000 tons of Allied cargo, had scuttled herself, thus ending the first surface challenge to British shipping.

That night Langsdorff, broken-hearted at the loss of his ship but taking full responsibility for her scuttling, shot himself.

Over the Christmas holidays, I saw this scenario played out on the silver screen, on a newsreel. It brought to life the drama that we had only heard and read about. It showed the *Graf Spee* blowing up. It panned to a view of the thousands of spectators on hand in the Montevideo harbour to watch the incident. One of the most moving sequences was Langsdorff's funeral with full military honours, the implication being that he had committed suicide rather than face disgrace for scuttling his ship. All of those scenes enhanced my feeling that I was witnessing the reality of war, and I was thoroughly excited and enthused by it.

Several factors surrounding the River Plate action later came to light. The German Supreme Command had requested an extension of the 72-hour limit and had been refused. The decision to scuttle the *Graf Spee* was not Langsdorff's—it was Hitler's. When the captain reported to the German Admiralty that he faced a choice of interning his ship or scuttling it because a breakout was out of the question, the Führer ruled out internment and ordered the destruction of the battleship.

Our interest in these events and in the war in general extended to the school's debating society. On one occasion, the motion before the House was "that the society is of the opinion that Russia is a greater menace to the world than Germany." I put in my two cents' worth by arguing that "Germany is a greater menace because Russia is blocked by the Dardanelles. Furthermore, the morale of other nations is greater than hers—all is not plain sailing in Russia, as some speakers have taken for granted. But she does have ample resources and is self-contained and has no need for expansion. Germany is by far the greater menace at this time." The House did not agree. The motion was carried 9–7. So much for my debating skills.

•   •   •

On January 23, 1940, my father became the director of recruiting for the RCAF in conjunction with the inauguration of the British Commonwealth Air Training Plan (BCATP). Canada was about to become what President Franklin D. Roosevelt called the "aerodrome of democracy," a training ground for aircrews from Australia, New Zealand, and the United Kingdom, as well as Canada itself—not to mention a neutral United States, thanks to a scheme that my father had concocted long before hostilities broke out.

Early in the year, the family moved to Sandy Hill in Ottawa, where my father was attached to RCAF headquarters. Our mansion, in which I had a room on the third floor, was at the corner of Blackburn Avenue and Laurier Street, one block east of Prime Minister Mackenzie King's house. My introduction to it came in April, during the school Easter holidays.

The Canadian capital was an exciting place to be in those days, and 5 Blackburn Avenue was no exception. It had been turned into something of an air force institution. Leth, our chauffeur and my confidant, now wore the air force blue, with three chevrons topped by a crown signifying his rank of flight sergeant. Leth pointed proudly to the air marshal's pennant flying from the left front fender of the family Lincoln—now a part-time staff car. Then there was my father's aide-de-camp, Paul Rodier from Montreal—a former Great War flying ace who held the rank of squadron leader—and his secretary, Margie Northwood, a strikingly beautiful girl from Winnipeg.

My father's office was located in the air force headquarters building on Bank Street downtown. In his office, a wide red ribbon across the map of Canada had been severed by a pair of scissors symbolizing his penchant for cutting red tape. His library/den at Blackburn Avenue served as an ex-officio command centre, with two telephone lines at the ready. (I found this very handy for making dates when the old man was on the other line ordering people about.) It was an impressive room, replete with his war trophies.

On one wall hung the propeller and hub—the "Blue Nose"—from his Nieuport fighter. Underneath was a wing tip from the Fokker triplane in which the Red Baron, Manfred von Richthofen, was killed. On either side were charcoal renderings by the noted American aviation artist Clayton Knight, himself a Great War ace, illustrating Billy Bishop in action at the height of his famous 12-day spree, in which he shot down 25 enemy planes, in May and June of 1918. A ledge beneath supported the windscreen from his plane, which had a hole in it made by an enemy bullet that had grazed his flying helmet. Below, on top of the bookcase, sat a German Parabellum machine gun, and a Luger pistol lay alongside it. In the hall hung a large gilt-framed full-length portrait of my father in dress uniform, by Alphonse Jongers. A showplace indeed, and I made the most of it to impress my young lady friends.

We had no problem making friends in Ottawa. The people were hospitable, going out of their way to make us feel welcome. My sister, who had attended Havergal in Toronto, now attended a private girls' school, Elmwood, in Ottawa. Our house always seemed to be full of visitors, both local and from elsewhere, some from faraway places. In particular, of course, were those with whom my father worked and was associated. I especially remember Bea and Gus Edwards. "Uncle" Gus, more formally known as Air Vice-Marshal Harold Edwards, was RCAF Air Member for Personnel. Then there was Charles Gavan "Chubby" Power, Canadian Minister of Defence for Air, as well as Ian Mackenzie, by this time Minister of Pensions and Health, and Homer Smith. Many a glass of liquid refreshment passed between my father and this latter trio.

Smith, a wealthy Canadian who lived in the United States, financed the Clayton Knight Committee, a clandestine operation conceived by my father to recruit Americans for the RCAF. It ran counter to the laws of neutrality; strictly speaking it was illegal to solicit American citizens to fight in a foreign war. The solution was to ensure that those being "recruited" were, in effect, volunteering. Early in 1940, my father visited the White House to assure the

American president that no rules would be broken. Roosevelt laughed and said, "I wish we could paint black crosses on Harvard and drop a couple of bombs on Boston. That would get us into the war soon enough." Of that meeting, my father also commented to me, "We had the best oysters for lunch I've ever tasted."

At the close of 1939, my mother, father, sister, and I celebrated Christmas at my grandparents' house in Toronto before entraining for Palm Beach in Florida to stay with Homer Smith. The Clayton Knight Committee financier was about to enlist in the RCAF as a flight lieutenant. He was to be indoctrinated in air force procedures as an aide to Group Captain Frank McGill, a World War I fighter pilot and CO of Camp Borden Service Flying Training School. Homer Smith talked grandly about hiring chefs from some of New York's leading restaurants to handle the messing at the station. He was generous to a fault, and his heart was certainly in the right place; he simply let his enthusiasm get the better of him. My old man wisely advised him to cool it and not get a reputation for throwing his weight around.

On quite another matter that arose during that stay I found my father's judgment very questionable, and had the temerity—or the stupidity—to tell him so. Visiting Palm Beach that holiday season were the multimillionaire mining magnate Sir Harry Oakes and his wife and family. One noontime Babes and I were hustled into the car and driven to the Bath and Tennis Club, where our parents were having lunch with Sir Harry and Lady Oakes. We were treated to the noon repast with their obnoxious daughter Nancy—a typically spoiled young girl of rich parents—one of her school friends, and her younger brother. Some treat. As I recall, Nancy was about 14 years old. I do remember—vividly—that whiny voice of hers that never seemed to stop. All she could talk about was the array of gifts she'd been given for Christmas. It was "Daddy this" and "Mommy that." And in that same self-indulgent tone I can still hear her smirking, smugly bragging: "Now I've got *three* radios in my room." Babes and I couldn't wait for the meal to end.

Afterwards we were driven to the West Palm Beach airport, where my father was to meet the noted American stunt pilot Roscoe Turner, complete with his fur-lined flying suit and his pet tiger occupying the rear cockpit. I let out a sigh and said, "Well, I'm glad that's over." I then proceeded to give a blow-by-blow description of that torturous hour and a half. But my old man would have none of it. He cut me off, sneering, "You just don't appreciate nice people." And that was that—well, for a while, anyway, as we shall later learn. I should have kept my mouth shut then and there. But I didn't. "Well, next time," I joked, "we'll have lunch with the old lady and you take the daughter." End of conversation—a grunt, then silence.

In the spring of 1940, World War II suddenly escalated with the German invasions of Denmark and Norway on April 9. A month later, on May 10, the Germans invaded the Low Countries and France, and Winston Churchill took over the reins as Prime Minister of Great Britain. There then followed in rapid succession the Dutch and Belgian surrenders and the miraculous British Expeditionary Force escape from Dunkirk.

At BCS we naturally followed these events with avid interest and excitement. For the first time, the schoolmasters, to the best of their ability—they could only repeat what the newspapers and radio were saying, though Crawford Grier was an ex–army major—briefed us in class on the military situation. The war was not to be overemphasized—we still had final exams to write. By the time the school term ended, Italy had declared war and the Germans had entered Paris. The French surrendered shortly afterwards. In Churchill's words, the Battle of Britain was about to begin.

At Ravenscrag in Muskoka, it became a nightly ritual for the family to gather round the radio and listen to the latest British Broadcasting Corporation (BBC) news bulletins from London. On August 17, No. 1 Squadron of the Royal Canadian Air Force was reported in action for the first time. The broadcast was punctuated with the sound of machine-gun fire. I was exuberant, agog with excitement. "Our guys are right in the middle of it!" I shouted. My father simply nodded, offering no comment. I had expected that he would be equally thrilled. But I did sense a certain wistfulness in his expression that perhaps concealed his true emotions: He might be feeling left out of it. Later I realized that he desperately wanted to be where the action was.

He didn't have long to wait. Within the next two weeks he flew to London, ostensibly to report on the progress of the BCATP to the British Air Ministry. What he was really after was an overseas posting, though he knew full well the powers that be in the RCAF hierarchy were not about to arrange one. In terms of seniority, being a temporary officer rather than a permanent forces one, he was at the bottom of the totem pole. Besides, they—and the Prime Minister, as well as the Minister of Defence, James Ralston, and the air minister, Chubby Power—were perfectly content to have him serve as director of recruiting, upon which the success of the BCATP depended to a large extent. But he was used to getting his way and would go to any ends to achieve it.

One of his Great War squadron comrades was Harold Balfour, the British Parliamentary Undersecretary of State for Air and a member of the British Air Mission that had arrived in Ottawa in October 1939 to negotiate the BCATP. My father persuaded Balfour to pull strings to get him an audience with Churchill. Nothing like going over everybody's heads—that never bothered my old man. "On principle, always go to the top" was one of the credos he lived by.

At the time I knew nothing of all this. One evening in early September 1940, as I was listening to the BBC, the radio commentator, after summing up the day's events in the war-torn skies over southern England, reported, "Tonight Air Marshal William Avery Bishop, known the world over as 'Billy' Bishop, has arrived in London."

.   •   •

I returned to Bishop's for what was to be my last year at school. Somewhat to my surprise I found I had been appointed a head boy. This bears some explanation. BCS at that time operated on a principle of teaching obedience to authority and how to exercise that authority and assume responsibility.

After our first year in the upper school, we graduated to the status of neutral, somewhere between being a new boy and becoming a senior. No standing really, no privileges particularly—nobodies, more or less—but at least no one badgered us. The following year (in my case I had to wait two years, having dropped behind because of my sinus illness) we were classified as seniors, a step up which did have its advantages. New boys had to defer to us, as we have already seen—a mild obeisance, addressing us by our surnames.

At the top of the BCS caste ladder were the prefects and head boys. The prefects were responsible for the discipline and general conduct within the student body. They also represented that body to the faculty. The head boys were dormitory lieutenants charged with overseeing the behaviour (out of class and off the playing field) of the dozen or so students occupying the dormitories. A prefect and a head boy occupied a cubicle within the dormitory that also served as a study for the latter. What with some privacy and a fag (new boy) to make my bed, shine my shoes, and carry out a variety of chores, life as a head boy was quite a change from the earlier years—enjoyable living, in fact.

Midway through the first term in 1940, I received special dispensation for a weekend off to visit my family in Ottawa, shortly after my father returned from England, fresh from the Battle of Britain. The experience seemed to have ignited the old warrior in him. We were treated to a first-hand description of what it was like to be on the receiving end of the London Blitz—albeit in style. "That first night when I heard the bombs falling and the ack-ack guns going off, I said to myself, 'This is War!'" Each evening, he told us, he would make his way up to the roof of Claridge's Hotel, where he was staying, for a grandstand look at the nightly bombing. There he had conveniently arranged for chairs, glasses, a bucket of ice, and a bottle of Scotch so that he could entertain guests and watch the "fun" through binoculars.

There, in the West End, people were exposed to danger more from falling shrapnel, as the flak defences shot at German planes, than from German bombs, which were directed mostly at the docks and industrial plants in the East End. Tin hats had to be worn by all people in uniform and by key personnel. One of my father's guests was Hartland Molson of the Montreal brewing family. He was flying Hurricanes out of Northolt aerodrome, northwest of London, with No. 1 RCAF Squadron, which my father had visited officially during his stay in England. After fighting all day, Hartland took the train into town to watch the battle from the ground. After the nightly performance died down, he, my father, and a handful of others repaired to my father's suite, where they drank into the early hours. Hartland had to break off to get back to the field to once more take up arms against the Huns later that day.

Ironically, the morning after my father told us this story, Margie Northwood, his secretary, phoned to say that a dispatch to RCAF HQ reported that Hartland had been shot down. Hit in the leg, he had bailed out, and on alighting, he had been driven to Canterbury Hospital. Because I knew Hartland from our early days in Montreal, where my father had persuaded him to take up flying, this news and my father's return from England brought the war into a new perspective for me. It was really beginning to hit home.

But I had mixed feelings about my visit home. My old man had always been the ruling figure in my life, even more so that weekend than before. This might be explained by the fact that his presence and the experiences he related to us (and to others such as Ian Mackenzie, Gus Edwards, and Paul Rodier) dominated the conversation—in fact, overshadowed the entire weekend. That was okay, it was to be expected. But I resented that he seemed singularly uninterested that I had been made a head boy in his absence and that I was getting along well on the football field as a substitute for the first team. (I omitted the fact that on the parade ground I ranked no higher than lance corporal.) I felt a bit left out. On reflection, I came to accept that my accomplishments didn't quite stack up against the dangers of being in the firing line of an actual war zone. But I was still pretty put out.

My father's description of his luncheon meeting with Churchill that had been arranged by the British Air Ministry had the veil of "military secret" about it. He related how he and the British prime minister were photographed in the garden at 10 Downing Street while dogfights raged overhead. All he would reveal was, "Our conversation was private—not for publication." It was not until many years later, after my father died in 1956, that I learned what actually transpired. I read about it in a book by Arch Whitehouse, a noted writer on World War I aerial warfare, called *The Years of the Sky Kings*. I checked out his report with Ralph Manning, a former RCAF historian and then curator at the Canadian War Museum in Ottawa. From what sources he had seen and could remember, although Whitehouse took poetic licence with the dialogue, Ralph was satisfied that the author had his facts essentially right.

As he had planned, my father requested an overseas posting, some sort of senior active command. As diplomatically as he could, Churchill assured him that what he was doing—recruiting aircrew for the BCATP—was the greatest contribution he could possibly make to the Allied air effort, but that he was welcome to visit the front line from time to time to see the fruits of his efforts.

I am not sure that really satisfied him. My mother every so often dropped hints that he would have much preferred to be overseas where the war was being fought. Meanwhile, I returned to school equipped with a piece of shrapnel from a flak gun shell—one of several souvenirs, including part of an incendiary bomb, that my father had retrieved—to be given to the headmaster with his compliments. Crawford Grier seem genuinely pleased and grateful. He said, "You know, I've still got a few pieces of that in my leg from the First War."

Graduates in uniform began to pay regular visits to the school. One of them was a flying visit—from Hartland Finlay, who was stationed at the Elementary Flying Training School in Windsor Mills, Quebec, about 10 minutes' flying time away. Defying regulations, Hart flew his Fleet Finch at about a hundred feet over the football field, waving to us as he repeated the stunt several times. He was lucky that someone didn't report him, as frequently happened when low-flying planes were seen over civilian areas so close to an airfield.

John Flintoft, a fellow classmate, was dazzled by the performance. He told me later, "I made up my mind then and there that it's the air force for me." After he left school he distinguished himself as a Typhoon pilot who was shot down and evaded capture.

Another RCAF visitor was Jay Ronalds, whose brother Leigh was in my class. Jay was stationed at the Victoriaville, Quebec, Initial Training School (60 miles north of Lennoxville), which was commanded by my Uncle Hank (my mother's brother), then Squadron Leader Henry Burden, DSO, DFC. I had never met Jay before, and neither of us realized that this was to be the start of a long-lasting friendship, as well as a strong business relationship. Before enlisting, Jay had worked for McColl-Frontenac (which by this time had been absorbed by the Texas Company in the United States) after leaving school. As he put it to me, "I worked for your father then. Now I'm working for him again." Hart's and Jay's visits were only two of many, and I could not disguise my envy while still being stuck at school.

Over the Christmas–New Year's holidays at the end of that school term (1940–41), I met the girl I would one day marry. Her nickname was Cilla, an abbreviation of Priscilla. The daughter of a prominent Ottawa lawyer, John Aylen, and his wife, Jean, a leading social organizer, she was everything I had heard about her and then some—a knockout.

It happened at a dance. She was sitting on the floor surrounded by admirers, wearing a lime-coloured evening gown that complemented her soft olive complexion. Her long, dark hair and brown eyes accentuated her Grecian features. And she had a beckoning, gleeful smile that lit up her face. She was the belle of the ball and I wasn't going to pass up the opportunity of pursuing her. I asked her for a dance, during which I persuaded her to go out with me the very next evening. She consented—"Provided you don't get drunk." Now wherever did she get that idea? She need not have worried. We celebrated our first date at the Château Laurier Grill. Under Ontario liquor laws, only beer and wine could be served, so I stayed sober.

For the rest of that holiday from school, to use the banal bromide of the day, we "went steady." One afternoon Cilla treated me to a swim in the indoor swimming pool at the Château. There were just the two of us, but afterwards we joined some others in the hotel cafeteria. "How did it go?" someone asked. "He's got skinny legs," Cilla replied. I said nothing; I was dazzled by visions of that pretty little bathing beauty, a potential pin-up girl. Small wonder the famous photographer Yousuf Karsh, for whom she modelled occasionally, called her his "outdoors girl."

As Cilla recalls, "I really don't remember much about all this except my dress. It was chartreuse chiffon, very sophisticated for a 15-year-old, and I wore it for years.

"But I want to get one thing straight. I was none of those things like 'belle of the ball,' and especially about being a Karsh model—Arthur always did like to exaggerate. My parents were friends of Karsh and my brother and I were regularly taken to his studio to have our pictures taken."

When I returned to school in January 1941, I found that I had been elected captain of the Tyros hockey team. To the uninitiated, this might seem like coming close to qualifying for the Hall of Fame. In truth, the team was made up of players who could barely skate, let alone shoot the puck. These were guys none of the other teams wanted, not even the Midget B class for which I finally qualified at the end of the season—soon enough to play three games.

I may have been only a lance corporal in the Cadet Corps, but all the same I was picked for the Special Squad, an exhibition team specializing in arms drill. At whistled signals from the leader we went through a series of drills—slope arms, present arms, and so forth. In March our squad entrained for Montreal to take part in a cadet rally. Held at an indoor arena on the northeastern slope of Mount Royal, the rally began with a march past. And who should be taking the salute, much to my surprise—and his own—but Bishop senior? Knowing that I was going to be participating, he had planned to attend purely as a spectator. But when he arrived, the senior army officer who was scheduled to officiate, ackowledging my father's higher rank, paid him the courtesy of asking him to take the salute instead. He looked very imposing in the air force blue with his impressive row of ribbons below his wings: the VC, DSO and bar, MC, DFC, Croix de guerre, Légion d'honneur.

Alas, our carefully rehearsed drill performance was a near disaster. When the crowd near the boards—mostly youngsters—caught on to our whistle-signalling system, they began confusing us by whistling themselves. Those nearest our signaller were able to keep to the routine, but the rest of us had to make out as best we could by trying to stick to our program. I thought the Sidge—our drill instructor—would throw a fit.

My final term at school, April, May, and June—I labelled "going Hollywood." In April 1941, my father and his aide, Paul Rodier, flew to Hollywood to discuss details of the forthcoming movie production *Captains of the Clouds* (a title taken from one of my father's speeches) with Jack Warner of Warner Brothers and Hal Wallis, the producer. The purpose of the film, the brainchild of the RCAF director of public relations, Joe Clark, was to dramatize the BCATP and sell the giant air-training plan to the Canadian public. The story was about a group of bush pilots joining the RCAF. My father combined the trip with a tour of the aircraft factories in the area that were turning out bombers for the RAF, the Douglas plant in Los Angeles and the Consolidated plants in Burbank and San Diego.

Shortly afterwards I was inundated with autographed pictures of movie stars from the Hollywood studios, which my father had arranged for while he was there. All very personal and sincere: "I'll be coming round the mountain Arthur—Kay Kayser" (the band leader). "To Arthur, a great guy, from his friend Jack Oakie" (the comedian). "All the best to you Arthur—Gene Tierney" (the glamour queen). Some were duplicates—in different handwriting! I tacked these Tinseltown handouts to the wall of my cubicle, which quickly became a Hollywood gallery visited by students and faculty alike.

A little later, to support the Canadian Air Cadet League campaign for funds, my father participated in a Celebrity Tour starring leading actors and actresses of the day—Anna Neagle, Herbert Marshall, Dennis King, Helena "Pixie" Picard, and others. One night the janitor came into the dormitory to announce that I had a phone call from Ottawa. I put on my dressing gown and hurried down to the pay phone located near the centre stairs. The call was from no less than Madeleine Carroll, the gorgeous blonde English star of the popular spy film *The Thirty-Nine Steps* no less—she was staying at our house.

One final scenario is worthy of honourable mention before closing this chapter. The head boy of the dormitory across the hall from mine was Joe Nixon. He and I prided ourselves that year on beginning to grow the makings of moustaches. But we were the only ones who knew it. The upper lip hairs were few and pretty light, only visible if you looked closely in the mirror, and even then you practically needed a magnifying glass. That simply wouldn't do, so we bought a vial of hair colouring from Norm Loach, the local pharmacist in Lennoxville, who assured us it would do the trick. If we followed the instructions on the label, we'd have real macho moustaches by morning.

So that evening we gave ourselves a treatment by daubing on the transparent liquid. Nothing happened. We went back to studying for half an hour. Still no result. This called for another treatment, even though the instructions specified a single application. Another half an hour. We peered anxiously into the mirror. No change. Another treatment then. Thirty minutes later, not an inkling. A couple more treatments and we were out of liquid. We went to bed hoping for the best—we were in the hands of the gods.

I woke up anxious to see our handiwork, and with a very sore upper lip. I looked in the mirror. My lip was bright red and swollen—terribly swollen—making it impossible to brush my teeth and hard to eat breakfast. Joe, who had a fair complexion, looked even worse. To everyone's delight except our own, we were compelled to live with looking like that the final two weeks of the term while we took our matriculation exams.

Chapter 3

"He Has Enough of the Devil in Him"

The Summer of 1941

On June 13, a week before the Germans invaded Russia, I celebrated my eighteenth birthday. While the world did not "hold its breath" as Hitler had predicted, in the case of that latter notable event, all that now stood between my self-appointed role as a potential scourge of the Luftwaffe were favourable final exam results. To qualify for air-crew training in the Royal Canadian Air Force, in addition to meeting the physical requirements, I needed my junior matriculation standing. Meanwhile, my parents decided that in the interim a little hard work wouldn't do me any harm—a change from my customary summer routine of loafing about in Muskoka, dating the girls at the Windermere House Hotel and the Rostrevor Lodge, and swimming and fitting in a game of golf or tennis here and there.

Ian Mackenzie convinced my parents that a stint out west would be just the ticket (he was Member of Parliament for Vancouver West). He duly arranged through his friend Colonel Victor Spencer of Spencer's Department Stores (Vic Junior was a friend of mine) that I would spend July at the family ranch at Lytton, B.C., 100 miles up the Fraser River east and north of Vancouver.

So, at the end of June I hopped a plane, leaving my family with visions of me cowpunching from dawn to dusk and getting "tough-ened up," to use Defence Minister Mackenzie's words. If they'd only known . . .

I was met at the airport by Vic's lovely sisters, Barbara and Diana, and that evening we drove up to Lytton. It was dark by the time we reached the town, which is on the east side of the Fraser. There was only one way across the river and that was over the tracks on the railway trestle, a rather jolting ride accentuated by hope that the train was keeping to its schedule.

Life at the Spencer ranch, as I quickly found out, was hardly roughing it the way my family might have hoped. The main house was spacious and comfortable and the meals were out of this world. Staying in one of the guest houses, which I had to myself, was like being at home. Indeed, the Spencers—the Colonel and his wife, daughters Barbara and Diana, and sons Vic (who spent that sum-mer working as a hand around the ranch) and John—treated me like one of the family.

This was cowpoking? Not bloody likely. True, I did spend time in the saddle—quite some time, as a matter of fact—and got to love horses. But it wasn't riding herd or roping steers. In fact the livestock were located at Clinton—70 miles further north—where I witnessed for the first time animals being branded. I was simply enjoying myself, having fun trotting and galloping about the property.

A lot of the time I spent lounging around the swimming pool with the others. I was also able to practise driving in the ranch pickup truck. This was a luxury denied me at home, where I was not allowed to use the family car—or any car, for that matter. This was the direct result of an incident the previous summer when one of our guests at Ravenscrag let me drive his car. In full view of my old man I failed to engage the clutch properly and hit a tree. Fortunately no damage resulted. However, from then on, my opportunities to learn to drive were severely restricted. There was an irony in this: When I was 12 years old, the old man had encouraged me to take flying lessons, but now I was 18 he wouldn't let me drive a car.

At the end of July I left Lytton after a thoroughly enjoyable stay with a wonderful family. It was a visit I have never forgotten, even though it never lived up to my family's expectation of a hard-working son's earning his spurs. Not to worry—I never revealed the hard truth, veiling it with embellished accounts of my ranching prowess, such as how I much preferred the Western saddle and descriptions—as gory as I could make them—of branding the steers: "all that hissing, with the smell of burnt animal flesh." Real cowboy talk.

When I arrived at Ravenscrag, my father, never lacking in show-manship, had turned our place into a designated RCAF seaplane base. The blue ensign was flown from sun-up to sundown from the flagpole on the point facing west across the lake. When my father was in residence, his air marshal's pennant was flown above it. For-tunately he was not at "the Point" on my return from out west. There was a little matter that needed to be cleared up and I hoped he wouldn't be around when the subject arose.

When I broached with my mother the subject of my school matriculation exam results, she let me down graciously by simply shaking her head. There was no need for discussion; I would have to take the year over again. When my father arrived by air force Grumman a week later—with guests film star Anna Neagle, her husband, British director Herbert Wilcox, and Pixie Picard, all part of the Celebrity Tour entourage—I had expected a dressing down, but he never even brought up the matter.

Anna Neagle seemed to project a regal aura around her. Perhaps I fell under the charismatic spell of her award-winning role as Queen Victoria, but I don't think so. Off-screen or offstage, Eng-land's leading screen star was every inch a lovely, diminutive, warm and affectionate grande dame. And she was fun. In the evenings at the cottage, to the accompaniment of my mother's piano, she would lead us in the popular songs of the time, includ-ing the patriotic war ballad "There'll Always Be an England."

She gave us pointers on how to pose for pictures, too. When the publicity news photographers arrived to take shots of my mother and father with Anna and Herbert, Anna advised, "Always point at something. It adds interest to the picture."

We had another lesson in picture posing that summer, this time from the movies. Forty miles from North Bay, at Four Mile Bay on Trout Lake, the bush pilot episodes for *Captains of the Clouds* were being shot. *En famille*, the Bishops flew by Grumman to the location, where we met all the stars—Jimmy Cagney, Alan Hale, Dennis Morgan (who proudly showed off a five-pound bass he'd just caught), George Tobias, and Brenda Marshall, as well as the director, Michael Curtiz. In our finest hour we were photographed with all of them and the members of the film crew.

During our visit we watched the shooting of a scene in which Cagney, the feisty central figure in the role of a bush pilot, tries to convince a potential passenger that he would be safer flying with him than a rival pilot because he provided a parachute; he then proceeds to show the passenger how it works. The scene took most of the morning to shoot because either Cagney fluffed his lines or Curtiz was unhappy with the take. When it was over I asked Cagney how long the repetition of his lines continued to haunt him. "Fortunately," he replied, "you forget them right away."

While that had been going on, my father and Alan Hale, a big, blustery, friendly fellow with a ready smile, had been enjoying a few snorts of whiskey in one of the cabins set up on the lot. My father must have told him about my western junket (I guess he must have swallowed my exaggerated reports of my ranching experiences), because the actor asked me, "Well, cowboy, how did you enjoy it?"

Two days later, on August 14, 1941, when I was enjoying a breakfast of bacon and eggs on the verandah of Ravenscrag, my immediate future was about to change. So was history. Fourteen hundred miles to the east, at Placentia Bay, off the Grand Banks of Newfoundland, Winston Churchill and Franklin D. Roosevelt were jointly issuing the Atlantic Charter, an unprecedented manifesto of intent between a technically neutral and a belligerent nation. It laid down both policy to be followed through war and political strategies to establish world peace.

Simultaneously my father handed me a document that, though hardly in the same Homeric proportions, was to determine the course of my life for the next four years. The RCAF had just issued a new recruiting policy that lowered the aircrew enlistment standards. To my relief and exultation, the education qualifications had been relaxed to "junior matriculation or the equivalent." *Equivalent.* That left enough leeway to meet the requirements, even with my poor grades.

In his character reference (two were required), Crawford Grier, my headmaster, testified, "He has achieved partial matriculation," adding, "He has enough of the devil in him to make a good fighter pilot." My other sponsor, Air Commodore Gus Edwards, wrote generously, "Mr. Arthur Bishop is well and favourably known to me. He is of good family, and I recommend him in the strongest terms as a conscientious and loyal youth with a high sense of duty."

On September 8, I walked into the RCAF recruiting station at the corner of O'Connor and Metcalfe Streets in Ottawa, where I was interviewed. I filled out the necessary forms, passed my medical exams, and was duly sworn in and handed a large brown envelope containing all my records. The recruiting officer shook my hand and said, "You're in the air force now." It was a proud moment, and one that Cilla remembers well: "I remember this vividly. His picture appeared next day in the *Ottawa Journal* showing him in front of the oil painting of his father in their house. I was very impressed that someone I knew was featured on the front page and I carefully cut it out and pasted it in my photo album."

Two days later I boarded the night train for Toronto to report to No. 1 Manning Depot, the air force induction and processing centre in the Coliseum building, located on the grounds of the Canadian National Exhibition.

Chapter 4

R125798

September 1941– January 1942

> . . . the kid was born into a military royal
> family. If he joined up . . . would he ever
> be treated as an ordinary mortal?
> —Robert Collins, *You Had to Be There*

On the morning of September 10, 1941, as I stepped off the train onto the platform at Union Station, I was greeted by an inhospitable-looking little character in the air force blue uniform. Staring belligerently at the brown envelope tucked under my arm, he snarled, "Recruit?" I nodded. "Follow me," he barked, not a whit friendlier. Without more ado I followed him outside the station, where a small white van with air force markings was parked. Pointing to the back seats he ordered, "Get in!" After I had complied, this nasty little fellow climbed into the driver's seat and we were off along Front Street to the CNE. En route, hoping to break the ice, I dared to venture, "What's the drill?" All I got was a half-growled "You'll be CB'd for the next 48 hours when you get your TABT shot. And boy, will that ever make you sick. You'll wish you were dead."* Welcome to the RCAF!

When we pulled up in front of the Coliseum building, my guide turned to me and announced unceremoniously, "Here we are." I got out and he drove off without even a wave; fortunately I never saw the miserable little son of a bitch ever again.

* CB'd—"Confined to Barracks."
TABT—tetanus–anti-bacteria–typhoid injection.

Once inside the Coliseum, the treatment differed perceptibly. When I handed over my documents, I was given a number— R125798—and the rank of a bona fide aircraftsman second class, or AC2 ("acey-deucy"), the lowest of the low; assigned a bunk (the lower of a double-decker); and ushered into one of the box seats bordering the bull ring, where the drills took place and at the end of which was a boxing ring. (The Ex had been closed for only a week and the place still reeked of horses and steers and their attendant manure.) I was told to go and have breakfast, then return to the box and await orders. Those orders were very simple: "Go and get a haircut."

For our first few days, we CB'd newcomers did nothing more than accustom ourselves to the place, along with the other 2000 or more air force recruits. Seated in the boxes, we listened to lectures from various flight sergeants on how to conduct ourselves as air-men. It was customary for the audience to blow up condoms and let them waft about in the air while listening to these orations. In the evening there was entertainment in the theatre—movies and guest appearances by performers such as the Happy Gang. And then there was the canteen—beer only—with the nickelodeon end-lessly playing "Bless 'Em All" to the accompaniment of our own bawdy version, "F— 'Em All."

Finally we were assigned to a flight with a corporal disciplinarian ("Dissip") in charge of drill. We were also issued uniforms and kits with sewing gear, toothbrush, hairbrush, and comb. We were ordered to attach our air force number to everything issued. This was to prevent theft, for which the penalty, we were told, was severe.

To emphasize that point, one evening the entire station was assembled in the bull ring arena. As the commanding officer and his aides made their way into the boxing ring, we all clapped and cheered; some even booed. The CO stepped forward and bellowed into the microphone, "Shut up, or I'll CB this station for three weeks." We then watched as a portly little prisoner with two enor-mous service police on either side was marched into the ring. His hat was taken from him with a flourish, the buttons were cut off his

tunic, and his sentence of two years' hard labour and a dishon-
ourable discharge for stealing was read to him. There was no cheering now, only shocked silence. I still wonder whether this was a
show put on simply to frighten us.

One evening I was summoned to the guardhouse. A reporter
from one of the newspapers wanted to interview me. I was well prepared for this eventuality—I had been forewarned. To avoid embarrassment all round, after the initial publicity announcing my
enlistment (which had recruiting value), the RCAF public relations
department had been ordered to place a moratorium on any further
publicity until—and if—I earned my wings. But this did not stop
the press from chasing stories. I had been instructed to say simply
that I was under strict military orders not to grant interviews or
make statements of any kind.

But this rule was bent somewhat exactly a week after I had
reported to Manning Pool and received my TABT shot (that little
prick of a driver had been right—it was an ordeal like enduring
three cases of flu all at the same time). My father visited the station
and we were photographed together by the *Globe and Mail* on the
front steps of the Coliseum—again for recruiting purposes. I must
have smelled like a stable—the bull ring still reeked of livestock
odors, which permeated our clothes. As the flashbulbs popped, my
old man said, "Son, you stink like shit!" Actually, though, I think he
was feeling quite proud at seeing me in uniform for the first time.

That fleeting publicity had no adverse effects. By this time all
the people in my flight, as well as the Manning Pool non-commis-
sioned officers (NCOs) and officers alike, knew who I was anyway,
and accepted me as any other acey-deucy recruit. Happily I found
everyone most considerate of my position; some even went out of
their way to make me feel comfortable. I in turn made every effort
to keep my nose clean while still joining in the fun. Being Billy
Bishop's son was something I had grown up with, and by that
time in life I prided myself that I was able to handle it, to take it all
in stride.

My Cadet Corps training stood me in good stead. In fact, I had an advantage over most of the recruits who had never experienced parade and rifle drill. Also, because I had played soccer in the prep school at BCS, when a soccer league was formed among the recruit forces in the Toronto area—including the Army, the Navy, and the RAF—I volunteered for the RCAF team. For a week we practised diligently every afternoon until the Saturday when the tournament was held. We won that contest, beating the RAF in the finals ("beating them at their own game," our warrant officer boasted proudly) to the delight of the Manning Pool NCO staff. We were rewarded with 48-hour leave passes and on the following Monday morning parade were formally presented with silver spoon trophies in front of the entire station.

About this time I attended my first pay parade. This was a novel, delightful experience for me. Other than getting paid for caddying occasionally at the Windermere Golf Club in Muskoka, I had never earned money before. Now I proudly collected my $1.30 a day and promptly went out and spent most of it.

At the end of September our period of orientation was over. Our flight was designated for future pilot training. It "went on draft" and was transferred to No. 1 Service Flying Training School at Camp Borden, 50 miles north of Toronto, for a spell of tarmac duty—what the noted author Spencer Dunmore described as "a typical service euphemism for airfield labourer." The students at this station were training on single-engine North American Harvards, their final course before receiving their pilot's wings. Among them was a friend of mine, Bob Hamilton from Toronto, who bore a striking resemblance to movie actor Jimmy Stewart. I would run into Bob occasionally on his way to or from ground school classes.

"The Harvard's a great plane," he told me. "You'll really enjoy it when you get to fly it." That seemed far off in the future for me at the moment. However, I promised that meanwhile, "I'll make sure your aircraft is good and clean." That was one of our tarmac duty chores, washing the bright yellow trainers, thus painted for visibility in order to avoid accidents and make them easy to find in the event of a crash in the wilderness. Other than that, sweeping out the hangar, and cleaning up here and there, our duties were strictly limited; no one wanted us fooling around with aircraft engines. Most of the time we played cards.

On one occasion, however, I drew night duty, assisting the ground crew during night flying training at a satellite field. I was filling in for the crewman who normally helped work the gasoline bowser (tank). On this particular night one of the students badly misjudged his landing and piled into the far end of the field, killing himself—not a pleasant sight. Clearly a case of pilot error. The sergeant in charge of our hangar asked ruefully, "What would have happened when the bullets started flying around?"

Tarmac duty filled in the time pleasantly, but it didn't bring me any closer to my goal of becoming a pilot. However, on November 15, 1941, my aspirations began to materialize when I was posted to No. 5 Initial Training School (ITS) at Belleville, Ontario, on the north shore of Lake Ontario. Belleville is not far from Trenton, where I had received my initiation into the RCAF three years earlier, together with Alf Dobell, who by this time was serving with the Royal Navy.

"Dirty Dave" Harding—who had flown my father and me to Ottawa three years earlier when my old man was promoted to air marshal—was the CO. The ex–football star placed heavy emphasis on physical training. Our barrack block and training centre were located in a school for the deaf and blind. Harding had a prefabricated gymnasium built and ordered all kinds of sports equipment, including a quantity of skis, though where we were supposed to ski in that flat part of the province was hard to fathom (we never did).

The training curriculum consisted of classes in navigation, meteorology, administration, aircraft recognition, airmanship, and flight theory, as well as algebra and trigonometry. In addition we were given basic Link Trainer (simulator) training and suffered through medical, air compression, and intelligence tests, although the last were somewhat cursory.

Our course was divided alphabetically into two flights, A and B. I was, of course, in A flight and, being B for Bishop, was appointed the class senior. My duty was to march our flight to and from classes. I thought there might be some sort of resentment over this, but my flight mates accepted it cheerfully and in good spirit. Not always the instructors, though. I remember marching the group from meteorology class on the ground floor to the navigation class on the top floor, only to be severely reprimanded by Flying Officer Tremblay, the navigation instructor, who pointed to his wristwatch and admonished, "Two minutes late, Bishop."

At the end of the first week of December we were given 48-hour weekend leave passes. I hitchhiked a ride to Ottawa, arriving at the house at dinner time, just in time to accompany my parents to the May Court Ball at the Château Laurier Hotel. Looking as gorgeous as ever, Cilla played a leading role as a chorine in the chorus of the floor show.

When we returned to ITS early Monday morning, we learned that the Japanese had attacked Pearl Harbor, bringing the United States into the war. The Americans in our class had joined the RCAF through the auspices of the Clayton Knight Committee, which my father had inaugurated. Overnight it had now become an unnecessary entity. They viewed this turn of events with mixed feelings. They had come to Canada to get into the fight. Now their own country was at war, leaving them with a sense of divided loyalties and obligations. At the moment, transfer to the U.S. Air Services was logistically out of the question. Later, many graduates of the BCATP did transfer to the U.S. Army Air Force, which also absorbed the RAF Eagle squadrons. But many of our adopted Yanks stayed to fly with RCAF bomber and fighter squadrons. In fact, when I finally graduated as a pilot, nine Americans in our course also received their wings.

•   •   •

I spent Christmas leave in Toronto with the rest of the family at my grandparents' house. When the furlough was up, I got thoroughly plastered at the Royal York Hotel before boarding the night train to Belleville. I flaked out the moment I took my seat. I had taken on such a load that some of the others had to shake me awake when we arrived at the other end.

I was in pretty ragged shape by the time we reached ITS. After a quick breakfast I was given my first Link Trainer test. It was a disaster—I had such a hangover I registered a big zero; I doubt if I could have navigated a kiddy tricycle. Luckily the instructor took pity on me. After I finished he said, "When you've recovered from your holiday bender, we'll try again." Next day, I passed muster.

We also had to endure a decompression test. The decompression chamber tested your reaction to lack of oxygen. Five of us were put through the exercise under the supervision of a medical officer (MO). We put on oxygen masks adjusted for 30,000 feet and the MO decompressed the chamber to the equivalent of that altitude. He then tested each of us individually. He removed the mask, briefly studied the man's reaction to being cut off from his oxygen supply, then hastily put the mask back on. The guy beside me simply passed out. The fellow across from me started to giggle before losing consciousness. I tried to beat the system by flailing my fists, banging them against my chest. What all this proved I still have no idea, except perhaps that you couldn't last long without oxygen at high altitude.

Academically I enjoyed the program immensely. For the most part I found it interesting and challenging. I had two soft spots—algebra and trigonometry—the former my nemesis and one of my main downfalls at school, and the latter a complete stranger to me. However, at ITS both subjects were studied at a pretty basic level, and with a little studying I managed to scrape through in both subjects.

In mid-January 1942 I was given a posting to Elementary Flying Training School to begin pilot instruction and was promoted to leading aircraftsman (LAC), with a raise in pay to $1.50 a day. I sewed the propeller badges denoting my new rank on the upper sleeves of my tunic during the train ride to Ottawa. I was beginning two weeks' leave, and I felt on top of the world.

Yet at this juncture I realized that I had reached a crossroads. I still had to prove that I had it in me to earn my wings and a commission as an officer. My father took a wait-and-see attitude. My mother, whom I accompanied to Palm Beach for the hiatus, was noncommittal. We stopped at New York for a cocktail party at the Park Avenue penthouse of Homer Smith who, with the demise of the Clayton Knight Committee, had wangled some sort of liaison job between the RCAF and the U.S. Army Air Corps. One of the guests was Hartland Molson, who had been wounded in the Battle of Britain but appeared none the worse for the experience. Casually standing there with one hand in his pocket, the other firmly clasping a martini, he was the embodiment of everything I aspired to—a true air-combat hero, fresh from battle.

From New York we flew to Palm Beach, a trip which in those days involved many stops along the way, all of which I slept through until we reached Jacksonville, Florida. There I got off the plane to stretch my legs. Wandering into the bar, I was mistaken for an RAF pilot by several U.S. soldiers, who greeted me as if I'd won the Battle of Britain single-handedly.

On display at Palm Beach was a German Messerschmitt 109 fighter that had been shot down over England. It attracted the many USAAC pilots in the vicinity, as well as RAF students from an elementary flying training school run by the Americans nearby. I used to join them in the evening in the posh Alibi bar and restaurant on Worth Avenue; we made friends with the cigarette girl, who lined us up with dates among the female patrons. One particular evening she pointed out a dark-haired girl sitting with some friends and suggested that I might approach her. "Do you know her?" I asked. "No," she replied, but she did know who she was— the heiress Gloria Vanderbilt.

Chapter 5

Fledgling

St. Eugene, Ontario, February–March 1942

> St. Eugene, I must say, doesn't sound like
> a very inspiring place. Where the hell is it,
> anyway?
> —Cilla, in a letter

St. Eugene was a crossroads farming community on the Ontario–Quebec border, between Montreal and Ottawa. No. 13 EFTS was typical of the elementary flying training school system of the BCATP. An outgrowth of the Canadian Flying Clubs Association and developed in the 1920s by the civilian aviation branch of the Department of National Defence, the system was operated by civilians under RCAF administration.

The instructors—both flying and ground school—were all civilians. Well, sort of. They were actually RCAF-trained instructors transferred from the air force to civilian status, who wore their own distinctive dark blue uniform and peaked cap. My mentor was Bill Tovell—*Mister* Tovell. However, the CO and Chief Supervisory Officer—Flight Lieutenant Joe Michaud—and the checking (testing) instructors were RCAF officers, and the disciplinarian was an RCAF flight sergeant.

Stuck out there in the boondocks, the station did have certain advantages. The food was prepared and served up as it would be in a hunting lodge. At Brownsburg, a town in Quebec to the north, across the Ottawa River, there was a munitions plant staffed by female war workers—and there were plenty to go around. And we were only an hour away from both Ottawa and the bright lights of Montreal.

At St. Eugene we trained on the Fleet Finch II. With a wingspan of nearly 30 feet, it could stay airborne for two and three-quarters hours and had a top speed of 104 miles an hour. The pupil sat in the front cockpit, the instructor in the back. They communicated through Gosport voice tubes that transmitted messages via earphones in the flying helmets. The most important factor in this communication—in the interests of safety and to avoid confusion—was to firmly establish who was in command of the plane. When the instructor turned over the controls to the student he would announce firmly, "You have control," which the pupil confirmed by replying, "I have control." When the instructor took over from the student this vocal transaction was reversed.

I made my first flight on February 3, 1942. After a week of dual instruction in "circuits and bumps" (takeoffs and landings), during which I logged exactly seven hours of dual flying time, I made my first solo. Though I'd practised countless takeoffs under the tutelage and watchful eyes of Bill Tovell, I remember my first solo effort as if it were yesterday; I felt as though I'd been given gossamer wings. Landing was a lot easier because it was wintertime and the field was covered with packed snow. Skidding on this smooth surface allowed for a margin of error, the wheels did not grip as they would on firm terrain or a concrete runway.

The next phase of pilot training was learning to master manoeuvres—putting the aircraft into a spin and recovering from it, making a slow roll, looping and rolling off the top. All these were executed at a safe height of 5000 feet. Over the next two weeks, under Tovell's supervision I practised these exercises in preparation for the 20-hour check, which pretty well decided whether you were going to continue with pilot training or be washed out.

To put the plane into a spin, you pulled back on the control column to lift the nose, closed the throttle on the left-hand side of the cockpit by drawing it back, which stalled the aircraft, then kicked the left or right rudder pedal, depending on which direction you wanted the aircraft to spin. Gradually the nose would fall forward and the aircraft would begin to twirl around as the ground began to spin before your eyes. Now, to recover. You reversed the controls, pushing the stick forward and kicking the rudder pedal in the opposite direction. Slowly the aircraft would begin to pull out of the dive as you eased the throttle back on.

Next, the loop—the easiest and most straightforward of all the aerobatics. You simply put the aircraft into a dive to pick up speed, pulled up and back until the aircraft was upside down, perpendicular to the ground, then pulled into another dive and levelled out.

The slow roll and the roll off the top were the most exacting of all the manoeuvres, calling for the highest precision. To execute a proper slow roll you had to concentrate on maintaining height. Say you wanted to roll to the left: You pulled the control column over in that direction and then, as the aircraft began to roll, you applied right rudder, using the right pedal. When the aircraft was upside down you pushed the stick forward so the nose wouldn't drop; then as you rolled out, you again applied left rudder, this time using the left pedal. Throughout you had to keep a steady hand on the throttle. The roll off the top was a combination loop and slow roll. At the top of the loop you rolled the aircraft out to a straight and level position, right side up. Again, the trick was to maintain height, keeping the nose up or down.

On February 26, 1942, the CO, Joe Michaud, gave me my 20-hour check, which I somehow scraped through, although my slow rolls and rolls off the top left a lot to be desired. At least I was given the green light to continue my pilot training. However, a week later Michaud called me into his office. He told me that my flying was satisfactory, but that I needed to pay more attention to the ground school training. I sensed where this was coming from, and my guess was right. As I learned from one of the ground instructors over many beers one night in the canteen, my father had been making inquiries. Because of my poor academic record at school, he wasn't allowing any chance of my flunking out in the service. It was only one of many times that he would be looking over my shoulder.

The next learning procedure in the air was known simply as INSTRUMENTS (according to my log book entry)—flying blind under a hood that covered the cockpit so that you had to rely on the various dials on the panel in front of you. The instructor in the back cockpit made sure you corrected any mistakes. The golden rule was never to trust your instincts in bad weather or in the dark, but always to rely on your instruments. Altogether I spent just over five hours under the hood. I also completed three hours of dual night flying.

This training was supplemented with Link Trainer practice. The Link was a simulator that enclosed you completely so that inside it was absolutely dark. The instruments were phosphorus-lit and the controls and pedals were as sensitive as those in an aircraft. You went through a series of exercises under the supervision of an instructor, who monitored your progress on a chart that registered your movements. We practised taking off, climbing, diving, turning, and landing approach. Some of the pupils disliked it intensely. I found it challenging and became quite proficient at it. During my stint at St. Eugene I spent 12 hours in the Link and was given a 93 percent rating on graduating, one of the highest marks in our class.

On March 21 I successfully passed my 60-hour test; two days later I also got a pass on the instrument test. In both categories I received an average rating, with the comment from Bill Tovell, "Needs practice on aerobatics." Though it hardly warranted thumbing my nose at my old man, I did manage to comfortably pass the ground school exams.

On March 26 I made my last elementary flight—and very nearly landed in hot water. Because my name began with B, as had been the case at ITS, I was appointed flight senior of A Flight. It was strictly a nominal designation. Other than leading the parade to ground school classes, it entailed no duties whatsoever. Before making that final flip, I had huddled outside the hangar near the chief flying instructor's office with Johnny Kuzak, the other flight senior. We decided to rendezvous over the Seigniory Club at Montebello, north of the Ottawa River in Quebec, some 40 miles east of the capital. This was strictly against regulations for student pilots, but because it was our last flight and we were being posted the next day we thought we could get away with it.

I started to taxi out to take off when I noticed Kuzak climbing out of his aircraft and lugging his parachute back to the hangar. I took off anyway and flew directly to Montebello, where I circled and circled, then did a few slow rolls, but there was no sign of Johnny. When I landed I was summoned into the chief flying instructor's office, where Jim Delaney tore a strip off me. He had overheard the conversation between Johnny and me. Stupidly, we hadn't noticed that the window was open. "Don't try a stunt like that again," the CFI reprimanded, "or you'll never graduate as a pilot."

Next day the tone was friendlier. Bill Tovell flew me to No. 2 Service Flying Training School at Uplands air base, Ottawa, where I would complete my pilot apprenticeship. There he wished me the best of luck. I was certainly going to need it.

Chapter 6

Flight Cadet

Uplands Air Base, Ottawa, Ontario—April 16–July 31, 1942

> He has the greatest name in military avia-
> tion to live up to.
>
> —*The Gazette*, Montreal

Uplands was the showcase of the British Commonwealth Air Training Plan. Originally designated as Ottawa's municipal airport (in which capacity it continued to serve all throughout World War II), in July 1941 it was the venue for a specially staged wings parade ceremony at which my father officiated for the filming of *Captains of the Clouds*. Uplands was a spit-and-polish station commanded by Wing Commander Bill MacBrien. Known as "Iron Bill," he was a graduate of the Royal Military College and the son of General William MacBrien, a former commissioner of the Royal Canadian Mounted Police. Iron Bill was a strict and unforgiving disciplinarian.

When I reported for duty in the spring of 1942, the station was a busy place both on and off the ground, with two Service Flying Training School (SFTS) courses going through at the same time. Our course, No. 53, shared an H-shaped barrack block with the course ahead of us, which was soon to graduate and be replaced by a new one. The washroom area that formed the crossbar of the H separated the two groups. I was assigned to B Flight, which was commanded by Flying Officer Ronnie Gibson. My instructor was F/O Bob Hyndman, a professional artist before enlisting in the

RCAF in 1940, who bore an uncanny resemblance to the movie star Henry Fonda.

My first flight was a familiarization exercise. I flew a Harvard, a powerful machine constructed of metal alloy, and I was terrified. Its tremendous speed—up to 212 miles per hour—awed me. I also wondered whether I could ever get used to the maze of instruments, the brake system, the locking tail wheel, and the variable pitch propeller. The biggest differences from the Fleet Finch were the retractable landing gear and the flaps used to slow landing speed; the elementary trainers, because of their low landing speeds, needed no such air brakes. In the case of the landing gear, when you were coming in to land, a red light glowed until the undercarriage was fully lowered and locked in place; then a green light went on. All this took a lot of getting accustomed to. But under Bob Hyndman's expert and patient guidance, my confidence grew with every outing. I also spent a great deal of time on the ground in the cockpit acclimatizing myself to the instrument panel. After just six hours of dual instruction in the air, I began to feel comfortable and confident. On April 22, 1942, I soloed the Harvard for the first time.

For the next few days I got along fine. Then, on my fourth solo flight in the Harvard, disaster struck—I ground looped. The difference between landing the light 2600-pound Fleet on packed snow and bringing in the 5600-pound Harvard onto a concrete runway was like comparing the docking of a canoe to the *Queen Mary*. Its narrow undercarriage and the fixed tail wheel gave the Harvard a tendency to swing to the left and shear off all or part of the undercart. Fortunately, in my case the damage was minimal. Ground loops were quite common with the Harvard, but they were neither popular nor excusable—they were still a case of pilot error.

Bob Hyndman recalls, "As his instructor I felt responsible for this prang [accident]. I could not only sympathize with him—I could empathize with him. I had ground looped the Harvard myself. Not as a student, but as an instructor!

"Fortunately, he wasn't too discouraged. Young Bish had a lot of determination. He loved to fly and had a special talent for it. I would say he was an above-average pilot."

There was no use brooding over the accident, and because it was a Saturday, that afternoon I went into town and had dinner with my mother, whom I told about the accident. That evening Cilla and I went to the Château Laurier Grill and I told her about it, too. Later, when my father learned about it from my mother, he simply said, rather bravely, "Well, it probably won't be his last."

Cilla recalls, "I remember the accident and feeling sorry for myself that he would probably be punished and kept on the station and wouldn't be available to take me out for some time. I guess that just about sums up my 16-year-old self."

The next day, Ron Gibson, my flight commander, took over the back cockpit and had me practise five consecutive landings. He was satisfied that I had overcome any tendency to repeat the ground loop, but I still had to appear before the chief flying instructor, Squadron Leader Brody Searle. I was expecting the worst, but he seemed quite understanding and lenient. He said, "Some people would prefer to train on twin-engines, Bishop. Are you one of them?" God forbid. "No, sir," I replied, "I'm confident I can master the single engine." (I hoped.) Dismissed.

From then on I worked hard on my flying, and with Bob Hyndman's encouragement and perseverance, on May 5 I passed the 20-hour test with "flying colours." Ground school was a different story, though. Interim tests showed I was falling well below the passing level. Three areas were dragging me down—algebra, trigonometry, and armament. I found all of them difficult, but if I didn't apply myself more diligently and catch up, I would be headed for trouble. I knew that pressure was coming from my old man. He was determined that I should qualify for a pilot officer's commission, if and when I got my pilot's wings. One-third of the class would qualify as officers based on flying ability and ground school marks. The rest would graduate as sergeant pilots.

Fortunately, one of the ground instructors, F/O Harry Duffy, was sympathetic to my cause and volunteered to spend evenings coaching me in my weak subjects. His consideration and willingness to give up his spare time proved to be my salvation. In the final results I ranked in the top third of my class. I had proved that I was capable of learning well enough when things really mattered.

I lived life to the full in those days. In the air I was in an element of my own. When we finished ground school and no longer had to study, we could make as many as three flights a day. When I took a Harvard up, I took great delight in relieving my full bladder at 1000 feet (regulation altitude for flying over Ottawa) through the "pisser" (a tube designed for that purpose)—right over Prime Minister Mackenzie King's house, which was on Laurier Avenue, down the street from our own house. I deemed it a test of accuracy.

Over our own house, I had a special treat for my mother as well. If she was working in the garden, I would fly over and pull the propeller pitch lever back from fine to coarse so that she could enjoy the awful screeching howl it would make. When I asked her if she could hear it, she'd chastise, "Of course I can hear the damn thing. Why don't you take your toy and go and play somewhere else?"

When not on duty we were free to leave the station, provided we returned by lights out (2000 hours, or 8:00 p.m.) during the week and midnight on the weekends. Every other weekend we had a 48-hour pass, which I spent at the house. Ottawa was a pretty exciting and lively place for aircrews in training in those days. There were the Château Laurier Grill and the hotel's tavern (men only), where at times it looked like half the air force was assembled. But the chief hangout, not only for trainees but for instructors as well, was the Standish Hall, in Hull across the river. Unlike Ontario outlets, where in those days only beer and wine were served, in Hull, under the freer Quebec liquor laws, you could buy anything you wanted.

Not far from the Standish Hall, but in sharp contrast, was Madame

Berger's, a restaurant that boasted the finest dining room in Canada's capital city area. I was present there that June when my mother and father hosted Harold Balfour, the British Undersecretary of State for Air, on his official visit to Ottawa while en route to Washington. During the meal he regaled us with an account of his visit to Moscow as a member of Foreign Secretary Anthony Eden's mission to confer with Stalin in mid-December of the previous year. His account was as enlightening as it was fascinating.

Up until the Germans attacked Russia on June 22, 1941, he told us, the Communists couldn't have cared less about anyone except themselves. They shared Poland with the Germans and watched with stony detachment as Europe was overrun and the British failed to set up a Balkan front. "Now they want every bloody thing—supplies and equipment and are demanding a second front—now!"

At the conference table, Lord Balfour recalled, the translator interpreted verbatim the words of the Russian leader, who spoke of himself in the third person: "Stalin waited to see how the Allies would make out. Stalin was playing for time, and when Hitler attacked, Stalin's army was stronger than the Germans expected."

Balfour put that statement into further focus: "The Soviet attitude is that it is up to us to support Russia in every way possible, although they did nothing to help us when our backs were against the wall. They're a tough lot. It's like dealing with a bunch of gangsters."

During this time at Uplands, No. 53 Course suffered its one and only fatality. A student named Wilmore* got lost across the border south of the St. Lawrence River and was killed as he tried to make a forced landing on a field in New York State. I was chosen for the burial party. It had turned extremely warm and practice parades were a real sweat, with the result that we became quite callous

* a pseudonym

about the entire affair. The student next to me, Tom Hyndman, who was a cousin of my instructor Bob, whispered to me, "All I can say is goddamn that bastard Wilmore!" When I started to veer off course during Link Trainer practice, the instructor warned me in a funereal voice, "Remember what happened to Wilmore." I had to agree with Tom.

When school finished that June of 1942, Cilla was spending part of the summer at her friend Joannie Creighton's family summer cottage on Lake McGregor in the Gatineau Hills, so I didn't see much of her toward the end of my SFTS training. Bob Hyndman suggested we beat the place up, meaning carry out a low-level flying display, which was strictly against regulations. We were all set to go when, on the afternoon before our scheduled beat-up, two instructors with pupils in the front cockpits were reported to be low flying in tandem somewhere in the area. Someone had phoned in the numbers of the aircraft, which were clearly visible in black on the yellow Harvard fuselage, and so the culprits were identified. The instructors were severely reprimanded—suspended, grounded, and confined to the station for two weeks. The pupils, whom their instructors swore were under the hoods at the time, practising instruments, were let off. That ended any aspirations to show off up in the Gatineaus.

As the class progressed, among the exercises we practised was formation flying. At least one instructor was always a member of the formation. On one occasion, which those of us involved never forgot, we formed a three-plane echelon to starboard, like the right-hand side of an inverted V. In the lead on the left was "the Hick," all by himself—why I'll never know. How he even got in the air force still mystifies me—he marched as if he were behind a plough. On his right, echeloned back by 30 feet or so, were Bob and myself, and to our right, distanced in the same way, were Ron Gibson and student Willy Cummings, from North Bay, Ontario. The plan, which Gibson had illustrated on the blackboard, was to form up once we got airborne, climb to 2000 feet, level off, circle the field twice to port, then peel off one by one to the left; the Hick first, then Bob and me, and finally Ron and Willy following behind the leader, down and away.

But the Hick got his flying mixed up with his ploughing; he peeled up—into us—instead of flying down and away in the opposite direction. I felt the control column suddenly hit me in the gut as Hyndman yanked back on the stick, just in time to climb over the Hick's Harvard. Gibson barely missed him as well. The Hick beat us to the ground, but not to the door of the pilots' room in the hangar. Hyndman won the race to get to him first, but Gibson did most of the shouting. Spectators at our wings parade a month later were spared the agony of watching the Hick marching and probably turning right instead of left from the lineup. He never did make it to graduation.

With the arrival of a new course, the circuit at Uplands Airport was virtually monopolized by newcomers who were busy practising takeoffs and landings. Some of us were diverted temporarily during the day to a nearby auxiliary field. Unlike Uplands, there were no runways at this field; we flew on and off grass. Nor was there a control tower monitoring student-pilot behaviour. This made it possible to practise getting airborne by simply raising the wheels instead of relying on the wings to lift the aircraft. If you misjudged your timing and the propeller tips scraped the grass and a little soil with it, they would escape damage, which would not have been the case on a concrete runway. I enjoyed this stunt immeasurably until one day, on returning to Uplands, I was greeted by Gibson, who beckoned me outside the pilots' room and steered me over to my aircraft. He pointed to the propeller blades—there was mud on the tips. "I was at the end of the field and saw you," he said calmly but firmly. "Don't do it again. You could end up in a heap."

Then dawned "Black Friday"—June 26, 1942. That morning I successfully completed a triangular cross-country flight to Picton, then on to Calabogie and back to Uplands, a two-hour exercise. As I entered the circuit, I could see that to avoid congestion the takeoff pattern had been altered. The aircraft were taxiing out to the far end of the runway, crossing over to the other side of the field and then up the taxi strip, turning left into the takeoff lane, which faced the control tower. There they waited for the green light from the signaller to take off.

After lunch I signed out for an hour of aerobatic practice in the Harvard and followed the prescribed route up the taxi strip to the takeoff lane. At the end of the strip I waited for the green light from the signaller. If there was an incoming plane, once it had landed, the procedure was to swing out onto the runway and take off fast, before the next arrival.

The light flashed green. I swerved left onto the runway and was at the same time lining myself up for takeoff when I collided with another Harvard, which I had not seen—nor expected to see—on my right. My starboard wing hit the other aircraft's port wing. I kept on going, but it soon became obvious that the Harvard was in no condition to fly. I pulled left off the runway onto the grass, turned right in the direction of our hangar, and waited until it was clear to taxi back in. There was no sign of the other aircraft. Where the hell had he come from, and where the hell had he gone? I soon learned the answer.

When I reached the hangar, Hyndman was standing there waiting for me. When I climbed out, he said, "I suggest you make yourself scarce. That was the CFI you banged into." Brody Searle, taking advantage of his rank, had taxied onto the runway straight from the control tower. He did not need a signal for takeoff. I spent the weekend drowning my sorrows at the Standish Hall, with full knowledge that come Monday I would be up on the carpet, even though—goddamn it!—it wasn't my fault. Searle had been generous last time, when I ground looped, but I knew that I sure as hell couldn't expect any sympathy this time around.

The instructors said nothing, but my classmates were sympathetic—all except one individual, who sneered, "When they realize who it is they'll simply dismiss the whole thing." On Tuesday morning I was summoned to Iron Bill MacBrien's office and stood before the CO, with the CFI on his right. I gave my version of the incident and then Searle gave his, insinuating that the collision had been my fault. What could I say? MacBrien said it instead: "These signallers are not infallible, Bishop. It's up to you to be alert." He then pronounced sentence: CB'd for a week, with one hour's pack drill each evening, and three weeks of washing planes for one hour every evening. (What was I supposed to do with my spare time?) Iron Bill then assured me, "This will not go on your record. Nor will it affect your chances of earning a commission."

That was a consolation. And there was another. When I reported to our flight sergeant in charge of ground crew, he dismissed the incident with a wave of his hand. "Consider it over and done with. It was that son of a bitch's fault anyway, not yours."

My father wired my mother, who was in Muskoka: "My reaction is that punishment instead of acquittal will help him much more with his own classmates and officers." He was right, with a single exception. Every night when I dutifully marched up and down the parade square escorted by a Special Police guard, with 40 pounds of bricks strapped to my back, Willy Cummings and most of the others took note. But not that sneering classmate, who never had the decency to at least admit that he was wrong. I don't think we exchanged a single word after that.

On Sunday, July 12, Iron Bill and his wife, Sue, were luncheon guests at our house. Our meal of grilled lamb chops was served on the verandah overlooking the garden. The meat was hot off the charcoal barbecue, which was quite a novelty for Canada in those days (my parents had adopted it from Palm Beach).

The MacBriens were duly impressed. Somehow the conversation got around to the family. "Well," my father mused, "it has certainly been an interesting summer so far, what with my daughter being asked to leave Elmwood School and my son running into the chief flying instructor." MacBrien gulped with some embarrassment, while my mother and Sue couldn't suppress a chuckle. After the MacBriens left, my father said, "I noticed as he was leaving that Bill had all your records in his pocket and was ready to trot them out. I think he was quite surprised that I hadn't asked to see them."

Ten days later, though, came the moment of truth—the wings test—which I passed quite easily, thanks to the thorough, painstaking flying training I had received from Bob Hyndman. With just over two weeks to go before graduating, we continued to practise our flying—as much as four hours a day.

One afternoon Gibson sent me to clean up the grounds outside the hangar, just around the corner from the pilots' room. I was busying myself when he suddenly appeared. "I just wanted to tell you you're getting your commission," he said. "Keep it to yourself, though. It will all be announced shortly." It didn't take long for the news to officially reach my father. My mother told me that when Iron Bill phoned to tell him that I was getting my commission and was going to be sent overseas as a fighter pilot, "He was so proud he sat down with tears in his eyes."

That Saturday night, with only a week left before our course ended, I ran into Iron Bill in the Château Laurier Grill. "I'll bet you're counting the days," he said kindly. Having had quite a few, I managed to slur, "And the hours, too, sshir."

During that last week of July our time was spent flying, all of it solo—I logged four hours on one day alone—and drilling in preparation for our wings parade, at which my father would be officiating. The officer in charge of the parade told us, "Now, as you march past, don't be intimidated. Just look the old boy straight in the eye," which brought a thunderous roar from the class. Willy Cummings shouted, "That's right, Bish, don't forget to look the old boy straight in the eye!"

On the Wednesday night our course closing-out dinner, attended by the entire class as well as all the instructors and even the CFI, was held in a private dining room in the Château Laurier, followed by a sojourn at the Standish Hall. Brody Searle brought along a tame goose on a leash. As I walked by—staggered might be a truer description—he said to me, "Keep your distance, Bishop. I don't want you damaging one of his wings."

When the big day—July 30, 1942—arrived, so did the rain. But the weather couldn't put a damper on this occasion. Our spirits were at an all-time high. The wings parade was held inside one of the hangars. We marched past and looked the old boy straight in the eye as instructed, then formed a line facing him, ranked from left to right in the order of our class ratings. One by one as our names were called out, we stepped from the line, marched to a point directly opposite my father, then marched forward to have him pin the coveted pilot's wings on the left breast of the tunic, just above the pocket.

When my turn came, I was so nervous I was sweating. The crowd must have sensed it, because there was absolute silence; you could hear that proverbial pin drop. As my father pinned my wings on me, he asked, "Where are we? In Ottawa?"—recalling my waking him from an inebriated sleep four years earlier, after the lunch celebrating his promotion to air marshal. I broke into a grin as I saluted and the crowd broke into applause.

Next day the *Ottawa Journal* described that moment:

The tense silence that overcame the large crowd of airmen and visitors as the air veteran pinned the wings to his flying, chip-off-the-old-block son mirrored the emotion felt by the two. When Arthur received his badge and the customary congratulations and stepped back in the ranks of the graduating class, the spectators burst forth in a thunderous ovation. The smile of the air marshal was the only indication of the pride he felt in seeing his son among the airmen who were soon to take up the fight he once took part in.

Chapter 7

Overseas Posting

August 15–October 1, 1942

> Between us we did our best to try and
> drink the ship dry.
>
> —Bill Olmstead, *Blue Skies*

I was now a pilot officer (P/O), serial number J13101, with an elevation in pay to $6.25 per diem and orders to report to the Y Depot in Halifax, Nova Scotia—the RCAF personnel embarkation assembly point for shipping overseas.

While I was on leave in Ottawa, Flight Lieutenant Ian Ormston was temporarily attached to my father's staff before taking up duties as an operational training unit instructor at Bagotville, Quebec. Ormy was fresh off operations as a flight commander with 401 Squadron RCAF (formerly No. 1 Squadron). He had flown more than 70 sweeps over Europe, had shot down several German planes, and had been awarded the Distinguished Flying Cross. To me he epitomized the fighter pilot of the day. It was a treat to be able to talk to someone near my own vintage who had been in combat. He gave me a graphic idea of what to expect: "The first time, the whole Spitfire trembles." And he offered this advice: "You haven't lived until you've been afraid."

During my entire training I had never discussed combat with my father; in fact, we never even talked about flying. But he showed great interest in Ormy's description of a sweep the squadron had made over Brest, in Brittany, France, in which one of his friends had been chased back across the English Channel by six enemy aircraft. "Six of them!" he emphasized. My father responded by telling us, "Once I got in the middle of 60 of them." Later Ormy said to me, "I'll bet your old man has plenty of stories to tell." I nodded, but in truth he never talked about those adventures until much later in his life. At that time, I simply could not relate his combat experiences to what I guessed lay in store for me. I had not even read his book *Winged Warfare*, in which he wrote at length about air fighting strategy and tactics.

Ormy accompanied Cilla and me on our last date before I left for overseas. The venue was the Standish Hall. Cilla looked particularly stunning in a white dress that did justice to her alluring summer tan. When we dropped Ormy off at Rockcliffe Air Station, where he was billeted, he said to Cilla, "Don't worry. He'll live."

When I reported to Y Depot in Halifax in mid-August, I enjoyed for the first time the comparative luxury of being an officer instead of an airman. I shared a room with one other recent graduate, an observer ("navigator" was a designation of the future), quite a change from a crowded, noisy barracks room. In the officers' mess, which was not unlike a private club, our meals were served by dining-room orderlies, in marked contrast to having to line up with plate in hand to have the food doled out. On the parade square we took our places in front of the ranks instead of among them.

During the two weeks I spent in Halifax waiting to be assigned to a ship, I met many Haligonians through Hartland Molson and his wife, Magda. At the time, Hartland was the CO of 126 Kittyhawk Squadron at Dartmouth, across Halifax harbour.

As the date of our embarkation for the British Isles grew near, we were given a lecture by an escort officer on how to conduct ourselves at sea. Shortly after boarding ship we would be given lifeboat drill. Although as part of a large convoy we would be well protected by naval corvettes and destroyers, there was always the danger of being torpedoed by German U-boats, particularly at night. In that event an alarm would be sounded and we would proceed to the lifeboat station to which we would be assigned. We were told to keep our lifejackets handy as well as our clothes. Most of the merchant vessels were armed against air attack, which was a distinct probability in what was known as the Black Pit, a 600-mile mid-ocean stretch over which, at that stage in the war, there was no air cover. Volunteers, of which there was no shortage among the air gunners with us, might be needed to man some of the guns. A stern warning was given: smoking on deck at night was absolutely forbidden under penalty of court martial. The slightest glow could be seen for miles by an alert submarine crew.

After lunch on September 1, 150 of us, mostly aircrew, marched through the city down to the docks, where we boarded the *Akaroa*, a New Zealand refrigeration ship carrying cargo from New Zealand and Australia picking up passengers in Halifax en route to Great Britain. The *Akaroa* had once been a luxury liner. The anteroom—in which there was a grand piano—the dining room, and the bar were richly panelled. There was a single passenger deck on which we were assigned to individual staterooms, where we were served by a steward who would wake us up with a cup of tea each morning and run a hot bath. The meals were out of this world. We were going to war in luxury and style.

That night we set sail. Some of us went up on deck after dark. The weather was clear and there were ships in every direction as far as the eye could see. This was one of the largest convoys that had crossed the Atlantic up to that time—nearly a hundred vessels of all types and sizes.

At breakfast next morning the subject turned to seasickness. It had been so calm throughout the night that most of us hadn't given it a second thought. But one character at our table kept worrying about it. Bill Olmstead, a former instructor with whom I had become friends, told him that the remedy was to go out and walk around the deck five or six times—backwards! I chimed in that I'd used that as a cure while sailing the Great Lakes, and it had worked. Bill and I could hardly keep straight faces, but our friend swallowed it—hook, line, and scrambled eggs. Sure enough, when we went outside after breakfast, there was this guy stumbling around the deck backwards, trying not to bump into anybody or anything.

As far as we could make out, the *Akaroa* was just astern of the lead ship in the centre column of the convoy. Behind us was a troopship. We knew full well how sharply their lot differed from our own. While we slept under sheets and blankets in our staterooms, those soldiers slept in three shifts of eight hours each in hammocks below decks. During the day we whiled away the time lolling about in deck chairs while those poor devils were crowded shoulder to shoulder above decks as they peered over the railings. One morning we woke up to find that the troopship was no longer there. In its place was a merchantman.

We feared the worst. One of the fortunes of war in convoys at sea was that, while of necessity the convoy moved at the speed of the slowest ship in the formation, if a vessel developed engine trouble or for some other reason was unable to keep up with the rest, the convoy continued on without it. The abandoned ship became a straggler, a sitting duck for Admiral Karl Doenitz's U-boat "wolf packs," which we later learned were shadowing us.

About a week out to sea, I was awakened by vibrations. They didn't last long and no alarm sounded, so I went back to sleep. Next morning others reported the same experience, and we soon learned the reason. Seated on deck after breakfast, we saw corvettes cutting in and out between the ships, executing sharp manoeuvres in a fairly rough sea. The vibration, we surmised, had come from the noise their propellers made when they rose out of the water. Actually, as we learned later, the corvettes had been dropping depth charges to scare off U-boats in the immediate vicinity. It must have done the trick, because there were no more "vibrations."

Several days later it began to get very cold, so when I went outside I put on my raincoat. As I was looking over the railing, I put my hands in my pockets to warm them and I felt an envelope in the right-hand one. I took it out—it was a letter from my mother, a very touching one, that she must have slipped into the pocket before I left. In it she wrote, "I want you to know that you have never been a burden to us and we will miss you. You will be in our thoughts constantly. May God keep you safe. Your loving Mum." It was a good thing I was alone and looking out to sea, because I was moved to tears.

In the evenings we were invited in turns to the captain's cabin for a drink. My turn came after we had been about 12 days at sea. The captain, a short, wiry New Zealand veteran of the seas, poured strong ones. He told us that we had narrowly escaped the wolf packs by detouring around Iceland, and that now we were sailing a more southerly route.

Our first port of call after leaving Canada was Londonderry, in Northern Ireland, where cargo was unloaded and the ship remained berthed overnight. Next morning we sailed down the Irish Sea, reaching our final destination, Bristol, after a 16-day voyage. We'd made it just in time; that evening, for once, was a quiet one—the ship's bar had run dry.

The following afternoon we entrained for Bournemouth. It was a pleasant journey through the rich green English countryside, which seemed untouched and oblivious to the war. I was comfortably seated in a compartment—a feature of British trains—with four others; it took about two hours to reach our destination. Bournemouth, on the south coast of Dorset, had in peacetime been a seaside holiday resort. For the duration it had been commandeered by the air force as a holding unit for BCATP graduates.

We were assigned to single rooms in one of the hotels, which had lost little of its sumptuousness. The accommodations were roomy and most rooms had private baths. We dined that evening in mess style—long tables with benches—but in the luxury of the hotel courtyard, complete with palm trees. The food defied everything we had been taught about wartime rationing in Great Britain. It left nothing to be desired.

After the meal I was summoned to the office of the popular CO,

Air Commodore Geoffrey O'Brian, AFC, a World War I fighter pilot and a friend of my father's. He had two sons flying fighters: Wing Commander Peter, a graduate of the RAF College at Cranwell and the only Canadian to receive that institute's Sword of Honour, and Pilot Officer Jim, who was on his way to the Middle East to join an RCAF Spitfire squadron. Geoff told me that he had just been talking to my father in London to tell him I had finally arrived. There had been some concern because of the length of our time at sea, which was much more than normal for convoys. During my time aboard the *Akaroa*, the old man had flown over to England, ostensibly at the request of Harold Balfour to straighten out problems between the air ministry and the RCAF overseas headquarters. To this day, however, I suspect that he wangled the trip so that he could greet me—that would have been typical of him.

Geoff O'Brian called in the warrant officer who had lauded our soccer efforts against the RAF team at Manning Pool, shortly after I joined up. He seemed genuinely pleased to see me and it was certainly great to see him again. Geoff then said that the WO had arranged for me to take the next train to London, and on arrival I was to hop into a cab to Claridge's Hotel, where my father was staying. I told him I would have to get my things first. Geoff winked at the WO, who said to me, "All taken care of, sir. They're packed and in the van. I'll take you to the station. But we better get going." I saluted Geoff and thanked him. "Give your father my regards," he said with a smile.

I shared a compartment with an RCAF padre and two British Army sergeants. The conversation centred around the Dieppe raid of August 19. This was the first I (or any of my fellow *Akaroa* passengers) had heard of it, although it had occurred before we left Canada. It still baffles me that we had no knowledge of this abortive assault on that coastal resort town of northern France. But I soon learned the grim details: Of the 4963 Canadians who took part, 907 had been killed, 460 wounded, and 1846 taken prisoner, although these figures were not made public at the time.

I reached London just after dark and went straight to Claridge's, where I was greeted by my father and Gus Edwards, now an air marshal and Air Officer Commanding in Chief, RCAF Overseas. A bed had been placed in a corner of the suite's living room for me; this was my home for the next five days. My father was scheduled for an audience with the King the following evening. However, his gold-braided cap had seen better days. It had an "operational look," as we used to say—a bit floppy. Gus told him he certainly couldn't wear it to Buckingham Palace and he'd better go out and buy a new one. But my father was just as determined that he was going to wear it to the palace, and to any other damned place he pleased.

Next morning he walked me through part of London's West End. Evidence of the German Blitz on London a year earlier was everywhere; hardly a block had been left untouched. In one place a Younger's pub stood proudly by itself; the buildings on either side had been levelled by the bombing.

As we marched down Bond Street my father saluted a short individual in a well-worn fedora and addressed him; "Good morning, sir." Sir? I'd never before heard my old man call anyone sir. I asked him who it was that merited such homage. "The king of Greece," he replied. We ended our morning's jaunt at Buck's Club, at the corner of Savile Row and Bond Street, where my father arranged a membership for me. It had been his favourite hangout when we lived in England.

We lunched in the resplendent dining room of Claridge's, where my father always had a corner table reserved for himself and his guests. On this particular occasion, the old man, his ADC, Paul Rodier, Percy Portlock, the resident director of the T. Eaton Company, and I sat looking out at a galaxy of luminaries, including General Jimmy Doolittle, famed for leading an air raid on Tokyo, and movie star Merle Oberon and her director husband, Alexander Korda, to name just a few. There was so much brass in the room—generals, admirals, air marshals—that as a lowly pilot officer I felt like I should be in the kitchen washing dishes rather than eating off them.

After lunch my father introduced me to Air Chief Marshal Sir William Sholto Douglas, AOC, RAF Fighter Command, a formidable-looking man who told me bluntly, "We've pulled a few strings to get you into Fighter Command, young man. Now it's up to you."

"Thank you, sir," was all I could manage to splutter in reply.

That night, while my father had his audience with the King (worn hat and all), I had dinner at the RAF Club on Piccadilly with Paul Rodier and an acquaintance of his, Wing Commander Harold Kerby, former CO of 400 RCAF Army Co-operation Squadron, and at the time attached to RCAF Headquarters staff. Kerby was engaged to a girl on the London stage and she had arranged to bring along two members of the cast from the theatre to join us for dinner. Later we went dancing at the 400 Club, one of many high-class London "bottle clubs," where you bought a bottle and poured your own drinks.

On the walk over from the hotel I was introduced to the Piccadilly commandos, prostitutes who lined the street from which they took their name. In the darkness of the blackout it was hard to see what you were buying. The solution was to take your lighter and ignite it right under the girl's nose. You had to be quick, because as fast as you lit up the commando would try and blow it out. The price was two quid (pounds), the equivalent of ten bucks in those days. At any rate, Kerby had warned me to give them a pass, "unless you want to come down with a dose."

Next morning, on quite a different level of discussion, my father told me about his visit with King George VI. They had talked of the times when Buckingham Palace had been bombed during the Battle of Britain in 1940. My father had told His Majesty that he thought it was a good thing. The King had replied, "Oh, you do, do you?"

My father said, "Yes, sir, I do. I think it showed people that you were sharing their danger."

"Well," the King answered, "perhaps you wouldn't have been so enthusiastic if you'd been here at the time."

That evening my father hosted a cocktail party in the suite. The guests included such notables as American generals Dwight Eisenhower, Ira Eaker, Carl "Tooey" Spaatz, Mark Clark, and Jimmy Doolittle. Also there were Alexander Korda, who had been knighted that afternoon, and Merle Oberon, Air Chief Marshal Sholto Douglas, Bill Stephenson ("the man called Intrepid"), and Leonard Brockington, the first chairman of the CBC and war advisor to Prime Minister Mackenzie King.

Two conversations remain fixed in my mind. The first was one between Doolittle and my uncle, Wing Commander Hank Burden. They had been friends in peacetime. "How does it feel to be a general, Jimmy?" Hank asked. "Terrible. No fun at all, Hank," Doolitle replied. "You can't fall downstairs stinking drunk anymore. If they try to promote you, turn it down."

The other conversation was one I had with Leonard Brockington. He had had tea in the lobby of the hotel that afternoon with a young lady who had been introduced to him as a sculptor. Apparently she was quite well-known for sculpting busts of famous people. "She told me she'd like to do a head of me," Brockington said. "Well," he smirked, "I told her it's like a coin, it has two sides. And *head* wasn't exactly what I had in mind."

The day before I left London, my father had lunch with Winston Churchill at 10 Downing Street. When he arrived, the Prime Minister said to him, "I understand your son has arrived in England with the air force." My father told him that I was staying with him at Claridge's. "Well, why didn't you bring him with you?" Churchill asked. Alas, another opportunity lost.

When I returned to Bournemouth I learned that I had been posted to No. 17 Advanced Flying Unit at Watton, in Norfolk, for a refresher course before going on to the operational training unit (OTU). On the way I stopped in London overnight. Paddy, the little Irish elevator man who always insisted on carrying one's bags himself, no matter how heavy, said to me, "And how long will ye be staying this time, *Master* Bishop?" Next morning I was up bright and early. Having said goodbye to my father, who appeared a little sad at our parting, I boarded the train for Norfolk.

Chapter 8

Advanced Training

Watton, Norfolk—October 1–November 13, 1942

> Flying: Average Plus.
> Navigation: Weak.
> —log book assessment entry

At the beginning of October I came face to face with the enemy for the very first time. When we changed trains at Newmarket, en route to Watton, we marched past hundreds of Italian prisoners of war. They had been captured in Egypt at the end of August, in the two-day Battle of Alam el Halfa, where General Bernard Montgomery's British Eighth Army had blunted the German–Italian advance. After the battle, General Erwin Rommel, the famed "Desert Fox," was invalided home.

They were a sad-looking bunch standing there, shivering in their desert uniforms in the damp, cold British fall. I was struck by how young they looked—some of them couldn't have been more than 14 or 15 years old—and they appeared frightened and bewildered. I felt sorry for them.

Watton was my initial exposure to a permanent force RAF officers' mess. It had all the style, elegance, and comfort of a posh country club. After the Great War, when "the founder of the RAF," Lord Hugh "Boom" Trenchard, won his fight to keep the air force independent, he began establishing the finest of amenities to attract recruits into the service. Soon officers' messes like the one at Watton started cropping up at RAF aerodromes throughout the country.

Basically the messes were of a standard two-storey H design constructed of brick or concrete. Upstairs were the bedrooms, each of which was shared by two officers. On the ground floor in the centre of the building were an anteroom (living room), dining room, and bar. At either end were squash courts. On my arrival I was struck by the ornate entrance—over the doorway was a portico and the walls were ivied.

I soon learned that I was the only Canadian officer in the mess. In fact, there were only two other Canadians on course at Watton, both of them sergeant pilots. Two courses were going through the station at the same time. I was assigned to Course No. 22, D Flight, which included several RAF officers and myself, but mostly RAF sergeant pilots. The other course was made up entirely of Australians who were taking their training in Great Britain, most of whom would be posted to squadrons in the Far East. Meanwhile, they immediately established how much they disliked England and Englishmen, and made no bones about it. "Cut the barrage balloon cables and let the place sink," was their favourite chant, "and all the Limeys with it." At night in the anteroom, when the tannoy (speaker system) on the wall bellowed out "The bar is closing," the Aussies would throw their drinks at it.

It didn't take me long to "put up a black" (make a mistake). After I got settled, that evening I teamed up with an RAF pilot officer, Trevor Evans, to explore the local pubs. By the time we reached the second one we were well lubricated. There were a number of very attractive girls in this establishment and Trev quickly began making time with one of them. I was left standing at the bar when a flight lieutenant got up from the table where he had been sitting with a very pretty girl and walked up and ordered a couple of drinks. He introduced himself as Ronald Kitchen, commander of D Flight—the one to which I had been assigned. I had enough

Dutch courage in me from all the ale I'd consumed to ask, "How about introducing me to your girlfriend?" He led me over to the table where his "lady" was sitting and said, "I'd like you to meet my wife." I bowed, shook hands—and left as soon as I could.

The following morning, badly hungover, I was making my way toward the hangar to report for duty, when Kitchen collared me and said, "I take a dim view of your asking to meet my girlfriend, Bishop." I apologized for the *faux pas* and he accepted, but he didn't entirely let me off the hook. From then on, whenever I encountered the Kitchens socially, he would jokingly chastise me with "This is the fellow who wanted to meet my girlfriend." He was a good type, though, and before the course was over we became close friends.

That morning he introduced me to my instructor, John Mara, a flight sergeant who had just completed a tour of operations on Spitfires. The first lesson was to familiarize myself with the Master, the single-engine twin-cockpit aircraft in which I would for the next two months train as a transition to the Spitfire. It was slightly larger and faster than the Harvard, but any resemblance ended there. The British instruments were different from the American ones on the Harvard. The cockpit was far more spacious, the visibility greater. One feature that could be turned on and off was the IFF—the Identification Friend or Foe. This was a critical device; if you did not have it turned on, particularly while flying over coastal areas, you would be picked up on the radar screens and identified as a bogie (enemy), in which case fighter stations in the immediate area and anti-aircraft batteries would be alerted to treat you as hostile. In the event that you drew fire, you could switch on the IFF, fire off a green Very light (flare), or do both, but it might be too late. On landing, if you failed to turn it off the battery would run down, earning you a fine of two shillings and sixpence (a buck and a half).

I had no problem adjusting to the Master; after only three hours of dual on October 6, 1942, I soloed. Watton had a grass field instead of a paved runway, and the Master had a much wider undercarriage spread than the Harvard, so I became quite proud of the smooth landings I was able to execute. Even night landings were a treat. In fact, my landings drew praise even from Kitchen, who complimented me, "Piece of cake, eh, Bishop?"

There was a marked difference in flying over England—a war zone—from what we had grown accustomed to at home. All of the aerodromes were camouflaged, although those with runways were easily identified. The nearest metropolis to Watton was Norwich, 20 miles slightly to the northeast. We were under orders to avoid the cities, which in any case had balloon barrages, particularly in poor (duff) weather, and there was plenty of that.

During the third week I was at Watton I got lost. I had been practising aerobatics and, coming out of a roll off the top, I found myself in cloud. I quickly dropped out of it but immediately became thoroughly disoriented. I guessed that I was about 20 miles southwest of the field, but none of the landmarks—roads, train tracks, or villages—looked familiar, even though I did my best to locate my position on the map. I started circling, but this didn't help, and I was getting worried because my petrol (fuel) was running low. With what I calculated to be about ten minutes' flying time left, I spotted a field with runways ahead of me. I made a circuit, noting the direction of the windsock, lowered the wheels and flaps, and landed. I taxied over to the control tower, parked the aircraft, and climbed out, to be greeted by an American air force officer. I saluted and he saluted in return, and I explained my predicament. He told me that the field was at Hardwick, and that it had just opened. The Americans were waiting for their Flying Fortresses to arrive from the United States. I checked my map and found that I was a mere 30 miles from Watton.

Because it was noon, the American invited me over to their mess, which was in a Nissen hut, to have lunch. First he sent off a signal to Watton that I had landed safe and sound and that after being refuelled I would be on my way. Before I left he loaded me down with American cigarettes, chocolate bars, and ladies' silk stockings, all of which were in short supply in England and would be welcome barter with the female population of Norwich. As I was loading the plane with all these goodies, two Spitfires landed, turned around, and took off again. This was the first time I had seen a Spitfire. They seemed so small, but tenacious looking, like wasps. I was fascinated by how swift and agile they looked. One of them waggled his wings to join in formation with the leader, as if it were waving at me. I was captivated.

After thanking my host I climbed into the Master, but the engine wouldn't start—the battery had gone dead. A mechanic wheeled over a battery ack and gave me the required boost to get the engine going. I acknowledged my thanks with a wave and was on my way. After I landed at Watton, I reported to Kitchen that the battery had gone dead and that perhaps it should be checked. "That's because you left the IFF on," he harrumphed. "And that'll be two and six."

As October came to a close, the weather took a turn for the worse. It got so bad that the field was flooded. The "met" people (meteorologists) forecast that it would not substantially improve for at least two weeks, so we were all given a fortnight's leave. I took the train to London, where I checked into the Park Lane Hotel on Piccadilly, a favourite hangout for Canadians. It was filled with army types and some from the navy, many of them old friends from BCS days.

On my last night, I had dinner with Percy Portlock, the Eaton's director, and two ladies at the Savoy Hotel. While we were dancing my companion steered me in the direction of Sholto Douglas—who she said was "such a dear"—and his party, who were sitting at a ringside table. I told her I'd met the air chief marshal with my father. "Fine, we'll go over and say hello." We did indeed. "You remember Arthur Bishop, don't you, Sholto?" The A/C/M, who was well into the champagne, gruffly acknowledged, "Of course, of course," without a clue, I'm sure, as to who this pilot officer was or wasn't—and couldn't have cared less.

By the time I returned to Watton in November, the church bells were ringing in celebration of the first Allied victory of the war: the defeat of Rommel's Afrika Korps at El Alamein by Montgomery's British Eighth Army. This was followed by the Allied landings in Morocco and Algeria. The names on the radio and in the newspapers and magazines featured the American leaders who had attended my father's cocktail party at Claridge's, but who at the time had meant nothing to me or, I guess, to anyone else not in the know. General Dwight Eisenhower was in command of forces in North Africa and his deputy was Mark Clark. Heading the U.S. 15th Air Force was Jimmy Doolittle.

The airfield at Watton was still under water, so we moved to a satellite field a few miles to the west, where the officers' mess was in a commandeered mansion. The emphasis was on formation flying. On my second flight after landing, I put the brakes on too suddenly while taxiing back to the dispersal tent with the wind to my back, and tipped the Master onto its nose, damaging the propeller. That brought me up before the chief flying instructor, who asked, "Is your father still in this country?"

"No, sir," I replied, not sure where this was taking me.

"What do you think he would say if he knew about this?"

I couldn't answer what I would like to have said—that he'd pranged a few himself in his day. Instead, I said what I thought my inquisitor would like to hear: "He'd say it was a poor show." Absolute balls, but it satisfied the CFI and I was rewarded with an instant "Dismissed."

I was thoroughly pissed off with the whole bloody performance. Why drag the old man into what after all had amounted to a very minor taxiing accident? Was I going to have to face this sort of bullshit every time something went wrong or whenever I made a mistake? When I reported this conversation to Mara, the instructor fumed. "What the hell has your old man got to do with it? That's way out of line, just goddamn mean." Kitchen agreed with him.

A few days later I said goodbye to Mara and Kitchen. With my course over, I was posted to an Operational Training Unit in Gloucester. There was no leave between courses, as our two-week hiatus had cut the AFU training short. After an overnight stop in London, I took the train to Aston Down.

Chapter 9

The Spitfire

Aston Down, Gloucester—November 29, 1942–January 24, 1943

> This officer tends to get quite drunk on
> small amounts of beer.
> —RAF report requested by my old man

At Aston Down all the flying instructors were combat veterans, many of them fresh from the air battles over Malta. The besieged Mediterranean island was a thorn in the side of the Axis; from it, British submarines and bombers constantly harassed shipping to North Africa. A mere 17 miles long and 9 miles wide, in the summer of 1942 Malta came under relentless assaults from fighter-escorted German and Italian bombers, which were flying out of Sicilian airfields, only 50 miles to the north, in battle formations of a hundred planes or more. While other battlefronts withstood two or three air attacks a day, Malta sustained as many as a dozen. Those who fought in both arenas said the blitz on Malta was an even tougher conflict than the Battle of Britain. The island held on, making possible victory in North Africa, thanks to the dogged resistance of its RAF Spitfire pilot defenders. These were the men who were going to teach us how to fly the Spitfire.

An exciting, fun bunch of guys, they opened up a whole new, wonderful world to me and my fellow trainees. Dual instruction being impossible because the Spitfire had a single cockpit, the initial step was to accustom yourself thoroughly to that confined space. This was accomplished using a cutaway grounded version—what

85

passed for a simulator in its day—so that mistakes would lead to no harm. On the left-hand side there was a small door that hinged outward and down to provide easy access when getting in and out. The cockpit itself was user-friendly—small but not cramped, and everything handy within easy reach. The bucket seat, which had armour-plating underneath and behind, comfortably accommodated the pilot as he sat on his parachute and dinghy pack, which were strapped to his buttocks from around his shoulders. The Sutton safety harness could be locked back for takeoffs and landings and released in flight to allow freedom of movement. The seat could be lowered or raised, to suit one's height. Also, the rudder pedals had three stirrup steps to choose from in order to accommodate the pilot's height and leg length.

The oxygen and air-pressure bottles were located behind the armour-plate at the back of the seat. These were accessible by releasing a locking pin so that the plate could be leaned forward. You fastened the oxygen tube to a tube on your face mask; the air-pressure bottle powered the brakes, guns, and flaps.

You trained yourself to take in the various instrument dials and gauges at a glance and to memorize the correct readings, so that anything out of line would jump out at you. The instrument panel held the air-speed indicator, altimeter, gyrocompass, artificial horizon, fuel supply gauge (upper or lower tank readings were obtained by pressing two buttons), oil temperature and pressure gauges, glycol coolant temperature gauge, and airscrew (propeller) RPM indicator. Then there were the two starter buttons; to "press tits," you would engage them with your index and middle fingers. Above them was the small tab that you flipped down to lower the flaps a full 90 degrees and flipped back up to raise them.

On the left-hand side of the cockpit, a quadrant housed the throttle, pitch, and fuel-mixture control levers. Above them was the radio transmitter (R/T) apparatus, a ratchet lever that you pushed forward to transmit and backward to listen in, through a microphone in your face mask and earphones in your leather flying helmet. The radio itself was stored in a compartment just aft of the cockpit on the port side, its antenna wire running from an aerial right behind the cockpit to the top of the tail section. Below the R/T lever were the elevator and tail trim wheels, and close to them, a map case.

On the right-hand side of the cockpit was a lever for raising and lowering the undercarriage. As a safety measure, a klaxon horn was installed that would go off when the throttle was pulled two-thirds of the way back, if on the landing approach the pilot forgot to lower the wheels or if, after the lever was in the down position, the undercart failed to lock fully into place. Nearby, another lever operated the shutters for the radiator, to control the glycol temperature. On the floor at knee level was a standard compass. At eye level, directly in front of the pilot, was the ring-and-bead reflector gun sight.

The gun and cine-camera buttons and the brake lever were all affixed to the round spade-handle grip of the control column. The cine-camera, located in the port wing, could be operated simultaneously when the guns were fired or separately when they were not.

While the Supermarine designers had taken pains to provide maximum comfort and ease of operation for the pilot, they had also kept his safety very much in mind. Between the fuel tanks, directly in front of the cockpit and the Rolls-Royce Merlin double-banked 1200-horsepower engine, was a firewall. In addition, the windshield was bulletproof—at the suggestion of Air Marshal Hugh "Stuffy" Dowding, the Air Member for Research and Development on the Air Council. When other members of the council initially scoffed at the proposal, Dowding had calmly replied, "If Chicago gangsters can have bulletproof windshields for their cars, I don't see why our pilots can't have them for their fighters." His prescience and insistence saved many a life.

The Spitfire demonstrated two important innovations in fighter aircraft construction and design. The sleek metal finish reduced drag through the use of sunken rivets. The "oleo" pneumatic undercarriage legs combined oil and air to provide a spring-like action that cushioned the impact of a heavy or bumpy landing.

But its most historical and memorable feature was the elliptical wing—the hallmark of the Spitfire—which gave it its classic graceful, bird-like appearance, like no other aircraft ever built. It had not been created, as might popularly be supposed, for aesthetic reasons—far from it. Reginald Mitchell, the Supermarine designer-genius who gave us the Spitfire, is quoted as saying, "I don't give a bugger whether it's an ellipse or not, so long as it covers the guns."* The ellipse configuration was simply the best solution for housing the eight Browning machine guns (and later two 30-millimetre cannons also), as well as the outwardly retracting wheels, while still keeping the wings as thin and strong as possible.

By operational combat standards, the Spitfires on which we trained at Aston Down were "clapped out." They'd seen better days. On the fighter squadrons the early model Mark Is and IIs had long been replaced by the improved Mark Vs. The OTUs took over the discards (at Aston Down we trained on Mark IIs). But those refurbished castoffs, though lacking in the higher power output, increased armament, and a few cockpit refinements that their successors enjoyed, still retained that aerodynamic quality that made the Spitfire the outstanding fighter aircraft of its day. As such, they were ideally suited as introductory trainers.

Viewed from the side on the ground, in silhouette the Spitfire sat at an angle of approximately 35 degrees from the tail to the propeller hub. From the cockpit, which was midway along the 30-foot-long fuselage, the pilot's forward view was obscured by the nose of the aircraft—while taxiing, you had to zigzag. For the same reason, when coming in to land at reduced speed, with the nose cutting off your forward view, it was necessary first to make a curving

---

* Reginald Mitchell, who had an impish sense of humour, also remarked when he learned that his aircraft had been labelled Spitfire—a name that became synonymous with air fighting excellence—"Just the sort of stupid name they would give it."

approach, looking out the port side to properly line up the runway. Prior to making a maiden flight in the Spitfire, we were given two hours' instruction on a Master to practise the curved approach.

On the gloomy, overcast afternoon of November 22, 1942, I flew a Spitfire—No. 9501—for the first time. While I taxied out to the takeoff point, my instructor, Flight Lieutenant Daddo-Langlois ("Daddy Longlegs"), bicycled out to monitor my three takeoffs and landings (for the record as "local experience"). Some people got very nervous on their maiden flight in the Spit, but I was far too busy going through the cockpit check to worry about anything else. I gave the thumbs-up to Daddy and opened the throttle all the way, quickly picking up speed. As the aircraft accelerated the tail came up and I suddenly had an unrestricted forward view. I gently pulled back the control column—and then I was flying.

Now I had plenty to do. First, I transferred the stick to my left hand to pull up the undercarriage with my right, and quickly realized how sensitive the elevators were fore and aft. The nose dropped. I overcorrected by pulling the stick back too far, as if I were riding a bucking bronco. You had to treat the Spit with respect under those circumstances. I closed the hood, put the pitch on fine, signalled through the R/T to Control that I was airborne, and made a gradual climbing turn to the left. When I reached 1000 feet and was on the downwind leg of the circuit, I straightened out parallel to the runway. For Daddy's benefit I waggled the wings. Unlike the elevators, the ailerons gave some resistance.

Now I concentrated on making a landing. I pulled the hood back and began curving in to the left with the runway in clear view. Then I started throttling off and put the flaps and wheels down. By the time I had lined up the runway and cut the throttle altogether, the speed had ebbed to 67 miles an hour—just above stalling—and the nose was blocking my view. I waited and waited—and waited. The Spitfire seemed to float, as if it just didn't want to come down. Then I felt the wheels touch and I began applying the brakes, coming to a stop about two-thirds down the runway. I pulled off onto the taxi strip and began zigzagging my way back for my second takeoff.

Daddy Longlegs must have been pleased; he gave me a thumbs-up as I wheeled onto the runway. This time when I changed hands on the control column after becoming airborne, I took more time and smoothed out my movements as I raised the wheels, closed the hood, and throttled back. I now felt in complete control, not just concentrating on what I was *supposed* to do next, but simply *doing* it. My landing was much firmer and took up less distance.

On my third circuit I was completely relaxed; the Spitfire seemed so easy to handle, my movements came automatically. It was unlike any other aircraft I'd flown and I was completely enamoured of it. It seemed to take over, as if it were part of me and vice versa. As someone once said, "You didn't fly a Spitfire. You wore it like a glove and waved it around." The airplane had a personality all its own; it was the answer to a fighter pilot's dream. Mark Maffre wrote, "Those who did not know her may wonder how mortal man can cherish an undying affection for her gasoline-reeking camouflaged memory. And no one can tell them." In my first 45 minutes as a Spitfire pilot I had become completely in tune with such sentiments.

That night in the mess, as the first one in our course to fly the Spitfire, I had to stand a round of drinks for the others—four Australian pilot officers (the rest of the course were sergeant pilots). Unlike those at the permanent RAF stations, the mess was a wartime structure. Built of wood, it was comfortable and well fitted out. Our quarters were separate huts. Because the rainy winter weather had left a lot of mud in its wake, duckboards had been laid down over the paths joining the buildings.

The atmosphere in the mess was a lot of fun—semi-operational, almost like being on a squadron already. The instructors treated us students more or less as equals; they were comradely, friendly, and very helpful. As noted earlier, most of them were recent veterans of the Malta battles. One of the exceptions was Leonard Watt, a flight lieutenant to whose flight I had been assigned. As a flight commander, Watty had just completed a tour of cross-Channel fighter sweeps and bomber escort sorties over German-occupied France, Belgium, and Holland.

One of the topics in the mess among the Malta people was George Beurling from Verdun, Quebec. Nicknamed "Screwball" because he applied that adjective to just about anything and everything, he had shot down 27 enemy planes, becoming the leading ace of the Malta battle before being wounded and invalided home. Beurling had taken his OTU training at Aston Down as well.

Beurling had refined deflection shooting—using angle of fire—to state of the art. Generally the Spitfire's armament was synchronized to concentrate the fire at a range of 300 yards. Beurling narrowed that down to 250. The reason for his success as an air fighter, quite aside from his accuracy with the gun, was his extraordinary ability as a pilot. The amalgam of this skill and his precision as a marksman was one that few could better or even try to equal. We practised deflection shooting at Aston Down on a drogue (target) towed by a Lysander over the Severn River. Our scores were nothing to boast about; certainly none of us was going to rival Beurling. Our gunnery officer at Aston Down, Flight Lieutenant Jack Charles, DFC, a Battle of Britain ace, advised us to concentrate on getting as close as possible on the enemy's tail in order to take direct aim.

My initial exercises with the Spitfire were aerobatics, the best way to get the feel of an aircraft. The plane was so responsive that they presented no problem. Remarkably, though, I found it difficult to put it into a spin. When I finally succeeded it was a very flat manoeuvre, so I decided to experiment with a flick spin—by closing the throttle, putting on hard rudder, and pulling the stick right back, all in one quick movement. This was more like it, violent but easy to correct, and a good way to get out of a dicey situation if someone was on your tail.

The main concentration of our training was on formation flying.

The outdated Vic (V) formation had long been dismissed as impractical and unwieldy. Its chief drawback was that the responsibility of keeping watch for enemy fighters rested almost solely with the leader. The other pilots were too busy concentrating on staying in position to look around. A practical solution was the line-astern formation: following the leader at a safe and manoeuvrable distance behind each other. It took some practice, particularly when the leader made abrupt changes in direction or went into a sudden dive or climb, but it was possible to keep a sharp lookout and still stay in position.

Between flying practices we were given lectures on various subjects. One of these was parachuting. The lecturer was Flying Officer Mike Graves, who had won the DFC in Malta, the son of Lord Graves, president of the BBC. One method was to open the door, step out onto the wing, and jump. An alternative was to kick the stick hard forward; the sudden thrust would throw you forward out of the cockpit. Or you could roll the aircraft on its back and simply fall out. In each case, you first had to pull back the hood, unfasten the Sutton safety harness, unhook the oxygen tube, and unplug the R/T chord. Above all, he reminded us, "It don't mean a thing if you don't pull that ring!"

Though Mike had never had to go over the side himself, he told us of the experiences of some of his friends. Some were quite macabre. Some Maltese had a habit of stealing the silk out of the parachute packs and replacing them with rags. Mike recalled seeing one of his mates jump: He pulled the ring, rags fluttered out, and the pilot fell into the sea. As a result, pilots were advised to check their packs before taking off. Beurling had a better solution. Whenever he saw a "Malt" anywhere near the aircraft, he let fly with several well-aimed revolver shots that would just miss the errant islander, but were enough to scare him away.

Mike also witnessed a "Roman candle." The parachute had caught fire before the pilot could get free of the aircraft; he descended with his parachute in flames. On another occasion, a chute failed to open properly for another unfortunate, who went down a "streamer." "I don't want to be morbid about this," Mike said, "but if that happens, you'd best snap open the harness and get it over with. This poor fellow took six hours to die."

Afterwards Mike asked Australian Johnny Maxwell and I how we thought his lecture had gone. Maxwell grinned. "That part about the guy in the streamer I found particularly appropriate, Mike. Nice touch that."

Another lecture was by the station intelligence officer. His subject was what to do if you were shot down over enemy territory. If you were lucky enough not to be picked up, you were advised to try to stay hidden until contacted by the French underground. However, if you were captured, you would be taken first to a *Dulag Luft* air force interrogation centre, where the Germans would use every method—cajoling, befriending, threatening—to obtain information. You were obliged only to give your name, rank, and serial number—nothing more. You would later be taken to a *Stalag Luft,* an air force prisoner-of-war camp. There was one consolation: You would be prisoners of the *Luftwaffe,* and thus could expect better treatment than at other POW camps.

Presumably all this "gen" (intelligence) came from eluders, escapees, coded messages from inside the POW camps, and so on—or so this know-it-all asshole would have us believe. He would parry our questions with a haughty "That's classified," "I'm not at liberty to answer that," or "It's a military secret," as if he was privy to inside information forbidden to us mere pilots. Well, this wing-less wonder wasn't doing any flying, so he wasn't liable to be shot down and try to escape or be taken prisoner. Over a few pints that night in the mess, Maxwell, Dave Gow (another Aussie), and I told him so and we demanded some straight answers. He had rank on us—he was a flight louie—but we didn't care. He reported us to the chief flying instructor, who told us, "I hear you've been having trouble with our poor old IO." He then grinned and walked away.

I had been at Aston Down for nearly a month when who should

arrive one morning but Wing Commander "Iron Bill" MacBrien. He was there to learn how to fly a Spitfire before taking a senior post with one of the Canadian fighter wings. I had my moment of glory when he began asking me about the aircraft, and I took a certain delight in briefly acting as the teacher instead of the pupil.

Thus far I had managed to stay out of trouble. Then came Christmas, and all hell broke loose. 'Twas the night before, and all through the officers' mess the creatures were stirring and whooping it up—myself, Gow, Maxwell, Mike Graves, and Jack Charles in particular. As things got under way, someone poured a beer over the IO's head, a gesture that was long overdue. He left in a huff, but the incident signalled a free-for-all in which the suds flowed both into mugs and over heads, until everyone was thoroughly drenched in brew. The orderly officer, probably on orders from higher up, closed the bar long before the usual hour.

But that was only a warm-up. A military tradition dictated that at noon on Christmas Day the officers would be guests of the sergeants' mess, following which we would repair to the airmen's mess and serve the other ranks their Christmas meal. By the time we had left the former for the latter, the aforementioned quintet from the night before was very much in the vanguard—and feeling no pain.

Afterwards we retired to the officers' mess for more libation and a sandwich lunch. In the afternoon, most of us kept the party going in preparation for Christmas dinner that evening. A few people had passed out, but by pouring jugs of water on them we woke them up for the meal, which, given the shape we were in, turned into a roisterous affair.

After dinner, some of us—including Graves, Maxwell, Gow, and me—staggered over to the drill hall, where a station dance was in full swing. I found the WAAF (Women's Auxiliary Air Force) airwoman I had been escorting regularly, and between refreshments we danced the hours away until the end of the party. I was walking my partner to her quarters when we stopped halfway and embraced. Suddenly I felt a jab in my back and someone was tugging my collar. Without turning around I said, "F— off!" and wheeled about in the same breath to come face to face with the senior WAAF officer. "I'll report you for this," she said, in no uncertain terms, and was off before I could mumble an apology. Meanwhile, my lady partner had fled.

I was in deep shit and I knew it. But I wasn't the only one. Next day the station adjutant, a smarmy, officious little man, took great delight in notifying Graves, Gow, Maxwell, and me that we were to report to Wing Commander Charles Lapsley, DFC, the station commander, at 0900 hours on Monday, almost as if he were meting out punishment himself.

We were called in one at a time. Graves was first to face the music, but there wasn't any. He was dismissed almost at once. With his record, he deserved no less. Gow's and Maxwell's turns came next. Other than a mild scolding about conducting themselves as officers and gentlemen, no sweat. Save the best for the last. I marched into Lapsley's office and saluted. His first words were exactly what I expected.

"Your father isn't still in this country, is he?"

Here we go again. "No, sir."

"You know you are very well-known around here. Not for anything you've done, but for who you just happen to be. You're usually fairly quiet until you get a few drinks in you. You should learn how much you can hold."

Pause for effect.

"You were making love to a WAAF, probably some airman's girlfriend. He could have hit you. Then, because you're an officer, he would be up on charge—instead of you. You could get the high jump for all this."

Lapsley then turned to the CFI, who was sitting beside him. The miserable little mole of an adjutant sat off in a corner looking pleased as punch.

"This officer is confined to the station for the next four days."

The CFI nodded. I saluted and said, "Thank you, sir!" (My training in after-caning manners at school was coming in handy.) Lapsley and the CFI looked quite surprised. It also took the smirk off the face of the adjutant. I suppressed a smile at having retaliated mildly. I made an about-turn and marched out the door. But I had a feeling the affair wasn't going to end there.

Watty, my flight commander, was eager to know how it had turned out. I related the interview word for word. "Old school tie," Watty snarled. "At least the bastard didn't ground you."

He could see that I was pretty sore. "C'mon," he said. "We'll go up and have a practice dogfight. Pretend I'm the station adjutant. That'll get it out of your system."

Some days later an RCAF flight lieutenant administrative type arrived from headquarters in London, ostensibly to check up on how the Canadians were being treated (there were only three of us on the station at the time). Iron Bill tipped me off that this had the earmarks of something more than just an ordinary visit, and warned, "Keep your feelings to yourself." Johnny Maxwell had a different suggestion: "Tell him you think the adjutant's a prick."

The F/L was pleasant enough. He asked how I was getting along, how I felt being in mixed company with the British, Australians, and New Zealanders. Would I prefer a posting to a Canadian squadron or a multinational one? I sidestepped most of his questions and avoided committing myself. I told him I was quite happy (which indeed I was, being in Watty's flight) and that I had made very good friends with two Aussie officers. I had the vague notion, however, that I was under a microscope.

Officially our course still had a week to run, but because I had completed my training by January 24, 1943, including battle formations, cloud flying, night flying, and high altitude (to 25,000 feet) flights, I was given a week's leave with orders to report back at the end of it for posting to a squadron. I packed my things and took the train to London, taking a room at the Park Lane Hotel, where I renewed acquaintances with many BCS old boys, all of whom were in the army. I felt very superior being a graduated Spitfire pilot while they were all still in training or on exercises, with no prospects of action in the near future. At noon one day, Bob Hamilton, whom I hadn't seen since tarmac duty at Camp Borden in November 1941, sauntered into the bar. His arm was in a sling. He'd pranged a Hurricane when he crashed into a fence on landing and was awaiting a new posting from the RAF squadron he'd been sent to when he graduated from OTU.

On the next-to-last day of my leave I was walking down Piccadilly just before lunch when I ran into Dave Gow and Johnny Maxwell. They were staying at the Piccadilly Hotel, which I found much superior to the Park Lane. We adjourned to the bar for a brief reunion. They had finished their course five days earlier, but that snotty little adjutant, whom Maxwell detested and who Gow said "had his finger in right up to the hilt," had screwed up their postings. So they had been waiting around the station, taking daily trips into town, which had little to offer except one or two country pubs and a single cinema. Finally they got their orders—they were being sent to the Far East. But they were still thoroughly pissed off with the adjutant. When I told them I had to report to him next day for my posting, Maxwell asked me to "give that little son of a bitch a boot in the ass for us."

When I returned to Aston Down the following day and reported to "that little SOB" for my posting, he asked me in that superior tone of his, "What about that spot of bother back around Christmas time? Is there anything more to be done about that?" He obviously enjoyed the moment. That spot of bother was none of his goddamn business. I ignored the question and demanded my posting. He backed right off and informed me that I was to report for duty to 401 Squadron RCAF—Ormy's alma mater. It had been taken off ops (operations) for a rest and remanning, and had moved from 11 Group RAF Fighter Command in Kenley, south of London, to Catterick in Yorkshire. I learned from some instructors who had been stationed there that it was a "wizard" station in every respect—

officers' mess, dispersal, and plenty of eager WAAFs—something to look forward to.

I didn't have to report there until February 9, so I had another week's leave coming to me. I'd had enough of the Park Lane Hotel and BCS old boys, both of which I found a bit too provincial. This time, with the help of Gus Edwards' secretary, Flight Officer Nancy Smith at RCAF Headquarters, I was able to book a room at the Savoy.

Chapter 10

Chez Savoy

February 2–8, 1943

Every possibility.

My first stop after registering at the desk was the Savoy's American Bar, where I found Jack Vaughan, who was married to a cousin of mine by marriage. Jack was on leave and also staying at the hotel. He was training for an intelligence officer's job in the Canadian Army and it was the first time I had seen him since leaving Canada. We had lunch together and then I checked into my room. A message was waiting for me to phone Nancy Smith, who told me that Uncle Gus would like to see me in his office next morning around 10 o'clock. I wondered whether my *faux pas* at Aston Down was about to come back to haunt me.

But when I arrived at RCAF Headquarters in Lincoln's Inn Fields, nothing was said about the incident. I learned from Uncle Gus that the RCAF Chief of Air Staff (CAS), Air Marshal Lloyd Breadner, had just arrived on a visit from Canada. He also told me that Bread's son-in-law, Jack Reed, was also staying at the Savoy, or would be later that day. Jack was with an RAF Coastal Command squadron. All of us were invited at noon the following day for cocktails at Lady Sholto Douglas's house in Mayfair.

I phoned the hotel and left a message for Jack Reed, then went off to Buck's Club for lunch. Afterwards I took in a Bing Crosby movie, *Holiday Inn*. On my way back to the hotel, I stopped in at the Chez Moi, an RCAF hangout that was around the corner from the Regent Palace Hotel. I found a few familiar faces from Uplands days and from the crossing on the *Akaroa*, including Bill Olmstead, from whom I learned the ship had been torpedoed and sunk on her return voyage to Australia.

When I got back to the Savoy, Jack Reed had checked in and we met at the American Bar. A group of ex–Eagle Squadron American fighter pilots, whose unit had been transferred to the U.S. Air Force, was seated around the big table. With them was the wife of one, Carole Landis, the Hollywood actress. After a few drinks, Jack said, "Follow me," got up and confidently walked over to where the film star was sitting, proffered his hand, and announced, "Carole Landis—Jack Reed. I'd like you to meet my friend Arthur Bishop." She was very gracious and shook hands with us. The American guys seemed to get a big kick out of it.

Back at our own table we compared notes on next day's event. Jack told me there would be a lot of brass at the cocktail party and then we were all being taken to White City Stadium for lunch and to watch the greyhound races. Air Commodore Critchley—of whom I had heard my father speak and who owned the racetrack— would be there, among others. This didn't ease my apprehension about meeting Jack's father-in-law, whom I had known from my days in Ottawa, after all the ruckus at Christmas at Aston Down. When I told him the story, Jack gave me a wry grin. "You think you've got problems. I sunk a goddamn Sutherland." Apparently he had struck a buoy while taxiing the huge flying boat into the harbour, and it had gone right to the bottom. So he was a little jittery as well. However, we drowned our sorrows and travelled over to Cracker's Club, not far from Chez Moi, but a little classier, for dinner. When we returned to the Savoy it was still fairly early, so we phoned up Jack Vaughan, who joined us for a nightcap downstairs before turning in, the other Jack and I all the while wondering what the morrow would bring.

At the cocktail party—Jack was right; it was teeming with

brass—the CAS pulled us both aside into a corner and said he wanted to have a word with us. Oh, oh, here it comes, I thought. But it wasn't like that at all. "You've both come a long way," Breadner said, "and I see every possibility for you. So I just want to wish you the best of luck."

Whew! And that was that. The afternoon was ours to enjoy, which of course we did, in luxury and style in the private members' glass-enclosed lounge at White City Stadium—drinks and food galore served to us like kings, waiters to take our bets. (But at the back of my mind was still a nagging notion that I had not heard the last of *l'affaire* Aston Down.)

That evening—from the sublime to the sleaze—found Jack and me in that basement den of iniquity Chez Moi, dodging spilled drinks and listening to the filthy stories of Maurrie, the fat barmaid. We graduated at dinner time to Cracker's Club, then afterwards enjoyed a leisurely stroll down Piccadilly to dicker over prices with the commandos. Oh! oh! oh! What a lovely war!

Two days later, the two Jacks and I decided to go and see *Casablanca*, the movie starring Humphrey Bogart and Ingrid Bergman that was winning raves from all the reviewers. But when we got to the theatre just off Trafalgar Square, the lineup for the box office was blocks long. I had downed enough Dutch courage before and during lunch to try and pull a little rank. I told Reed and Vaughan to wait while I made for the side door. I knocked on it and an attendant opened it and politely asked, "What can I do for you?"

I answered, "My father, Air Marshal Bishop, is a friend of the manager's and he told me to ask for him."

"I'll go and tell him," the attendant said, and closed the door in my face.

I waited a bit tremulously, not quite sure how all this was going to turn out. Suddenly the door swung open and the manager, all smiles, put out his hand and said, "This is a great honour."

"There are three of us," I explained, waving at Reed and Vaughan.

"Fine," he said, and all three of us dashed through the door as quickly as possible. Reed and I had front-row balcony seats, while Vaughan had to settle for the stairs in the aisle. It was worth it—a memorable movie.

I did not have to report to 401 Squadron until noon of February 9, but I took the overnight train. That would get me into Catterick early in the morning, giving me plenty of time to freshen up before making my entrance and a proper impression.

Chapter 11

Sprog

Catterick, Yorkshire—February 9–May 29, 1943

> . . . slow stuff beside the swift "Spit" son
> Billy is flying.
> —*Windsor Star* photo caption

No. 401 Squadron RCAF was an elite fighter outfit with a proud heritage. The only Canadian squadron to fight in the Battle of Britain, it was originally formed as No. 1 Squadron at Trenton, Ontario, on September 21, 1937, the nucleus of its personnel coming from the fighter flight of No. 3 (Bomber) Squadron. Under the command of Flight Lieutenant Brian Carr-Harris, it flew Armstrong-Whitworth Siskin biplane fighters. It moved to Calgary, Alberta, in August 1938, with Squadron Leader Elmer Fullerton as its new CO, and was re-equipped with Hawker Hurricane monoplane fighters in February of the following year.

At the outbreak of World War II on September 10, 1939, the squadron mobilized under Squadron Leader Ernie McNab at St. Hubert, Quebec, moving to Dartmouth, Nova Scotia, in November. There, on May 20, 1940, prior to going overseas, it was amalgamated with No. 15 (Fighter) Auxiliary Squadron of Montreal. At the same time it was also augmented with personnel from Nos. 8, 10, and 11 bomber reconnaissance squadrons.

On June 9, squadron personnel sailed for England, where on August 26, 1940, flying from Northolt RAF fighter field near London, No. 1 became the first RCAF squadron to engage the enemy, the first to score victories, and also the first to suffer combat casualties and win awards for gallantry. March 1, 1941, found the squadron at Digby in Lincolnshire, by which time Squadron Leader Paul Pitcher had taken over as CO. It was renumbered 401 as part of RAF policy to number all RCAF squadrons in the "400 block" series to avoid confusion with their own—a measure in which the Canadians had no say whatsoever.

On June 18 the renumbered squadron flew its first offensive mission, a Channel patrol that proved uneventful. On August 8, it scored its first victory as 401 Squadron, when Flying Officer Eugene "Jeep" Neal shot down a German Junkers 88 twin-engine bomber on a coastal patrol off Skegness. Hit by return fire, he managed to crash-land safely, without injury, in a wheat field near Horncastle.

A year and a half later, at noon on February 9, 1943, that same Jeep Neal greeted me warmly with a stein of beer in the anteroom of the officers' mess at Catterick. As the new commanding officer, he welcomed me to 401 Squadron. "I had a telegram from Ian Ormston this morning, who sends you his regards," were his first words to me. He made me feel right at home.

He explained to me that the squadron had only recently moved from Kenley, south of London, where it had been engaged in fighter sweeps over France They had been flying Spitfire IXs, the answer to the Luftwaffe's Focke-Wulf 190s. At Catterick they had taken over Spitfire Vs from 403 RCAF Squadron, which had previously occupied the station. The aircraft were in disrepair when 401 had taken them over two weeks before I arrived; many of them needed new engines.

In the last two months of 1942, 401 Squadron had lost three pilots, who had been shot down over the Continent. Another had bailed out over the Channel and had been badly injured. Two or three had been taken off ops, having completed their tours. Two others had been transferred to another squadron as flight commanders. The remainder were badly in need of a rest. To bring the squadron up to its full strength of 26 pilots, "sprogs"—untested pilots like myself—were being posted to the unit to fill the ranks. The job of Jeep, the two flight commanders, and the other experienced pilots was to mould the squadron into a first-class fighting unit. No one was better qualified to head up such an assignment than Jeep Neal. After six months' leave in Canada at the finish of his first tour (during which he got married), he was well rested, full of vim and vigour, and raring to go.

When we went into the dining room for lunch I came face to face with Willy Cummings, whom I hadn't seen since our wings parade at Uplands the previous July. Jeep introduced me to other members of the squadron, among them Gib Coons, Thomas "the Snerd" Ibbitson, and the two flight commanders, Dave "Bitsy" Grant* (A Flight) and Scotty Murray (B Flight).

After lunch Jeep drove me down to stores, where I was issued with a flying helmet and goggles, flying boots, and a "Mae West" life jacket. Next stop was the parachute section, where I received my 'chute. We then drove over to the offices, passing the sergeants' mess on the way, where I met the adjutant, John Orpen, who had been with the squadron since 1938, and the intelligence officer, "Spy" John Sancton. Afterwards we drove around the perimeter of the field, across the runway, and over to dispersal. It was located near some woods at the edge of the far side of the aerodrome, where the WAAFs were quartered. I was given a locker, in which I stored my gear, then was introduced to the members of the squadron who were not up flying—a mixture of officers and sergeant pilots.

I also met the squadron engineering officer, Rusty Bragg, and four senior members of the ground crew: "Whizzer" White, "Gunner" Gunn, and Jackson Moffat, all of whom had been with the squadron since its arrival in England in 1940, and Willy "No Neck" Worrell, who would spend most of his time with the 401's four-plane detachment at Thornaby, near the east coast of Yorkshire. At the coastal command station, our four pilots and Worrell had a

---

* In those days anyone named Grant automatically earned the nickname "Bitsy," after the famous tennis player of the same name.

shack that served as a dispersal in which they slept and sat on readiness, taking turns in pairs from dawn to dusk. They took their meals in the officers' and sergeants' messes. The pilots were rotated, taking a week's stint at a time.

On the way to the Angel pub after dinner for the squadron bash, I walked with Willy Cummings, who told me he had been with the squadron for only a week before the move to Catterick. He had flown only once or twice—not enough time-in to take part in any sweeps. When they learned I had been posted to the squadron, rumours flew thick and fast—for one that I'd already been promoted to flight lieutenant. "I set the record straight," he said. "I told them, 'Hell, I trained with this guy.' But I also said that you weren't exactly a shrinking violet."

I asked him if he thought anyone had heard about the blacks I'd put up at Watton and Aston Down for my various indiscretions. He didn't think so. I said, "Tonight I'm going to take it easy. I don't want to screw up on my first night with the squadron." It was a wise decision—I was about to be tested.

Before the speeches got under way we sat around drinking and talking as I got fully acquainted with everyone. From the corner of my eye I noticed Scotty Murray pouring rum into a glass of beer, suddenly changing it from amber to deep brown. Willy had caught it too; he nudged me as Murray came toward us with his own beer in one hand and the darkened one in the other.

"Now that is just an ordinary beer, Bish," he said. "Put it down and try this one." I knew when I was being challenged. "Okay with me," I replied, took the glass, and deliberately, slowly downed it all. A look of amazement came over Murray's face.

Willy laughed. "That showed you," he said. "You didn't think he could do it, did you?"

The speeches were about what you would expect. The squadron diary expressed it this way: "The Angel witnessed the good fellowship of 401's officers and senior NCOs. S/L Neal, F/Ls Murray and Grant, F/O Bragg and P/O Cosborn all got up to voice pride and faith in our past and future as 'the best darned outfit in England.'" What struck me most was the way in which Jeep encouraged this *esprit de corps* with remarks like "That's what I like to see—rivalry between flights" (this after Bitsy and Scotty had embraced each other). And following Slim Cosborn's accolade, "Damned right we're best!"

We were all allotted bicycles as a means of transportation around the station, and when I wheeled over to dispersal next morning, Bitsy advised me that I had been assigned to his flight. "You must have lost the toss," I joked. "That remains to be seen," he replied with a grin. I knew this was deliberate on Jeep's part, and I was highly flattered. Bitsy, who had been an outstanding instructor before going overseas, was one of the finest, most accomplished pilots ever to fly a Spitfire. He could practically make it talk. I could not have been placed in better hands.

I made my first flight that morning: several takeoffs and landings under Bitsy's watchful eyes. When I got seated in the cockpit I was taken with how much fresher-looking everything—the instruments, the levers and controls—seemed compared to the clapped-out Spitfires we'd been flying at OTU. When I got off the ground and closed the hood, it was a treat to see how clear the Perspex was compared to the scratched hoods I'd been used to.

My performance met with Bitsy's approval. He told me to take off again and have a good look around the immediate vicinity to familiarize myself with the surroundings. "Don't worry about getting lost. You can always ask for a homing [through the R/T]. They [the controller] will give you a heading that will bring you right back to base."

The weather was clear, with only a few scattered clouds, so I climbed to 2000 feet and began a wide circle to port. There were plenty of landmarks in the area: the village of Catterick, the Great Northern Road, and the Aire River, which divided our field from

Scorton aerodrome, where a Beaufighter night fighter squadron, 219 RAF, was stationed. I had no trouble acclimatizing to the general topography, and after an hour landed feeling very comfortable and satisfied. "Good," said Bitsy. "This afternoon we'll try a little formation flying and you can get in some cine-gun camera practice."

I had been with the squadron for just over a week when Bitsy put me down for a three-plane tail chase with two NCOs—a Pole, Flight Sergeant Giles, and Warrant Officer Muirhead, who had joined the squadron just a day earlier. Giles would lead as number one in the line-astern formation and Muirhead was to fly as number two, while I brought up the rear slot. We took off after lunch, climbed to 6000 feet, and soon found ourselves above a solid cloud layer at 3000 feet.

Suddenly Giles made a sharp turn to starboard. Muirhead was slow to follow, and by the time he'd gone into his turn, Giles had banked steeply over to port. I had throttled back to stay a safe distance behind when Giles went into another turn to the right. By this time Muirhead was completely out of position; from where I sat the two Spitfires resembled a pair of gulls criss-crossing past each other. Then, a second later, they collided.

Giles's aircraft dived straight down to the left in a spiral and disappeared into the cloud. Descending fast in a shallow dive, Muirhead flashed by my right wing tip, his own port wing sheared off at the root. He was staring straight ahead when the cloud layer swallowed him.

I got on the blower fast: "Red Three calling, Red One and Two have collided. I'm over ten-tenths cloud and can't see whether they bailed out or crashed. I haven't a clue as to my position. Give me a vector."

"Reading you loud and clear, Red Three," came back the controller's reply. "Vector one-six-zero."

When I landed, Bitsy and Gib Coons were standing by as I taxied in. Both planes had been reported crashed near Northallerton, on the Yorkshire moors. A cannon shell had gone through the window of the chief constable's office. "What happened?" Bitsy asked. I explained as best I could, though it had all occurred so fast.

"Do you think Muirhead was showing off?" he queried.

"I dunno," I replied. "But I bet that right now—up there, wherever they are—Giles is giving him shit."

"In Polish," Gib cut in.

"Bishop," Bitsy said, "if you get killed, I'm going to kick your ass. From now on you'll do your tail chasing with Gib here." Thus I became Gib's wingman, an assignment he accepted in his usual cheerful, enthusiastic manner.

The crash party found both aircraft buried deeply in farmland, with wreckage strewn across fields over a distance of two miles. The bodies were not on the ground. Muirhead's was recovered from 4 feet deep, but attempts to recover Giles were abandoned—his body was 18 feet below the surface of soft sand.

Gib Coons recalls, "For a while after our first flights, on landing Jeep would pull me aside and ask, 'Well, how's Bishop doing?' I told him he was getting along fine. 'He just needs to build his confidence.' What prompted all this was that the RCAF HQ in London were constantly pestering Jeep on how the Air Marshal's son was getting along. I later realized that this overzealous overkill arose from concern over the welfare—not to mention behaviour—of Billy Bishop's son. It wasn't fair to him or to the rest of us personally involved.

"Bish was no different from any of the newcomers to the squadron. He was understandably apprehensive at first, what with the old man's record hanging over his head. But he fitted right in and became just one of the rest of us."

Another exercise Gib and I teamed up for was air firing. These practice flights took place over the North Sea off the coast near Thornaby, where our detachment stood on readiness. The targets were drogues towed behind Lysanders flown by pilots who had been taken off ops for "lack of moral fibre" (LMF). Although they wouldn't fly on ops, they weren't totally out of danger; there was always the chance that a practice shell might go astray. I deemed it poetic justice to aggravate this state of affairs.

Gib Coons remembers, "As we made a curving approach into the target, Bish said, 'I've got his tail right in my sights. Just a short burst—nothing too serious.' Then he let go a bunch of tracers, but they were well short of the target. But it was enough to frighten the guy in the back of the Lysander out of his wits. He began screaming, 'I'll report you guys for this.' Which he did. Bitsy laughed it off: 'The yellow bastard deserves a scare!'"

Two days after the Giles/Muirhead fiasco, on February 19, I had another adverse experience. This time, fortunately, it was without serious consequences. For night flying practice we flew from Scorton aerodrome, across the Aire River, where the 219 Beaufighter squadron was stationed; the runway was much longer than our own and the control tower was geared to night flying takeoffs and landings.

On my first night flight I got lost, and even with a homing vector I couldn't seem to make out Scorton in the dark. I kept circling, but to no avail. Finally I made out an aerodrome with small landing lights along the sides of the runway. Since I was getting low on fuel, without signalling or anything else I put my wheels and flaps down and proceeded to land.

It wasn't one of my better efforts. I kept swerving to the left and ended up slightly off the runway, with the wheels stuck in thick mud. I tried to throttle my way out of it, but the Spitfire refused to budge, and the tail was projecting onto the runway. Finally I shut down and climbed out. A couple of irate airmen came running forward, shouting at me to "get that goddamn butterfly the hell out of there."

They had good reason for concern, as I quickly learned. Suddenly a huge aircraft came speeding down the runway, passing me with a great *whoosh* and a roar—a four-engine Halifax bomber. I'd landed at Leeming, the home of 406 RCAF Squadron—no place for a "butterfly" with heavies plunking down right behind me. With the help of the two "erks" I managed to get the Spitfire clear of the runway. I left it there and trundled over to the officers' mess, phoned Scorton, and told them where I was. They said to hold and wait for instructions. After few minutes Jeep came on the line. "Are you okay?" he asked. I assured him I was and explained what had happened. He told me to wait right there and he would come and get the aircraft himself. When he arrived he sent me home with his driver and flew the Spitfire back to Scorton himself. All in a night's work. But I felt like an idiot.

This was not to be our only association with the Canadian bomber squadrons. One of our exercises was bomber affiliation: working with the crews in No. 6 Group to allow them to practise defensive tactics against enemy night fighters. At the same time it gave us a chance to hone our own cine-gun camera skills. The main evasive manoeuvre was corkscrewing—weaving from side to side in a rolling sort of dive. In daylight (and all our bomber affiliation practices were in the daytime) it was easy for us to follow the bombers, no matter how skillful the skipper or second pilot. But in the dark, this evasive action had proved successful time and time again. These exercises also allowed the air gunners to practise with their own camera guns. Before and after practices we would sit down and discuss them with the bomber crews at their airfields at Croft, Dishforth, or Leeming, which were only 10 minutes' flying time away.

We were very much aware that on any given night our bomber friends were facing the real thing, enemy night fighters and flak—not to mention the risk of collision. At lunchtime in the anteroom of the mess we listened intently to the regular BBC noon radio bulletins on the news of the war. At this stage, in March 1942, the German advance had stalled in Russia. Although Stalingrad had surrendered at the beginning of February, Kurst and Rostov had been recaptured by the Russians. Rommel's Afrika Korps in

Tunisia was sandwiched between the Americans in the north and the British to the southeast. North Africa was on the verge of being liberated. But it was the almost nightly bomber raids over Germany that riveted our attention. At one lunch hour the room was stunned by the announcement "Ninety-three of our aircraft failed to return."

A few days later, when Cummings and I flew over to Dishforth for fighter affiliation practice, we felt as if we'd arrived at a ghost town. Room after room in the officers' mess was being emptied of the belongings of those who had gone missing. The distraught surviving crews were awaiting aircraft and aircrew replacements.

On March 1 we went on "active service" ourselves, when four of us were scrambled for an hour-long convoy patrol off Whitby, on the east coast. It was disappointing. As I recorded in my log book, there was "nuttin' doin'."

March was a month of changeover for 401 Squadron. Several of the veterans, their operational time expired, were posted home for a rest, while newcomers filled their places. Among the arrivals were an instructor from Uplands with whom I had a passing acquaintance, Bob Hayward (known as "De Bub" for his Newfoundland accent); Bob Hamilton, whom I had last seen on leave in London at the Park Lane Hotel bar; Jack Sheppard, who had flown a Hurricane catapulted off the deck of a merchant ship as aerial convoy protection on the Murmansk Run to Russia; Bill McRae, Bob Buckles, Robert "Tex" Davenport, Don Wilson, Ray Lawson, Walter "Johnny" Johnson (a former BCATP instructor), and Tom Koch, who became my roommate. On April 2, Scotty Murray was posted home to Canada as an instructor. Replacing him as flight commander of B Flight was "the Snerd,"* Ibby Ibbitson, who was from the Prairies. When he was drinking, the Snerd demonstrated an incredible tolerance for imbalance. The more he consumed, the farther he would lean forward, often to as much as a 30-degree

* named after ventriloquist Edgar Bergen's dummy

angle to the floor, and would still be standing and carrying on a conversation, no matter how incoherent.

On March 13, I had been with the squadron a little longer than two months, during which I had logged 62 hours' flying time, when Willy Cummings and I were given a week's leave. That night we took the train to London and checked into the Regent Palace Hotel. A story going the rounds about this establishment was that one night two cats were copulating on top of a fence outside when lightning struck them dead, knocking them, still locked in the connubial act, to the ground. One of the hotel guests, having witnessed this scene from the window, called down to the desk and reported, "Your sign just fell down."

Over the next two days we made the rounds, Chez Moi, Cracker's Club, and the Park Lane Hotel, where I ran into my old school chum Peter Holt, in whose family plane I had made my first flight, a decade earlier in Muskoka. Peter was with a bomber squadron and had already made two raids over Holland, so we treated this "operational type" with due reverence. Sadly, this was the last time I ever saw Peter.

Willy and I soon tired of London. Through a friend of mine who worked at the American embassy, we were able to arrange accommodation at the Royal Anchor, a stopover inn at Liphook, on the Surrey–Hampshire border south of the capital, halfway to Southampton. This establishment was famous as the trysting site of Lord Nelson and Lady Hamilton. In the bar, in which oysters were the specialty, there were accoutrements from his warship, the *Victory*, including a large lamp that hung from the ceiling.

In that same bar we met a Canadian army lieutenant who was stationed nearby and who had fallen in love with the English way of life. He told us that he intended to stay in England after the war. I wondered how many other Canadians felt the same way—none in our squadron that I was aware of. I still often wonder whether or not that man's dream ever came true.

There wasn't much to do at Liphook except relax, enjoy the food (which was exceptionally good, given that there was strict rationing) and the drinks, and roam the countryside. We did manage to get in a couple of games of golf, which, while not a threat to the records of Bobby Jones or Walter Hagen, proved to be an interesting experience. Back in 1940 great precautions had been taken throughout the south of England to prevent airborne landings by parachute or glider. Golf courses, of which there was (and still is) a plethora, were the most likely targets for such operations, and great pains had been taken to obstruct them. Although golf courses continued to exist throughout the war, steel posts were everywhere. Ditches had been dug. Barbed wire was strung across the fairways. Spikes had been placed on and around the tees and greens. The bunkers had been deepened. For the golfer it was an obstacle course—a real challenge.

When we returned from leave, the pictures that the public relations people had taken of our squadron earlier had begun appearing in the Canadian newspapers. One of the stories read

London, March 29. (BUP).—Pilot Officer Billy Bishop has joined a Canadian Spitfire squadron somewhere in northeastern Britain, it was revealed here today.

Another showed a picture of Willy, Adjutant Orpen, and myself standing in front of one of our aircraft. Part of the caption stated,

Bishop's father . . . shot down 72 enemy aircraft during his career in the last war in his famous Nieuport fighter—slow stuff beside the swift "Spit" son Billy is flying.

Bob Hamilton never let me forget that one. Frequently when I would come down after a flight, he would walk up to me and ask, "How is that *swift* Spit that son Billy flies?"

Somehow the news also leaked out that "[Bishop] has been christened 'Hairless Joe' by his fellow pilots." True enough. Pictures taken during those days inevitably showed me as badly in need of a haircut. But the real credit belonged to the ground crew, who not only tagged me with the nickname (after the hairy caveman in Al Capp's *L'il Abner*), but painted a likeness of the cartoon character on the side of the Spitfire I usually flew.

On April 11, I took my turn with the four-pilot readiness section at Thornaby, a one-week stint. The town did not lack for female companionship: it teemed with girls from the munitions plants. But on this occasion it was Peggy, the blonde barmaid at one of the pubs, who attracted the attention of my wingmate. She asked him to escort her home, telling him, "Bring your friend along for my sister—she's a good sport." The girls lived with their father, so Peggy sold us each a bottle of gin with which to ply the old fellow and put him to bed early to get him out of the way.

It turned out that "Pop" had quite a capacity, so it was quite late and we were all pretty sloshed by the time he bid us good night and went upstairs. The sister and I went into the kitchen to make some tea, leaving wingmate and Peggy alone in the living room to finish off what was left of the gin.

When the tea was ready I picked up two cups to take into the living room. But when I looked across the serving counter into the room, I changed my mind. Wingmate and Peggy were making out on the floor with great gusto, the former's naked backside rhythmically bobbing up and down—what a shot for the cine camera! I put one of the cups on the counter and quietly took the other into the living room. In our practice dogfights we had been taught that timing was everything, and this was no exception. I waited for the exact *instant critique* to make my move, then smacked wingmate smartly on the bare ass and in my best cockneyfied accent said, "'Ave a cup of tea, lad!"

On the day before I was to return to Catterick, my Spitfire's undercarriage got stuck and refused to go down, so I was forced to make

a wheels-up landing. Although I had followed the established landing procedures, I still made a botch of it. As the horn kept blowing
and the green light failed to go on, I struggled with the undercart
lever, which was in place, thinking I could maybe shake things
loose. But no luck. I climbed to 5000 feet and went through a
series of aerobatics, including diving steeply, then pulling up
sharply. Still no dice. Finally, the last resort: press down on the CO_2
bottle lever to force the gas into the chambers. But that didn't work
either. I prepared to land with wheels up.

I made two cardinal errors. First, I failed to radio to control that
my undercart was stuck, and second, I landed on the runway
instead of the grass. Landing as I did was decidedly more danger-
ous and could do more damage to the plane. On my final approach,
red flares from the control tower shot off all over the place. I
ignored them, scraping along the runway and creating a horrifying
shriek, sparks flying in all directions. Finally the Spitfire screeched
to a stop. As I climbed out, the crash truck raced up. When Willy
Worrell, our ground crew chief, arrived on the scene I explained
what had happened. He telephoned Catterick and was informed
that Rusty Bragg, the engineering officer, was on his way over in a
Tiger Moth to examine the aircraft. I was ordered to fly back to Catterick and report to the CO.

I realized that, because I had failed to report the problem over the
R/T, I would be under suspicion of simply forgetting to lower the
wheels. I told Jeep that, had that been the case, as soon as I saw all
those red flares I would have gone around again. Also, I said, I did
push down the CO_2 bottle—further proof of my innocence. Jeep
was most sympathetic and told me to forget all about it. Bitsy said
the same thing. The strange outcome of the whole affair was that
Bragg could find nothing wrong with the undercarriage apparatus.
Case unsolved. Probable cause: gremlins.

Tex Davenport and I made a joke of the incident that even Jeep
got a kick out of. Some days later, after he and I had been practising
tail chasing and were on the downwind leg of our landing

approach, I called Tex on the R/T and said, "Remember to put your wheels down." To which, as planned, Davenport came back with his Texas drawl, "Ah cain't heah what you all are sayin'. There's a horn blowing in mah ears!" We were hoping to get a rise out of the control tower, but our ruse didn't work. The controller couldn't interpret that thick Texan accent.

My old man was still keeping tabs on me, it seemed. Early in May Jeep pulled me aside and we took a short drive in his car. He had just returned from receiving his DFC at Buckingham Palace, and during his brief visit to London he had called on RCAF Headquarters. Nancy Smith, Gus Edwards' secretary, had informed him that the AOC-in-C would be visiting 6 Bomber Group RCAF headquarters at Allerton Park, south of Catterick, in two days' time and that he would like to see me. Jeep sent me down to HQ with his driver the next day.

On arrival at Lord Mowbray's imposing 75-room baronial mansion, which the RCAF had appropriated for the duration, I was escorted to Uncle Gus's office by an orderly sergeant. Standing outside the door was a group captain wearing the DSO and DFC, who I later learned was Johnny Fauquier, the famous RCAF bomber pilot known as "the King of the Pathfinders." We did not meet on that occasion—it was strictly business. In between tours Fauquier was temporarily attached to Air Commodore George "Brookie" Brooks's HQ staff. But one day Johnny would marry a cousin of mine and we would become best friends.

Uncle Gus greeted me cheerily and warmly and said that Nancy sent her regards, mentioning that he had recently heard from my father. Then in a friendly fashion he inquired, "Behaving yourself?" (prompted by my old man, no doubt). I replied, "I think you should ask my CO about that, sir." After all, I wasn't about to own up to pranging a Spitfire wheels up or tell him about our caper with Peggy the barmaid and her sister. He then asked me if there was anything I needed. I told him that I was very happy with 401 Squadron, that they were a great bunch of guys, and that my CO and flight commander were showing me every consideration.

Several days later Willy Cummings and I, along with Norm Maybee and Ken Woodhouse, were selected to attend a British Army assault demonstration exercise several miles from our field. When the army van arrived to pick us up, the lieutenant in charge stepped from the vehicle and regarded us haughtily, scowling at Maybee and Woodhouse, who wore sergeant's chevrons on their sleeves, then growled, "Only officers."

I blew my stack. "Wait a minute, my friend," I fumed. "These guys are pilots just like us. If they don't go, we don't go." Willy nodded in agreement.

"Suit yourself," he snarled, climbing back into the van. "In our regiment we don't mix officers with the ranks."

That did it. "Well, we do," I bristled. "So just fuck off at the high port."

When Willy and I had received our wings, it was generally accepted that, as a rule, the top third in the class earned commissions while the rest were promoted to the rank of sergeant—cut and dried. But I had been a member of a fighter squadron for three months. During that time Jeep Neal had marshalled his unique leadership skills, with the help of his flight commanders, Bitsy Grant and Ibby Ibbitson, as well as the veteran Gib Coons, to knit together a cohesive, fraternal team—a brotherhood, if you will. I saw things quite differently now. In that environment, class distinctions were decidedly out of place.

I sensed a certain injustice in a system that created such disparity. We were all called upon to do the same job, to take the same risks, to put our lives on the line. Yet the officers enjoyed markedly better accommodation and higher pay: $6.25 per day for a pilot officer versus $3.95 for a sergeant. (I had recently been promoted, as a matter of course, to flying officer, and my increase in pay exaggerated this difference.)

It is to Jeep's credit that he prevented any dissension over what I considered to be a delicate issue of unfair inequality, and he still maintained a remarkably high state of morale. Eventually most of our sergeant pilots were commissioned, though they had to earn their spurs first, so to speak. Not everyone—officers and NCOs—measured up to squadron standards, what the CO and flight commanders expected of them. So there was some weeding out, several postings off strength for a variety of reasons: incompatibility, unsuitability, casualty potential, and, in one case, LMF.

One of my more hairy experiences at Catterick was another night flying incident. As I was taking off from Scorton, both my R/T and air pressure failed. That meant I had to land without flaps or brakes. What's more, with my radio out of commission, I couldn't let the controller know of my predicament. I was strictly on my own and I knew it wasn't going to be easy.

Without the benefit of flaps to slow my speed, my glide angle on the final approach was virtually nil. Because I had no brakes, I had to touch down as close to the end of the runway as possible with the throttle off, hoping I would slow down sufficiently to avoid going right off the far end. What was scary was that I knew there were trees on either side of the approach corridor, trees that I couldn't see in the dark. In addition, I had to keep a sharp watch for other planes in the vicinity.

My first attempt failed miserably. I simply couldn't get the Spitfire to sit down and behave itself—it didn't want to land. It kept ballooning, like riding an air pocket that won't allow you to land, giving me no choice but to go around again. My second, third, and fourth endeavours were no more successful. I decided to take drastic measures, otherwise I'd be up there all night—figuratively speaking, of course.

So on my fifth try I started well back and had the nose high with lots of throttle, keeping me at just over 67 miles an hour, barely airborne. As I crossed the end of the runway, I switched off the ignition, held the stick back, and waited for it to stall. I was no more than five or six feet off the deck when the port wing fell. I tried to correct quickly just as the aircraft hit the runway. It was still rolling, so I pulled off the runway onto the grass. I then pressed the starter buttons to get the engine going again and taxied over to the control tower. When I climbed out I was absolutely soaked with sweat. That was my effort for the night—and my last night flight at Catterick.

During our last two weeks in Yorkshire we acquired a mascot—a stray goat. The station adjutant was a dour, grumpy old RAF type by the name of Henniker Gottley. So we named the goat after him—Henniker *Goatley*. Henniker kept getting tangled up in the rope we used as a leash, prompting Jeep to say, "Look at that, getting all screwed up and confused and not knowing what he's doing. Goatley, a perfect name for him."

That night, Jeep drove Henniker in his car over to the officers' mess and dragged him inside, going in search of the adjutant, whom he found reading *The Times* in the anteroom. At the sight of a goat being hauled into the mess, Gottley harrumphed a couple of times, but he was absolutely nonplussed when Jeep pulled Henniker toward where he was sitting and announced in a loud voice, "There you are, Henniker. Meet your namesake. A striking likeness, don't you think?"

We were due to move south to join 11 Group RAF Fighter Command at the end of the month. Since joining the squadron in early February, I had amassed a total of 130 flying hours. This intensive extra training equipped us much better for operations than if we had gone into combat fresh from OTU. As a result, we were full of confidence.

Before leaving Catterick, Willy Cummings and I had a week's leave coming to us. We managed to bum a lift with one of the Beaufighter pilots at 219 night fighter squadron at Scorton to fly over to Grange, a seaside resort on Morecambe Bay, on the south coast of Westmoreland. From there we planned to take the train north to Lake Windermere, in the Lake District. But not before I added one more gaffe to my growing string of discredits.

It occurred just before lunch on May 20, the day before we went on leave. A replay of my earlier nemesis: the undercarriage refused to go down. I went through the same rigamarole as I'd done earlier—aerobatics, diving, climbing, stall turns, the whole kit and caboodle, with no better result—the wheels wouldn't budge. I used the only option left and banged down the CO_2 bottle lever. No luck there, either. Now I proceeded to repeat my earlier mistakes. I made a circuit to execute a wheels-up landing—without advising control through the R/T—and chose to pancake onto the runway instead of the grass. How clueless can you get?

Red flares erupted all around as I belly-flopped onto the concrete, sparks flying in all directions. As I climbed out I could see Jeep's car hurrying to the scene from dispersal. I expected him to tear a wide strip off me. Well, I deserved it. But to my astonishment, he only asked if I was okay—typical of him to concern himself more with the pilot than the misdemeanor. I nodded affirmatively and he simply said, "Hop in," and drove over to the mess.

We marched smartly straight to the bar, where Jeep ordered two drafts. "Let's find someplace private," he said and we found a couple of chairs in the foyer, where there was no one else around. After we got settled and had taken a couple of sips, he put his hand on my arm and in a warm, consoling tone said, "I want you to take the afternoon off. Go into town and forget this whole thing. I know and Bitsy knows that you've been trying harder than anyone else, and you can do with a break. The leave will do you good."

After this compassionate understanding I felt better. I went to my room, changed out of battledress into my uniform, and walked into town. I spent the afternoon enjoying myself with some of the patrons at the Angel, a favourite squadron hangout, returning to the mess at dinnertime.

The following afternoon Willy Cummings and I went over to Scorton. From there, Flight Lieutenant Dan Willson, DFC, a night fighter ace, flew us west to Grange in his Beaufighter. We checked into a resort hotel, a white wooden structure with a red roof on top of a hill, with a covered open verandah running the width of the building that offered a spectacular—and peaceful—view of the bay. After dinner we were joined for drinks on the verandah by a pair of administrative officers from RAF Headquarters at Whitehall in London.

When we got around to introducing ourselves by name one of them said to me, "Bishop? Are you by any chance . . ."

But before he could finish, Willy broke in with, "The very same!"

At this the fellow looked a little perplexed. "Oh," he replied, "I read a report on you that passed through our office on the way to your own Canadian air force headquarters." The way he said it left me with the distinct feeling that he was hiding something.

Willy butted in. "What did it say?"

"Oh, it was fine," was the reply. "Nothing to worry about. It was fine. Fine."

Sounded kind of phony to me, like a cover-up. It left me wondering how long my Aston Down "spot of bother," to use that little prick of a station adjutant's words, was going to be around to haunt me—and how far afield. As far as 5 Blackburn Avenue, Ottawa?

Next day we took the train to Ambleside, a small, sleepy town at one end of Lake Windermere. This is a very picturesque part of England, with its lakes and hills and rolling countryside, particularly at that time of year. Because of the shortage of fuel there were no motor boats, although we did manage to commandeer a rowboat for a look around. There really wasn't much to do except explore the countryside. We were about the only guests at the country inn where we stayed. However, we did have a restful, relaxing holiday and returned to Catterick (via Willson's Beaufighter) fully refreshed.

I flew my last flight in Yorkshire on May 27, 1943—a scramble. Enemy aircraft had been reported inland from the North Sea, near Middleborough. It turned out to be a false alarm. When we spotted the "bogies" they turned out to be a pair of Canso flying boats whose pilots must have forgotten to turn on their IFFs.

That night a farewell party was held in the officers' mess; 219 Squadron were our guests. The highlight of the bash was the building of a human pyramid to allow De Bub Hayward to display his artistic talents by painting the squadron's mark on the ceiling, which read "THE GRAND ORDER OF THE PURPLE ARSE-HOLE." He was able to finish it just before the pyramid collapsed, leaving a visiting cousin of Bitsy Grant's with a sprained ankle and a black eye, and sending one of 219's pilots to hospital with various strained tendons.

Next morning we bid a formal farewell to the station from the air before proceeding on to Wellingore, in Lincolnshire, where we would dispose of our planes and board a Harrow transport aircraft to our new home at Redhill, in Surrey, south of London. After taking off we formed up in line abreast, then at a low level swept across the length of field in a salute. I was on the far port end of the formation and had to pull up smartly or collide with the officers' mess. *Vale* Catterick. Fond memories!

Chapter 12

Baptism of Fire

Redhill, Surrey—May 29–August 7, 1943

> F/O Bishop has the real sympathy of his
> fellow pilots in the latest series of mishaps
> he's suffered and we hope his ill fortune
> will turn for the better.
>
> —401 Squadron diary

The first of these "latest" incidents took place only two days after our arrival at Redhill. On this occasion I was simply a spectator-passenger. Another pilot, Tex Saunders, and I had been dispatched to Wellingore to pick up some documents that had been left behind when we passed through there on our way south. On the first leg I flew the Tiger Moth from the rear cockpit. We picked up the material and reversed places; Tex took over to pilot the return trip.

We had just taken off when the aircraft veered sharply to starboard. I put my left foot on the port rudder, but it wouldn't move; the starboard rudder was also stuck. Tex pulled up, narrowly missing a concrete gun emplacement at the edge of the flying field. Then he switched off and we plunked down into a freshly plowed farm field, the wheels burrowing into the mud. The Tiger Moth pitched forward and turned upside down.

Without thinking, I pulled the safety-harness pin loose and promptly landed head first in the mud. I was lucky it was wet and soft, otherwise I would have broken my neck. Tex too was guilty of doing exactly the same thing. We collected ourselves and walked to the officers' mess, carrying our parachutes. Tex phoned Jeep to tell him what had happened. The CO instructed us to get back to Redhill as best we could.

Two days earlier, 416 Squadron, commanded by Squadron Leader Robert "Buck" McNair, had arrived at Wellingore to form part of the Canadian Digby Wing (12 Group RAF Fighter Command). Among the pilots was Ian Ormston, whom I hadn't seen since Ottawa. From him we learned that there was no air transport available to get us back to Redhill. He suggested we hitch a ride by truck transport to London—there was a British army camp nearby—and take the train from there. We stayed overnight at Wellingore and arranged a ride the next day. With our flying gear and parachutes, we presented quite a sight at the railway station in London. When we boarded the train to Redhill, someone asked if we'd been shot down. It made us feel very operational.

We had inherited the Spitfire Mark VBs that had belonged to 421, the "Red Indian" Squadron. (That unit had been posted to the Kenley Wing under Wing Commander Johnnie Johnson, DFC, where it was flying Spitfire Mark IXs.) The VBs had each been christened with a Native name. The one that Tex Davenport and I shared—YOK—had "Strong Bow" painted on the side. Four-two-one Squadron had been "adopted" by my father's company, McColl-Frontenac Oil; affixed to the nose of each Spitfire was a decal of the "Red Indian" company trademark.

There were no runways at Redhill; to make up a wing, we shared a grass aerodrome with 411 Squadron. That unit, which had occupied the station since early April, was commanded by Squadron Leader Dal Russel, a Battle of Britain ace who had been one of the first RCAF pilots to be awarded the DFC in World War II. The airfield commander was none other than my old friend Iron Bill MacBrien.

MacBrien advised us that our chief role would be close bomber-escort work at top altitudes of 15,000 feet, which necessitated that the wings of the Spitfires be clipped. This detracted from the aircraft's graceful elliptical appearance, but at those heights we needed considerably increased manoeuvrability. Also, to improve engine performance, the impellers (blowers) had to be cropped. On June 2, the squadron flew to Cranfield, near Cambridge, to implement these modifications, which would take two days. In the meantime, we took off en masse for two days of celebration in London.

When we returned to Cranfield, my aircraft wasn't ready, so I had to wait over until the next morning, when I flew it back to Redhill for our own ground crew to give it the once-over. After lunch, our flight crew chief, Whizzer White, asked me to air test it, so at mid-afternoon on June 6, I took off to put it through its paces.

I had been in the air for about 40 minutes, everything running smoothly, and was heading in the direction of the field at 1000 feet when I was suddenly jolted by an explosion. The aircraft started to vibrate so violently I couldn't read the instrument panel. Flames were licking around the fuel-tank cap in front of me.

I decided to bail out. I unfastened the safety harness, shoved back the hood, and started to climb out on the wing, with my R/T still plugged in. But looking down I realized that I had lost so much altitude that I was far too low to risk parachuting, so I climbed back into the cockpit. The safety straps were blowing back behind me, so I couldn't reharness them. I had no choice but to try and make it to the field, even though I was losing height fast. The airplane was shaking so badly I had trouble holding the stick steady. I put the wheels and flaps down, and then a high-pitched voice broke into the R/T: "Aircraft coming toward the field—you're burning!" As if I didn't effing know it.

With the aircraft shaking like mad and pieces of metal flying across the port wing root, I tried to maintain height as best I could by putting on as much throttle as I dared, hoping for the best. Then two poplar trees appeared abruptly dead ahead and there wasn't a thing I could do about it. I shut my eyes and thought, I've had it; so this is what death is like. Then everything went blank.

The next thing I knew I was sitting at the end of the airfield across the road from where *Strong Bow* rested on its belly, flames licking the top of the engine hood. A gang of my fellow pilots who had seen the crash, led by Jack Sheppard, were desperately trying to get through the barbed wire that protected the field. Then, from a house only a few feet from where the Spitfire lay, someone came running out with a bottle of brandy, which he offered to me, relieved that I hadn't crashed into his house. I took a quick swig, rose to my feet a bit shakily, and shouted to the guys across the wire, "I'm okay! I'm okay!"

Just then Jeep drove up in his car with Doc Thorn, our medical officer. Doc gave me a quick examination, looking for broken bones, but I didn't feel any the worse for wear. I didn't have a scratch, not even a bruise—and the shot of brandy must have soothed my nerves. Then the fire truck arrived—better late than never, as usual—and doused the flames.

I knew I would have to fill out a report. But what could I say? How could I report something I couldn't explain? My parachute and helmet were in the aircraft; the hood had slammed shut. The miracle was that the plane was still in one piece, although there was a large hole on the port side of the engine. It had obviously blown a piston rod, the cause of the explosion. The trees must have knocked the undercarriage off, and that had probably saved my life. If the plane had tipped over onto its back, I would have been trapped inside with it still burning, not a comforting thought. I have never, even to this day, been able to arrive at a solution to this puzzle. The only theory I can advance is that my mind blanked out between the time the trees came up to greet me and when I came back to the real world sitting beside the road. Why, without my safety harness on, I wasn't hurt by the impact when the plane crashed on its belly is unexplainable.

Several days later a bowler-hatted little cretin of an official from the Rolls-Royce company in Derby arrived at Redhill to interrogate me. I didn't like him and the officious little bastard didn't like me either. Fortunately the interview took place in Iron Bill's office and MacBrien took my side. An example:

RR: How often did you check the oil pressure?

Me: Every two minutes or so.

RR: That's impossible.

MacB: Any pilot graduated from the British Commonwealth Air Training Plan is trained to check his instruments with a glance every two minutes.

I had learned that Rolls-Royce had a policy of rewarding pilots who managed to bring their aircraft back following engine failure or battle damage—with a silver penknife as a souvenir. But Bowler Hat wasn't buying it: "You didn't get wounded or even hurt," he sneered. To which I replied, "No thanks to you bastards." End of interview.

(*The possibility that there might have been sabotage when the engine was undergoing modification at Cranfield could not be ruled out, and was given serious consideration. These fears proved unfounded, however, when the aircraft was examined after being fitted with a new engine and undergoing repairs to restore it to flying condition.*

In 1975 a young English writer called on me in Toronto. His mission was to research the history of Redhill aerodrome, and he'd read about my accident in the official RCAF history. I filled him in on the details and suggested he might want to look into the reason it happened. His sleuthing of that incident of 32 years earlier indicated that faulty metal had been used in the piston rods. He would not reveal his source and I didn't press him, but obviously there had been some sort of cover-up.)

Tex Davenport and I were given a new YOK Spitfire. On my first flip the R/T went u/s (unserviceable), cutting the flying time down to five minutes. Two days later, on June 13, 1943—my twentieth birthday—I made my first operational flight. It was a ramrod: a Boston twin-engine medium bomber raid on the fighter airfield at Lille, in northern France, close to the Belgian border. At the briefing we were told that our two squadrons would act as close escort, 411 on the starboard side and our squadron on the port side. Our altitude would be 15,000 feet. Above us, somewhere between

25,000 and 30,000 feet, two squadrons from the Kenley Wing would be providing top cover.

When we took off at 1030 hours the weather was sunny and clear. Our squadron flew in three sections of four in line astern. Jeep led the centre Red section and Ibby the Yellow section to starboard, with Bitsy leading our section, Blue, on the port side. I flew as Bitsy's number two.

We rendezvoused with the bombers at Dungeness, on the English coast, and remained on the deck as we proceeded across the English Channel in the direction of the Pas de Calais. Halfway across we could see the French coast and I was certain that we could be seen from there, too. Then we climbed at full throttle as a humming sound came over the R/T, a signal that we had been picked up by German radar. We reached altitude before crossing inland between Boulogne and Calais, where I had my first look at enemy anti-aircraft (ack-ack) fire. It didn't frighten me, but it certainly surprised me, erupting out of the blue but nowhere near our formation. To play it safe, Bitsy began weaving our section, but more to keep a sharp lookout for Huns than out of worry about the flak.

The bombers maintained a steady course throughout. When we reached the target, they made a wide circle, so that after completing their bomb run they were aiming west, toward the French coast. There was a lot of heavy flak from Lille, but it was some distance away from us and chiefly aimed at the bombers. There was more ack-ack over the airfield, and at times it was very heavy.

Nevertheless, our bombing was accurate. Having dumped their loads, the Bostons poured on the coal, making for the Channel. We were about halfway to the coast when a single Focke-Wulf 190 came racing down in a dive. It flattened out about 250 yards behind the rearmost bomber and opened up with its cannons. Jeep said later, "That Boston looked like it was firing off a peashooter compared to the 190's guns."

However, the Boston's fire must have been more lethal than it looked. The German fighter broke off its attack after getting in only a few bursts and dived for the deck. No one followed—we couldn't match the 190 in a dive. We continued on without incident and broke off from the bombers midway across the Channel and returned to base.

I was feeling pretty proud, relieved, and excited all at the same time. After nearly two years since joining up, I had at last been in combat. I had not been nearly as scared as I thought I would be. I was too busy trying to stay in formation and keeping a sharp look-out to give much thought to fear. In fact, I found the experience both enlightening and exciting, and I earnestly looked forward to the next sortie. My blood was running high.

That afternoon we were ordered to patrol an area south of our field on a line running roughly between Maidstone in the east to Guildford to the west. Bogies had been reported over the Channel heading north at 5000 feet. When we scrambled I approached the assignment with a sense of exhilaration. This time we were over our own turf. But it turned out to be a false alarm.

That night we celebrated my birthday with a pub crawl. Jeep lent me his tunic for the evening. I was flattered. Even though I appeared to be a very young-looking squadron leader with a DFC, the locals were none the wiser. At each pub we visited my first two drinks were on the house.

The following morning Tom Koch and I boarded an air force bus to take us to Dutton Homestall, the East Grinstead estate of John Dewar and his wife. As in many such establishments, the owners had moved into a single wing for the duration and had lent the rest of the estate to the air force as a leave and recreation centre for officers. Among others of the dozen or so there that week was Squadron Leader Charlie "Maggie" Magwood, DFC, the CO of 403 Squadron, with the Kenley Wing, who was on sick leave recovering from the flu.

The Dewars had been friends of my parents, and when they

learned I was staying at the rest centre, they invited Maggie and me to their wing of the house for cocktails. Visiting that afternoon was Ian MacLean, from BCS days, who was with the Canadian Tank Corps and was stationed nearby. Next morning Mrs. Dewar told me Ian had informed her that Peter Holt had been killed on a bombing raid over Holland. She was not sure whether she should tell me, for fear it might upset my holiday, but Maggie had assured her that we were accustomed to that sort of news.

East Grinstead was the home of the famous "Gash House," the hospital where Archie McIndoe was working his miracle plastic surgery on his "guinea pigs"—airmen who had suffered burns, some hideously. One form of therapy was to accustom them to being seen in public in order to overcome self-consciousness about their appearance. Tom Koch and I were in a pub when three of these patients came in and sat down at the table next to us. All of them had facial scars that would take time to heal, and perhaps were something they might have to live with permanently. But we were the ones who were self-conscious, and these guys realized it. They went to great pains to make us feel at ease, treating their misfortune as a joke. One even called another "Scarface"!

One afternoon our detachment received a special visitor in the form of Wing Commander Johnnie Johnson, commander of the Kenley Wing. He was sporting the DSO as well as the DFC, and had run up a score of 24 enemy aircraft destroyed. As Mrs. Dewar remarked, "He's shooting a plane down for breakfast every morning." His name was periodically in all the papers as his score mounted. He had driven down to Dutton Homestall to see how Maggie was getting along, accompanied by Harry Dowding, one of the latter's flight commanders.

I was flattered that my misadventure with *Strong Bow* had come to Johnson's attention. When he congratulated me on what he called a "good show," I said, "I wish you would tell the Rolls-Royce people that." He asked if we were still flying in line-astern formation. When I replied in the affirmative, he said, "Well, we're using the finger-four [a variation of flying line abreast], which is much more flexible and much more offensive." What could I say? As a lowly flying officer with a single op under my belt and a pretty tame one at that, I was hardly in a position to agree or disagree, let alone comment.

When I returned to Redhill, Bitsy Grant had been given command of 416 Squadron at Digby and Ian Ormston replaced him as commander of our A Flight. Two days later, in the late afternoon of June 21, we flew to Martlesham Heath, on the east coast, for an early morning mission. We were to escort a squadron of Mitchell medium bombers for a raid on the docks of Rotterdam, on the Dutch coast.

To summarize the ensuing action, already described earlier, in the early morning mist our top cover failed to show up and we were bounced by a gaggle of 190s, one of which a Mitchell shot down. Ormston, with whom I was flying number two, was about to open fire on another 190 when one of the other Spitfires cut him off, forcing him to pull up so sharply I couldn't follow. Finding myself alone, I made for the deck in a spiral dive, then headed across the Channel at full throttle, passing between a pair of Focke-Wulfs speeding back to Holland in the opposite direction.

When I landed back at Martlesham, Ormy greeted me with a sigh of relief: "I thought I was going to have to write your parents one of those letters," he said. Unlike my first sortie, which I looked upon as something of an adventure, this time I was scared—damn scared, and not afraid to admit it.

Shortly afterwards we were bewildered by the arrival of a Royal Navy Fleet Air Arm instructor accompanied by a crew of two able-bodied seamen. We soon learned that we were about to take a course in deck takeoffs and landings. This left us wondering what it was going to lead to. Jeep, with his customary sense of enthusiasm and drama, said, "The next two weeks could very well change the entire course of our lives."

But what it mostly proved was that we weren't cut out to be aircraft-carrier pilots. An area the same size as a landing deck was marked off on the field with white tape. We were supposed to take off and land within its perimeters. From the air it looked like a postage stamp.

Figuratively speaking, on my first takeoff I splashed into the drink. I took up too much room and went over the end of the "deck" before becoming airborne. My landing wasn't much better; I went right off the end again. Even with practice I didn't improve, and I wasn't the only one. Two things need to be said: First of all, our "carrier" was stationary. Had it been moving into the wind at full knots, our relative takeoff speed would have dramatically shortened the distance needed for both takeoffs and landings. Secondly, the later Seafires enjoyed the benefit of arresting gears. After a fortnight our navy instructor packed up and left, probably in disgust, because nothing ever came of this exercise.

In between deck-landing practices, we flew another ramrod, this time from Bradwell Bay, on the coast, as close escort to Lockheed Ventura twin-engine medium bombers that were attacking installations at Flushing (Vlissingen), on Walcheren Island in the Netherlands. After the briefing Hayward said, "Our target is a military secret, but . . ." Then De Bub pantomimed pulling a lavatory chain. The outing was uneventful; although there were a few FW-190s lurking about around the target area, they gave us a wide berth. This time I found the flak uncomfortably close and felt a bit twitchy.

One afternoon a North American Mustang arrived, piloted by Dave "Bitsy" Grant, who had come to say hello to his friend Tom Ibbitson. He was with 400 Squadron, stationed at Dunsfold, in Surrey, no more than 15 minutes' flying time from our field. The station was commanded by my uncle, Hank Burden, DSO, DFC, a World War I fighter ace. Now a wing commander, he was, according to Bitsy, highly popular with the reconnaissance pilots. Grant had made quite a name for himself as a train-buster, having destroyed 18 locomotives, all of them at night from over France. "Nothing to it," he said.

A few days later I received a letter from Hank inviting me to fly over to Dunsfold for dinner. I discussed this with Jeep, who said he would put a crew on standby for my return. When I landed at Dunsfold I parked near the control tower and was greeted by Hank, who took me up to the officers' mess. We were joined there by Bitsy, who, I realized, had initiated the invitation.

I received a mild scolding from my uncle. He said that he had seen my godmother, Princess Louise, and had detected royal displeasure that I had not been to see her or even called her since arriving in England. I put it in the back of my mind to correct this oversight when time and circumstances permitted.

After dinner, Bitsy and I asked Hank for permission to stage a dogfight; he would be witness to test the merits of the Mustang versus the Spitfire. He agreed, "as long as you stick to the regulation 1000 feet." The result was exactly as we had suspected. The Spitfire could out-turn and out-climb the Mustang. But the latter was more effective in a zoom—a dive down, then a zoom up out of range. After we broke off I made a slow roll—a bit under regulation height, and flew back to Redhill.

About this time the station padre decided we needed some religion, and arranged a church service. I can't recall that we'd had one since I joined the squadron. It was held on the grass outside the dispersal hut. The sermon was not what we had expected or liked. As a group of fighter pilots putting in time between flights, we presumed the padre would provide us with some inspiration for what we were doing. No bloody way. Instead he castigated us for our coarse language and told us that in all his years in the service he had never encountered an outfit that used such filthy language so much and so often. We came away resenting both him and his uncalled-for remarks. Who the hell did this sanctimonious asshole think he was?

Some days later, because the weather was duff—cloudy and drizzly—we were inside the dispersal hut. Jim Murchison and I were battling it out over a game of table hockey when he suddenly broke off, got up, and said, "Hold it for a minute. I've got to take a shit."

The padre, who I noticed for the first time was sitting right next to me, admonished, "Do you have to announce it?"

Ormy, with a wide grin, turned to him and countered, "Well, Padre, he didn't know you were here. Next time when you come through the door, fart three times and we'll all know you've arrived." A couple of guys clapped, whereupon the insipid little twerp stomped out of the hut, never to be seen again. Good riddance—justice had been served.

On June 29 I saw the vaunted American Flying Fortresses for the first time. Spitfires would escort them to the maximum of the fighters' turnaround range and from there on they were on their own. That evening we picked them up at Cabourg, on the Normandy coast just east of the Orne River, to escort them home. There was no enemy activity, not even any flak, and over the Channel they presented a majestic spectacle, the sun casting a golden glow on the uncamouflaged silver wings and fuselages of these magnificent Goliaths. As Jeep prophetically put it afterwards, "the sight of things to come."

Our next sortie was escorting Mitchell bombers to an industrial target in the heart of Amiens. Before we reached the city, the controller warned us of "30-plus bandits above." They chose to strike just as we reached the target. It was a mixed bag of FW-190s and Messerchmitt 109s, my first glimpse of the latter. As Dal Russel's 411 Squadron Spitfires broke into the attack, Jeep instructed us to "pull in closer to the bombers and protect them."

In the engagement, 411 shot down one of the 190s but lost one pilot (shot down) and another aircraft (damaged, although the pilot made it safely back to Ford aerodrome on the Sussex coast).

•   •   •

At this time the major news for Canadians was the invasion of Sicily on July 10, 1943, in which the First Canadian Division, under the command of Major-General Guy Simmons, played a starring role. Back in the south of England, major restructuring was taking place, with the formation of the Second Tactical Air Force RAF under Air Vice-Marshal Sir Arthur Coningham. All RCAF fighter and reconnaissance squadrons were being absorbed into 83 Group of the TAF. The plan was for this group to support the British Second Army in the planned invasion of Europe—the second front.

At Redhill, Dal Russel was elevated to the rank of Wing Commander Flying of the newly named 126 Wing. (He was replaced as CO of 411 Squadron by Charlie Semple.) The addition of 412 Squadron, commanded by George Keefer, DFC, a veteran of the air battles in North Africa, brought the wing up to triple-squadron strength. Our airfield commander was Wing Commander Jimmy Walker, DFC and two bars, another desert veteran, who replaced Iron Bill MacBrien. (The Kenley Wing, under Johnnie Johnson, had been renamed 127 Wing and comprised 403, 416, and 421 squadrons, commanded by Hughie Godefroy, Buck McNair, and Charlie Magwood respectively.)

One morning in mid-July, I got a phone call from Wing Commander Gus Nanton, a close friend of the family. Gus was an escort officer for RCAF drafts sailing overseas and was in London at the Dorchester Hotel. He asked me if I could get away for a night and he'd book a room for me. After I got the okay from Jeep, I phoned him back and said I'd take the afternoon train into town. I met Gus in the hotel bar and we settled down to some serious drinking.

He told me that my father had had a severe attack of pancreatitis, but that he had pulled through and was fully recovered. Both my parents were anxious to know how I was getting along, which was a polite way of telling me that I should write more often. I admitted to having been a delinquent correspondent, but I just didn't seem to find the time to write at any great length. I didn't think my lim-

ited operational experience was anything to write home about anyway, with only four what we loosely called sweeps under my belt.
But Gus insisted on hearing about them in detail and asked me to
write them down so that he could take them back home.

He then asked me what I did for excitement, so I promised to
show him. After dinner I took him to one of my favourite haunts,
the Coconut Grove bottle club on Regent Street, of which I was a
member. We finished off a bottle of Scotch that had my name on it
and Gus bought me a new one, in which we made quite a dent. I
got completely carried away, and as we were leaving, followed my
usual ritual of making a pass at Molly, the miniskirted cigarette girl
who always stood by the door. By the time we got back to the hotel I
was in no shape to write that letter to my mother and father. I fell
right into bed.

When he got back to Halifax, Gus penned my mother the following note:

Dear Margaret:
    . . . Arthur is very cheery and looks awfully well—his side-
burns suit him too. Will tell you all about it when I see you.
                                                    Love, Gus

My father had obviously heard quite a different version of my
get-together with Gus:

Gus tells me that you are fine and happy but that your
language is not something Aunt Florence [great-aunt Lady
Eaton] would quite approve and that your behaviour was
somewhat obstreperous.

I asked Doc Thorn what the hell he meant by obstreperous.
"Drunk and disorderly, probably," was his only comment.

On July 15 we made another sortie as close escort to medium
twin-engine Bostons to bomb Poix airfield. Bob Hamilton's aircraft

and one of the Bostons were hit by the flak, which was heavy and accurate. Several FW-190s attacked from above, diving right through our formation. One of 411's pilots managed to damage one of them. Hammy's aircraft was still flyable, but the Boston had to limp back across the Channel on one engine, though it put down safely on an airfield near the coast.

Five days later we flew to 15 Armament Practice Camp at Martlesham Heath for a 10-day air firing course. Our shooting was not something that was liable to worry the Luftwaffe's chief, Reichsmarschall Hermann Goering, or to keep him awake at nights. In fact, it was pretty dismal. Even Bill Klersy, who had recently joined the squadron and who was highest in his class for marksmanship during his OTU course, scored a couple of goose eggs against the drogue targets. I shot away the tow line on three different occasions by leading the target too far, sending the drogues fluttering down into the sea, much to the chagrin of the Lysander towing crews, who had to land and get a new one each time.

On an afternoon off I spent the time in town basking in the sun at the local public swimming pool with wall-to-wall swimmers and sunbathers, including a host of local lovelies. That night I dined in the local hotel, joining an American lieutenant who was a Flying Fortress second pilot (the Yanks always referred to them as B-17s, their factory designation). His aircraft had crashed in a field close by after being badly damaged over the target, the Focke-Wulf aircraft factory in Bremen, Germany. The crew had been lucky there were no injuries. He told me it was his seventh mission, as the Americans called their raids. That left him with 18 more to complete his tour of 25 trips.

He was curious to know all about the Spitfire; his squadron had heard a great deal about it but had never seen one. The Fortresses were usually escorted by P-47 Thunderbolt fighters, nicknamed "jugs." A week before we flew to Martlesham, Lieutenant-Colonel Don Blakeslee, commander of the USAF Debden fighter group and erstwhile member of 401 Squadron, had flown down to Redhill to renew acquaintances with Jeep and Ormy. The Thunderbolt was a massive-looking machine. I remember thinking how large the cockpit seemed compared to the Spit, and noted that the instruments were the same as those in the Harvard on which all of us had trained. Blakeslee said, "It sure can dive, but the lumbering son of a bitch can't climb."

In my own small way I repaid Blakeslee's courtesy in showing us the Thunderbolt. I invited the Fort pilot, who was staying at the hotel where we dined, to Martlesham next morning, and showed him the Spitfire cockpit. He seemed fascinated as he watched the takeoffs and landings, but he would not have been so impressed had we revealed our practice scores.

The night after we returned to Redhill from Martlesham, on July 31, Ibby Ibbitson was riding his motorcycle in the blackout when he collided with a jeep. He was rushed to hospital, but even Doc Thorn's skill as surgeon couldn't save him, and early next morning he succumbed to internal injuries. This was a great loss for the squadron. The Snerd had been highly popular with pilots and ground crews alike. We all missed his "leaning tower of Pisa" stance that he demonstrated so ably during our drinking bouts.

As part of the transfer to the Tactical Air Force, we learned that we would be moving to a primitive airfield further south in Kent, where we would live and operate under canvas. This was part of a process of toughening us up for what the future held in store—our introduction to "hard living." But the news wasn't all bad; we would receive a hard-living allowance.

The squadron made one last sweep before we moved, but my part in it was logged "DNCO"—duty not carried out. Over Ashford, on our way to the British coast, the Spitfire suddenly began to vibrate. I throttled back slightly and the vibration stopped. I wondered whether I had been imagining things. But halfway across the English Channel, between Dover and the French coast east of Calais, the vibration started all over again, this time somewhat more pronounced. I throttled back and it stopped, but when I eased the throttle ahead, the shaking started once more. We were getting close to France, and I thought if I had to jump right then, at least I'd end up in the drink and could be picked up by the Air-Sea Rescue Service. That would be all right, but a little farther on and I would have to hit the silk over enemy-occupied territory. No thanks! I made a 180-degree turn and headed back across the Channel, with the throttle back just enough to prevent the craft from vibrating.

To the west of Ashford, a grass airfield appeared in my path. Without bothering to make a circuit, I lowered my wheels and flaps and landed, taxiing over to what looked like a small dispersal hut beside the field. I switched off and unbuttoned my face mask as a ground crewman walked over. I climbed out of the cockpit and described my problem and asked him if he would check to see what was wrong. He took my place in the seat and started up the engine while another crewman unscrewed the panel covering the engine on the port side. They put it through a brief run-up, then the man in the cockpit turned the engine off and said they couldn't find anything, suggesting that when I got home I should ask to have the engine put through a thorough maintenance check. Since Redhill was now only minutes away, I got back in the Spitfire and took off, hoping for the best.

On alighting I was greeted by Willy Worrell, who asked why I'd turned back. I gave him a rundown on what had happened and told him what the mechanic at the airfield had said. I could see he was a bit leery. Any green pilot turning back was naturally treated with suspicion—but in this case it didn't last long.

After the rest of the squadron had returned and we were loafing about the dispersal hut, Worrell dashed inside looking quite excited—or perhaps relieved. "You're a lucky guy," he said to me in his high-pitched voice. "We pulled off all the engine panels, then cranked the prop counter-clockwise [opposite to normal rotation], and the engine spewed out glycol in every direction. A few more miles and you'd have ended up in a field again." And if I hadn't turned back?

Five days later, on August 7, we flew to our new home in Staplehurst, in Kent. I wasn't too unhappy to leave the memories of such incidents behind me at Redhill.

Chapter 13

Hard Living

Staplehurst, Kent—August 7–October 31, 1943

> Unless you've had someone on your tail
> trying to kill you by shooting at you, you
> haven't the faintest idea what I'm talking
> about.
> —Wally Floody, 401 Squadron pilot and
> chief engineer of "The Great Escape"

Staplehurst lies directly south of the ancient city of Maidstone—
famous for its public baths—in the heart of the Kentish apple and
hop country. Our airfield (officially 126 Airfield, which was also our
wing designation) was a farmer's field with two steel-mesh runways. We lived and operated under canvas. Food was prepared in
field kitchens. All the workshops and equipment were housed in
specially built trucks so that we could break up and move to
another field on short notice, mobility being an essential element
of a tactical air force.

We rapidly adapted to our new living and working conditions—
with a few exceptions. Our tents were in a picturesque orchard that
offered shade from the hot summer sun, so when we retired they
were pleasantly cool. De Bub Hayward, Willy Cummings, and I
shared a tent and found the canvas cots quite comfortable. But we
all found it hard to get used to shaving in cold water out of canvas
wash buckets. However, we managed.

The pilot dispersal was adequate. We could stash our flying gear in a large tent, which also served as a shelter on rainy days. Some chairs had been appropriated from the Redhill dispersal and brought to Staplehurst by truck for relief from the "hard living."

If there was a single outstanding drawback, it was the food in the officers' mess. If we didn't have the worst messing sergeant chef in all of England, I am certain that only his counterpart at the Aldershot military prison could have run him a close second. On the first morning at breakfast, when I asked if I could have some cream and sugar in my porridge, his haughty reply was, "Sugar and cream is in the mush, sir!" The other meals weren't a whole lot better. The alternative was to take our evening repasts at one of the local pubs.

However, after our performance on the first night at Staplehurst it was a wonder they would serve us, or even let us in the door. We had been warned that the local cider was a lot more potent than it tasted, but we chose to ignore this well-meant neighbourly advice and proceeded to guzzle it down in great quantities as if it were mere apple juice. It soon took effect, and it didn't take long for us to collectively disgrace ourselves in the eyes of the local populace as an undisciplined, unprincipled bunch of boors. Some of the townsfolk expressed their resentment at our behaviour with what was not entirely a non sequitur: "Up until now we've been left alone. Now you've come here, it will bring the Germans."

We deserved our hangovers the next morning. I was not the only one to climb into the cockpit of my kite, connect the oxygen tube, and turn the dial up to 10,000 feet in order to clear my head. This practice was frowned upon by Doc Thorn, who predicted all kinds of nose, throat, and sinus problems. Fortunately for everyone concerned, we offered apologies and the local citizenry quickly overlooked our misconduct—after all, it was in everybody's interest to get along with each other. We soon developed a mutually warm relationship.

Two days after our arrival we made our first sweep from our new domicile, as escort to Marauders of the 9th U.S. Air Force on a mission to bomb the Luftwaffe fighter field at St. Omer. Cloud obscured the target, so the bombers had to dump their bombs into the sea on the return flight. This was standard procedure to avoid random bombing that might endanger the French populace.

Five days later, on August 15, 1943—a date that remains etched in my memory—I came as close to getting written off as at any time during my tour of operations. Right after lunch the entire wing flew to Predannack, on the south coast of Cornwall, a forlorn, rocky part of the world. There we were joined by 127 Wing for a sortie to provide fighter support to Westland Whirlwind "whirlybombers," whose mission was to attack the submarine pens at Brest, across the Channel in Brittany. Our formation consisted of 127 Wing flying top cover, with our wing underneath, stepped down by squadrons 412 and 411, with ourselves as low men on the totem pole. I was flying number four in Yellow section, led by Ormston.

When we were over the target the R/T crackled with shouts that made little sense to me, or perhaps I just wasn't listening—as tail-end Charlie I was too busy concentrating on keeping a sharp lookout above and behind me. Just in time I saw an FW-190 diving straight down at my tail, great red flashes erupting from the leading edges of his wings and nose. His gunfire missed me by a hair as I broke sharply to port in a climbing turn. The enemy aircraft flashed by and—thank God—kept on diving. After turning 180 degrees, I found myself all alone (when had that happened to me before?). Ahead I could make out a pair of Spitfires, so I put on full throttle to catch up.

When we landed, Jeep and Ormy ran over just as I was climbing out of the cockpit and asked, "Did you get hit?" I shook my head—not a scratch. "Grisle" Klersy* said, "Boy, you nearly went for a shit just then." Notably, neither side scored in this brief encounter. Our

*The nickname "Grisle" derived from a pair of comic strip characters in the *Daily Mail*: Pee Wee, a conniving little mastermind, and his huge, bear-like guardian, Grisle. "Grind him up, Grisle," Pee Wee would command with an evil look, rubbing his hands together. When we mimicked them, I was Pee Wee and Klersy was Grisle; for him, the name stuck.

wing had been bounced by 30-plus 190s, who simply took potshots as they dived right through us.

Three days afterward I was assigned as Jeep's number two. Our role once again was close escort to American Marauders—36 of them this time. The weather was frightful. Over Dunkirk, Jeep and I got separated from the rest of the squadron—which, of course, he was leading—and found ourselves in heavy grey clouds. It got so dark that I just concentrated on sticking to Jeep like glue, ignoring everything else. All of a sudden, a bunch of Flying Fortresses appeared above us—flying upside down—the whole bloody lot of them! Of course, it was an illusion. It quickly became apparent that *we* were the ones who were upside down. Jeep immediately pulled into a steep dive and I followed, right on his tail.

As soon as my aircraft became vertical, the armour-plate behind my seat started pressing against my back, pushing me forward toward the instrument panel. It had come loose, and it was heavy. I braced myself, holding the control column firmly between my knees to steady my dive, with my feet on the top rudder pedal bar and my hands on the top of the instrument panel. With all my strength I forced the panel back as far as I could and held it there. How long I could have maintained that status quo, I'll never know—because my back was aching furiously. But after what seemed like an eternity, Jeep, whom I had managed to keep in sight, finally pulled out of the dive and I followed. As we levelled out, the pressure behind me eased—a weight literally being lifted from my back—and I pulled up alongside the leader. "Red One," I called over the R/T, "my seat's come loose. I'd like to land and fix it."

"Okay," came the reply. "We'll land at Manston."

But another mini-ordeal still lay in store for me. When we touched down at the coastal aerodrome and rolled across that rough grassy terrain, the armour-plate kept slapping against my back—ouch!—until we came to a stop. We both shut off and climbed out to inspect the problem. It was simple. When my rigger (airframe mechanic) had unbolted the armour-plate to push it forward and open the oxygen bottle right behind the seat, he had forgotten to lock the spring bolt back into place.

(The incident was one that Jeep and I long remembered. Thirty years later, at a cocktail party at Bob Hamilton's condominium in Toronto, Jeep, who was in a sentimental mood, said to me, "You stuck with me among the Forts and I'm never going to forget it.")

Our sweeps concentrated mainly on escorting the U.S. Marauders to various targets in northwestern France, chiefly German airfields, and their anti-aircraft defences had been heavily strengthened in response. The size of the American formations gradually increased until they numbered as many as 75 bombers on any given raid. The master bomber called the shots. Once he was satisfied he had the objective properly sited, he gave the signal "bombs away," and the entire formation unloaded their missiles, plastering the target in a matter of seconds and ensuring instant mass destruction.

The downside was that if the master bomber's aim was off, every bomb from the entire formation would also go astray. On one occasion just such a misjudgment occurred on a ramrod to bomb the airfield at Lille (the "milk run") for which we flew close escort. All the bombs went awry. The flak was vicious; two of the bombers went down, one of them straight into the field. On our way back to the coast the Marauder commander called up our wing leader, Dal Russel, and asked, "Did you all see one of my boys hit the field?" Some smart aleck in our formation replied, "It was about the only thing that did hit the field."

When we landed, the usually imperturbable, mild-mannered Dal Russel was furious. At the debriefing he admonished angrily, "That was uncalled for and unfair. These people are new at this game and it's our job to do all we can to help them. I want the person who made that remark to see me personally and privately after this meeting."

We never did learn whether or not anyone stepped forward or, if he did, who it was. But several afternoons later it befell Willy Cummings, to whom I was flying wingman, and me to atone, in a way, for our confrere's impropriety. The milk run again, but this time the bombs were squarely on target. One of the Marauders, which was damaged by flak, began losing height and the crew became so disoriented that it veered off in a westerly direction instead of heading north to make for the Channel.

Jeep ordered Willy and me to break off and escort the stricken bomber. We formated on either side of the aircraft, which by this time had levelled off, and we switched over to the same R/T channel as the bomber. Willy got on the blower and told the pilot to correct his heading by turning to starboard and to follow us. "Wilco," came back the reply, the standard American acknowledgment, an abbreviation of "will comply." We learned that the bomber had lost its port engine. Our job was to see it safely across the Channel, ward off any enemy aircraft that might attack our lame duck, and fly cover if it had to ditch in the drink.

We flew slightly above and ahead of the Marauder, hoping no one would intrude on the tranquility of what was a beautiful summer evening. The sky was clear, and from 5000 feet the sea was a deep azure blue, tranquil and calm. It was so serene and peaceful that I felt lucky to be alive, fortunate to be a fighter pilot as I reflected on the wonderful life we led. One minute we would be over an enemy airfield dodging flak and fighters, concentrating so intently on the job at hand that there wasn't time to be scared. Later we would be entertaining some lovely at a local establishment, the recent dangers and excitement forgotten—which brought me abruptly out of my reverie, right bang into the present. I had a date for dinner at eight.

I had been squiring a local maiden who was serving with the Women's Land Army at one of the nearby farms. I not only enjoyed a warm relationship with her, she also kept me supplied with fresh eggs, of which there was a severe shortage in wartime Britain. On this particular evening I was to meet Julia at one of the local pubs that we frequented, and she did not like to be kept waiting. According to my watch it was now a few minutes past seven, and we were proceeding at half throttle, the English coastline still not in sight. If the Marauder ditched, I'd had it. I was becoming increasingly impatient as we lumbered across the Channel. The moments seemed to drag, and in an effort to keep my priorities straight, I kept praying that the bomber wouldn't have to ditch, or I'd never get to the Dragon's Arms on time. First things first, after all.

After what seemed an eternity, we finally crossed the coast just east of Dungeness, where the Americans said goodbye—"Thank you, little friends"—leaving us at last on our own. "I'm going through the gate,"* I told Willy. "I'm late already."

"Don't panic," he called back. "I want to get laid, too. Here we go!"

With throttles wide open we made it to Staplehurst in minutes. I dumped my flying helmet and 'chute in dispersal, rushed to my tent, where I changed from battledress into uniform, and ran all the way to the Dragon's Arms. It was half-past eight by the time I walked into the bar and found Julia sitting in a corner, a scowl on her pretty face.

"What kept you?" she asked in a not-too-friendly tone.

"I got held up in the traffic," I answered.

"There isn't any traffic," Julia scoffed. "And at least you could have shaved."

"Didn't have time," I explained lamely.

"Excuses! Excuses!" Julia said.

But it is amazing how a few ciders, a bottle of red wine, and dinner can turn a frosty start into a great evening.

On August 23, Wing Commander Keith Hodson, DFC, took over duties at 126 Airfield from Jimmy Walker. Keith had been CO of

---

*On the early Spitfires, a guard on the throttle quadrant—the "gate"—prevented the pilot from pushing the throttle to its limit, except in the case of an emergency. At full throttle the engine would run for only a few minutes before burning out. Later models were able to dispense with this precaution.

401 Squadron before Jeep took command, then for a brief period became Wingco Flying of the Kenley Wing. Keith was highly popular with all ranks and occasionally led our squadron on sweeps for old times' sake. His command fell under the jurisdiction of Iron Bill MacBrien, who had taken over 127 Airfield, now stationed at nearby Lashenden, also under canvas. Iron Bill had been promoted to the rank of group captain with responsibility for both 126 and 127 airfields. This was not a particularly popular appointment. He rarely flew on operations, and many former instructors with the group—such as Bob Hyndman and Hart Finlay, and most particularly De Bub Hayward—had served under him at Uplands and held less-than-fond memories of that servitude.

One evening Iron Bill appeared in our mess after dinner. I was not witness to the original discussion, but after a brief argument MacBrien ordered Dal Russel to bed. The usually even-tempered Dal stomped angrily out of the mess. Then it was De Bub's turn, with Jeep, Willy, Grisle Klersy, Sheppard, Hyndman, and me well within earshot. Hayward was just well enough oiled to lay it right on the line. To MacBrien he said, "You know, at Uplands I used to refer to you as 'Iron Bill.' But over here, as far as I'm concerned, you're 'Tin Willie' until you prove yourself a man."

"Tin Willie" was either too stunned—or too hammered, or both—to respond. His only rebuttal was, "I've got to make a speech before I get too drunk."

De Bub, like a dog with a bone, refused to let it drop. "Well, in my opinion," he ventured, "you've already had it."

Tin Willie! The name stuck.

During the summer of 1943 our escort sorties were of a moderate nature, rather mundane and routine, though we did encounter enemy fighters on rare occasions and there was always the danger of flak. But the medium-bomber raids were serving their purpose. To deter enemy defence preparations against the inevitable Allied invasion of Europe, the Allies had to constantly disrupt communications and destroy ammunition and fuel depots, as well as airfields and military installations. In addition, these forays supported the work of the underground and helped to maintain civilian morale. But from a fighter standpoint, it was our counterparts in the 127 Airfield wing, with their high-altitude Spitfire IXs, who were seeing all the action. However, this situation was about to change—slowly, but dramatically.

On August 17, 367 Flying Fortresses of the U.S. 8th Air Force penetrated deep into Germany to bomb the ball-bearing factories at Schweinfurt and Regensburg. The commander-in-chief of the American Air Forces in Europe, General Carl "Tooey" Spaatz, described the raid as "one of the most significant and remarkable air battles of the Second World War."

Even with long-range fuel tanks, Spitfire and Thunderbolt fighters were limited to escorting the bombers to the German border. Beyond that the Fortresses were on their own, and the Luftwaffe threw everything it had against them. But despite heavy—yet acceptable—losses of 20 percent, the raid set the pattern for daylight missions to come. From that date on the Luftwaffe began husbanding its fighter strength behind the German border to cope with what they recognized as a growing menace.

Starting from that very date, the Allied High Command began laying elaborate plans for an operation to entice the German fighters in huge numbers away from the daylight raids on the Fatherland toward the west. The objective was to take the pressure off the USAF and deliver the Luftwaffe fighter arm a decisive blow. The code name was Operation Starkey.

The number of medium-bomber raids increased. Between August 26 and September 7, I flew on five different escort sorties myself (three of them on the milk run to Lille). Wooden dummy aircraft began sprouting all over southeast England on farm fields and other sites presenting what looked like a mass buildup of air power, but purposefully easy to detect by enemy aerial reconnaissance. All of this was designed to create the impression that an invasion of the Continent was imminent. On the evening of September 8, Tin Willie gave us the word.

Shortly after midnight a flotilla of invasion craft escorted by warships would set sail across the English Channel from Dover in the direction of the Pas de Calais between Boulogne and Calais. But it would have no intention of landing there or anywhere else on the French coast. This was the essential element of the hoax. After it reached a point three-quarters of the way across the Channel, the flotilla would turn around and return to the embarkation port.

To complete the deception, just before daybreak, medium bombers would hammer at installations along the Pas de Calais coastline and directly behind it. By daybreak the "invasion fleet" would have reached a point halfway across the Channel, where it would be clearly visible. By this time, presumably, Goering and his commander of the German fighter arm, Generalleutnant Adolf Galland, would be propelled into action and all the defences along *Festung Europa* would be placed on full alert. Spitfires would form an umbrella over the "invasion area" and a full-scale battle would ensue, by which time the "invasion fleet" could return to Dover, its mission in the scam having been accomplished.

But, Tin Willie warned, his expression appropriately dour and grim for a commander who was about to unleash us into what promised to be one of the great aerial battles of all time, reprisals could be expected. Gunners with the RAF Regiment had already been brought up to full readiness on all airfields and small trenches were being dug around the dispersal areas. Winding up his briefing, MacBrien solemnly warned us that we could expect casualties as high as 50 percent. He wished us luck and ordered us to bed early so that we would be well rested for the morrow.

When we retired to our cots there was an orange on each pillow (the invasion of Sicily was at last paying off). The condemned men at least ate heartily before turning in, which is more than could be said for the usual breakfast the next morning. Fog blanketed the field so thickly we could hardly weave our way over to the mess tent to enjoy our usual plate of mush. Adding insult to injury, it was cold—the burners weren't operating properly. But then, neither was anything else.

By mid-morning the mist had thinned a bit, but not enough for takeoff, and there was a heavy overcast. We sat around like any other day, playing cards and shooting the shit. I wondered what it was like aboard the invasion fleet mid-Channel. Truth was, I couldn't have cared less. Obviously Operation Starkey was a dud. Great expectations had come to nothing, Sicilian orange or no Sicilian orange. Only our spy, Intelligence Officer John Sancton, kept the old Operation Starkey spirit alive as he wandered to and fro, waiting for God-knows-what, incongruously clad in his helmet, with his revolver at his waist and his gasmask bag over his shoulder. "Who's he going to shoot?" Hammy asked. Good question. It sure as hell wasn't the Luftwaffe.

By early afternoon the weather had cleared sufficiently for us to take off on a ramrod to Courtrai. But the weather turned so bad that by the time we reached North Foreland we had to turn back. Much later in the day, another sweep succeeded in getting through to the same target, but there was no sign of the German Air Force—no flak, no nothing. The Germans obviously hadn't been taken in by the deception; in fact, they probably hadn't even been aware of it.

That evening we skipped the usual Sicilian orange and imbibed on cider and ale instead. We felt we'd been had. As far as we were concerned, Tin Willie and his goddamned Operation Starkey could get stuffed. We were thoroughly pissed off. We resented bitterly that he didn't even have the guts to show his face and explain himself. Looking back, in the shape we got ourselves into that night, I think it's probably a good thing he didn't.

In fairness, this nonsensical farce was not of MacBrien's making. He was just as much a victim of circumstances as the rest of us. The powdered egg on his face belonged rightly to those on high who conceived the idea in the first place. In restitution, on the following day the powers that be unashamedly issued a 24-hour stand-down for all fighter groups. "The RAF Rests," as the daily press headlined this historic drama. Good public relations? More like propaganda.

I made two more sweeps over the next four days, bringing my total operational outings to 19 before going on a week's leave. When I arrived at Victoria Station in London, I ran into Wing Commander Lapsley. It seemed like only yesterday that I had stood before his desk at Aston Down to be disciplined for my New Year's Eve *faux pas*. This time he was much friendlier. He greeted me warmly, asked how I was getting along, and gave me a lift by cab to Buck's Club, where I checked in to arrange for hotel accommodation. With the influx of Americans, rooms were scarce in London at that time, but the club secretary was able to secure one for me at the Goring Hotel (having been renamed since 1939 from the original Goering—as in Hermann).

After registering at the hotel I called in at the Eaton's office on Regent Street, where I kept a trunk that I had brought over on the *Akaroa* full of fresh underwear, socks, shorts, and canned goods such as butter, condensed milk, bacon, and sausages—items that were strictly rationed in the wartime U.K., the meat being almost nonexistent.

Percy Portlock, the Eaton's resident director, was out of town, but his secretary told me that my Uncle Hank Burden was in the city, and gave me the phone number where he could be reached. He was staying with Beverley Shenston, an aeronautical engineer from Toronto who was with the British Air Ministry. He had been the aerodynamicist member of the Supermarine Aircraft Company design team that produced the Spitfire. I called Hank from the office and he invited me to join him and Shenston at the Carleton Club that evening for dinner.

It didn't take long for the table talk to get around to the Spitfire, since we were old pro Hank (26 enemy planes to his credit in World War I), embryo ops type me, and Shen, architect of my trusty steed, YOK. I ventured the opinion that in this current show, the Spit was the way to go.

"You are certainly to be congratulated," I told Shen. "It's like riding a polo pony. You become a part of it—and vice versa."

"It really is the most beautiful machine," Hank commented. ("Machines" were what the World War I types called their airplanes. We referred to them as "kites" or, more formally, "aircraft.")

"The elliptical wing was something that just happened," Shen said.

"Wasn't it copied from one of the German Heinkel planes?" I asked.

"No," was his answer. "Almost from the beginning we chose it because aerodynamically the induced drag created by producing lift was lowest with that shape of wing. We wanted the lowest possible wing-thickness-to-chord [surface area] ratio while still maintaining the strength we needed. But near the wing root it had to be thick enough to accommodate the retracted undercarriage and the guns. In fact, R.J. [Reginald Joseph Mitchell, the Supermarine's chief designer] said to me, 'I don't give a shit whether the wing is elliptical or not, so long as it covers the guns.'"

"So it wasn't copied from other aircraft, as I've heard?" I asked.

"Absolutely not. The ellipse was simply the shape that gave us the thinnest wing possible into which we could still stuff all the things we needed to."

As an afterthought he added, "But there was an innovation I did copy from the Heinkel transport—the countersunk rivets that gave the metal skin its flush, smooth look. In fact, I indulged in quite a lot of correspondence with Ernst [Heinkel]. He was most cooperative. I wonder if he realized he was providing us with helpful information for a fighter that would one day be shooting down some of his bombers."

Then Shen quickly changed the topic of conversation. In the next breath he asked, "Where are you spending your leave?"

I replied that I hadn't given it much thought, only just having arrived in London that morning. "I guess I'll just have to tough it out at the Goring until something better comes along," I said.

"You want to keep a sharp lookout so that you don't trip over all those crutches in that place," Hank said with a grin.

"I'll do better than that," Shen piped up. "I've got some friends that I'm sure would like to have you stay with them. I'll phone them right now and set it up."

He left the table and was back in no time at all. "It's all arranged." he announced. "Take the Oxford train tomorrow morning. Here's the address."

Enroute to the university city, I shared a compartment with three American officers. One of them happened to notice my name "F/O W.A. BISHOP" painted prominently in white on my suitcase (according to RCAF instructions for overseas drafts).

"Are you any relation to the flyer Billy Bishop?" he asked. I never knew where that question was going to lead to. At the time I found such unexpected questions, out of the blue, particularly from strangers, embarrassing. I preferred to avoid any such identification; I guess I was still trying to play it down. "No," I replied.

"Oh," he said. "I met the old gentleman once when I was in Quebec City." Fair enough, but I didn't care to pursue it and stuck with my earlier resolution to deny any kinship.

I spent four days in the delightful city of Oxford. The family I stayed with could not have been friendlier or more gracious. They seemed genuinely interested in what I was doing, and even more interested in making me feel right at home, at which they certainly succeeded. They seemed particularly curious about "The RAF Rests" headline in the daily press, and they got quite a charge out of my suggestion that a better headline would have been "The Big Hoax." This was my first real experience with British hospitality, and I thoroughly appreciated and enjoyed it. In those peaceful surroundings for those few days, the war seemed so remote to me that it could have belonged to another world, another time.

I spent the rest of my leave staying with Gus Edwards at the house he had recently commandeered on the edge of the Duke of

Richmond's estate in London, adjacent to a golf course. A discussion we had that was close to Gus's heart was the Canadianization of the RCAF overseas. "It was something your father championed from day one," he said. It brought to mind a letter my father had written in 1918 as a staff officer, which read

Under the present circumstances, Canadians in the RAF, although doing remarkably well, are certainly not doing as well as if they were in a Canadian Corps for the reasons that (1) They are in a great many circumstances working under senior officers who do not understand them. (2) They are also working with officers who do not understand them or often appreciate their different point of view. (3) They have not the personal touch with their country which branches of the Canadian Corps have and consequently are not inspired by direct connection with the country they are fighting for and the people back home.

Oh, Canada! Unwittingly, perhaps, this letter may have given rise to an issue that became a bone of contention from almost the very outbreak of World War II. The controversy would last nearly until the cessation of hostilities—a see-saw issue, bitter at times, between the Canadian government and the chiefs of the RCAF on one hand and the RAF and the British Air Ministry on the other—made worse by indecision at home in Canada. And at the very centre was my host, Uncle Gus Edwards himself.

At the time I was staying with him I had no idea of the complexities of this situation. However, as a graduate of the British Commonwealth Air Training Plan (BCATP) and a six-month veteran of an RCAF squadron, I could readily share his sentiments. As pleasant as my RAF advanced training was, after mixing with the British, Aussies, and New Zealanders, joining a Canadian squadron was like coming home.

The Empire Air Training Scheme was first presented to the

Commonwealth countries on September 28, 1939. The British asked that Ottawa finance the scheme, and at the same time had the gall to demand that all trainees be enlisted directly into the RAF. In Whitehall's opinion, RCAF units would be superfluous—unnecessary.

This high-handedness—virtually treating Canada as once more a colony—did not sit well with the Canadian War Cabinet. Particularly riled was Prime Minister Mackenzie King, who was a strong advocate of forming as many RCAF squadrons overseas as possible in the shortest possible time. He angrily denounced the British approach. Canadians enlisting in the BCATP would become members of the RCAF—period.

King stipulated in Article XV of the BCATP agreement, which dealt with national identity and affiliation, that "Canadian personnel from the training plan will, on request from the Canadian government, be organized into Royal Canadian Air Force units and functions in the field." However, this was easier said than done. Canadianization produced its own problems.

Unlike recruits who joined the army or navy, the air force recruit was not assigned to a combat unit, that is, a regiment or ship of Canadian origin. The RCAF enrollee could not be posted to a squadron overseas until he had completed training in Canada for his chosen vocation. In the early stages of the war, he would more likely be assigned to an RAF squadron, because few RCAF squadrons were in operation in the United Kingdom in relation to the number of graduates arriving overseas. (By the end of 1941 there were only 15 RCAF squadrons operating overseas *vis-à-vis* a disproportionate total of nearly 12,000 personnel, 6,800 of whom were aircrew.)

Complicating this issue was the status given to RCAF Headquarters overseas—that of a liaison office. When Air Commodore Leigh Stevenson took over in October 1940, he was instructed by the Canadian Chief of Air Staff, Air Marshal Lloyd Breadner, to hand over all administrative responsibilities to the RAF, and that "as a matter of national policy all RCAF personnel should be integrated into the Royal Air Force."

The CAS and other senior air force staff officers, who were looking to cut dominion administrative costs, were far more concerned about the problems and ramifications of the giant training plan than they were about overseas operations, which they considered to be the RAF's responsibility anyway. In view of Mackenzie King's determination to have a strong overseas RCAF fighting force, that policy was doomed to a short life.

The inevitable shakeup came a year later. On October 24, 1941, Air Vice-Marshal Harold "Gus" Edwards, former air member for personnel, assumed the office of Air Officer, Commander-in-Chief (AOC-in-C) RCAF Overseas. His deputy was Air Commodore Wilf Curtis. They made a formidable pair, well qualified to carry out Minister for Air Charles "Chubby" Power's mandate to "put the RCAF on the map . . . make the Canadians known . . . get as many squadrons as possible with Canadian aircrews and Canadian commanding officers."

Breadner underscored this dictum with his own instruction to "convey to it [the British Air Ministry] in the strongest possible terms the Canadian Government's desire to use Canadians in Canadian squadrons and keep continued pressure to this end. Our policy must be to build up Canadian squadrons as quickly as circumstances permit."

It proved to be an uphill battle. Edwards' initial optimism on taking over his new post of AOC-in-C quickly turned to despair by the fall of 1942. The first indication of the Air Ministry's continuing resistance to Canadianization came when it failed to inform RCAF overseas headquarters that RCAF squadrons would take part in the Dieppe raid in August 1942. Edwards may have been overreacting, but this illustrates the RAF's attitude all the same. The following September, an RCAF communiqué stated that an RCAF bomber squadron had taken part in a raid on Frankfurt without the loss of a single aircrew. Intended for Canadian consumption, it neverthe-less found its way into the London papers. The Air Ministry was not amused.

Then the controversy was extended to the home front, when Edwards told a group of visiting Canadian journalists that "some people are talking a lot of bloody nonsense about splitting the Empire. If Canadians who see it from that point of view want to be mugs all their lives, that's their business. I see no reason to oppose Canadianization." When asked what papers he was referring to, he singled out the Montreal *Gazette* and the Toronto *Globe and Mail*, infuriating the owners of both.

Breadner signalled to him from Ottawa: "Your statement to Canadian editors . . . is causing considerable furor here." At the same time, he was told to retract his statement in order to avoid a crisis with the RAF and the Air Ministry. He did, saving his job and smoothing feathers all round.

But Edwards stuck to his guns all the same and kept badgering the Air Ministry to speed up the Canadianization of airmen over-seas. In particular he singled out Air Marshal Sir Bertrine Sutton, RAF member for personnel, and Air Marshal J.J. Breen, the direc-tor of general postings.

By the time of my visit with Uncle Gus—mid-1943—the RCAF already had 33 squadrons overseas, and by year's end it would climb to a total of 40. A job well done. His health failing, Gus was replaced as AOC-in-C, RCAF Overseas, by Lloyd Breadner.

I returned from leave to Staplehurst at the beginning of the last week of September. The first sweep I flew when I got back was a wing ramrod escort to medium bombers to Amiens, led for some inexplicable reason in Wingco Dal Russel's absence by a squadron commander from one of the other squadrons. Jeep was thoroughly pissed off—understandably so. From a seniority standpoint he should have been leading, and I for one considered it a slight, an insult. On landing after a completely uneventful sortie, Jeep was greeted as usual by our intelligence officer, John Sancton, for the CO's report.

"Sanc," Jeep snarled, "Sergeant Blackburn could have led that sweep."

"Who," I asked the IO, "is Sergeant Blackburn?"

Sanc smiled and replied quietly, "He was a pilot we had who landed with wheels up three times in a row." That said it all.

Next day Ormy went for a swim. When his engine quit halfway across the Channel, he bailed out and was quickly picked up by an Air-Sea Rescue Walrus seaplane. Unfazed by the experience, he was back in the mess in time for lunch. On the following morning he was given command of 411 Squadron, the former CO having completed his tour.

There was news from the home front. In a letter Cilla wrote that "Tony thinks I would love London." Tony?

"Probably some Aussie with a couple of gongs [medals]," Jeep consoled me (thanks a bunch, boss).

I had my own idea, which I expressed by return mail: "Who is Tony? Some civilian in a green sportscoat?" I had to wait for over a year to receive an answer to that question—and then in person, and in no uncertain terms.

As Cilla recalls, "I wasn't about to honour that cocky so-and-so with a reply. He could damn well wait until I saw him. Meanwhile, I screwed up his letter and put it away in a box until I got a chance to face him with it."

The other bulletin from home was a verbal one, which also called for reciprocal action. Willy Cummings and I had hitched a ride to a pub in Seven Oaks for a date with two girls we knew. Also in the bar were Dal Russel, George Keefer, the CO of 412 Squadron, and Ormy, celebrating the latter's appointment as CO of 411, along with Freddy Green, the newly installed CO of 416, who was on his second tour. He had recently returned from a stint as an OTU instructor in Canada, and while on leave he had dined at my family's house in Ottawa. I asked how my parents were, and with a grin he said, "Your father said, 'I hear he is drinking a lot.' " *Well!*

How to retaliate? Circumstances played right into my hands. At the time the newspapers were full of stories about the arrest of Count Alfred de Marigny, who had been charged with slaying his father-in-law, Sir Harry Oakes. Marigny's wife, Nancy (née Oakes), was reported to have fled to Mexico. (You'd have thought that she could at least have shown up at the Bath and Tennis Club in Palm Beach for a lunch interview just for old times' sake.) It was too good an opportunity to miss.

I cabled my parents: I NEVER REALIZED UNTIL NOW HOW IMPORTANT IT WAS TO KNOW SUCH NICE PEOPLE UNTIL I READ IN THE PAPER ABOUT HARRY OAKES MURDER STOP I'LL DRINK A TOAST OR TWO TO THAT.

Earlier that year my mother and father had been staying in Nassau, during which time an incident took place. Although it in no way related to the Oakes murder, it is not entirely out of context, because the letter my mother wrote in reply to my telegram included the following anecdote.

At the time the Duke of Windsor was the Governor General of the Bahamas. My parents were invited to Government House for dinner, a formal occasion at which my father wore uniform. It turned out to be a pretty shattering experience, as my mother related to me:

The Duke was late coming downstairs, and when he did appear he was quite drunk. When we sat down I was on his right and he spilled his glass of wine on the table and nearly on me as well. The Duchess, who is not the beauty some make her out to be— her head is too big for her body for one thing—kept referring to the Queen as "that woman."

Billy finally had to tell her: "Duchess, I am serving the Queen in this uniform, and if you persist I will be forced to ask your permission to leave."

The Duke then turned to Billy and said "I see you're wearing your medals [ribbons, to be correct]. I left mine in Paris." "Well sir," Billy replied, "I imagine Goering's wearing them now." The Duke took umbrage. "Absolutely not. Goering is a fine gentleman!" Billy's answer was, "Yes, and a fine enemy too !"

Truly an evening to remember.

Our wing remained at Staplehurst until the middle of October, by which time, with autumn in full stride, life under canvas was less than comfortable. We'd wake up to damp, chilly mornings that the breakfast of mush did little to warm.

Lounging about when we weren't flying, we kept the chill off by taking a jerry can with the top cut off and filling it with sand and precious 100-octane airplane fuel to make a fire. We also managed to keep warm by sawing logs for firewood. A picture taken by the PR people of me chopping a piece of firewood found its way into the Canadian newspapers with the following caption:

Keeping Fit
Flying Officer W.A. Bishop, Ottawa, smiles as he swings a
hefty axe in the battle of the firebox, a continuous campaign to
keep warm at an RCAF fighter base in Britain.

This brought a missive from home—a chuckle this time from my mother, who wrote:

You didn't fool anyone, dear. You might know how to swing a golf club but you certainly don't know how to wield a "hefty axe." Never mind, I won't tell anyone.

Love, Mum

Our operations for the remainder of our stay at Staplehurst followed the same old routine, flying as escort to medium bombers with very little or no action other than the usual flak. One sweep, however, did provide a few minutes of excitement. It took place on October 3, when we flew a withdrawal mission for 12 Bostons whose objective had been Beauvais, with Jeep leading the wing. When we reached the rendezvous point over France, there was no sign of the bombers, so we withdrew.

En route, Al Studholme's aircraft was hit by anti-aircraft fire from a flak train below us. It made a large hole in one of his wings but he managed to get home safely. When we reached the French coast, a dozen or more FW-190s bounced us from above. Jeep's voice came over the R/T loud and clear: "Let's get out of here, fellas!" Meanwhile, as we broke around into the attackers, one of the pilots from 412 Squadron shot two of them down.

Our last sortie before moving from cider country occurred five days later and was memorable only for what it never achieved. I noted in my log book: "RAMROD TO LILLE. Close escort to 72 Marauders. 10/10 cloud all over France. No Flak. No fighters. No target. SMART!!!" When I was making this entry I accidentally sprayed a few ink blotches onto the page. One day I opened the log to find a notation from Bob Hamilton: "These ink spots represent flak no doubt." (I swore I'd get even with him some day.)

A week later we were on our way to our home for the next five and a half months—Biggin Hill, the most famous fighter station in all of England.

Chapter 14

On the Bump

Biggin Hill, Kent—October 13, 1943–March 30, 1944

> You're going to get shot down. Then
> what's old man Bishop going to say?
> —Buck McNair,
> Wingco Flying, 126 Wing RCAF

Located on a windswept crest of the North Downs overlooking the Weald of Kent to the west, Biggin Hill was a mere hour's drive from Piccadilly Circus. While autumn mists hung low in the valleys on either side, "Biggin on the Bump" was often left clear when all other airfields in the south of England were socked in.

In 1916 it had been chosen as the ideal site for an airfield from which to conduct aerial wireless experiments; there were no sources of electrical interference and its altitude helped increase the range of wireless signals. But even more significantly from another standpoint, it occupied a unique position for guarding the southern approaches to London in defending the capital against air attack.

In May 1917, Biggin Hill's strategic importance became obvious when the Germans launched the first of their Gotha bomber raids against London. In January 1918, two Home Defence squadrons were transferred to Biggin Hill, a portent of its future role as a key fighter sector station.

A generation later, during the Battle of Britain in the summer of 1940, the station took on historical significance as the most prominent of all the fighter fields, producing such RAF aces as Sailor Malan, Michael Crossley, Brian Kingaby, and Tony Bartley (also the husband of actress Deborah Kerr). The Germans attached such strategic importance to the Bump that on Friday, August 30, on two different occasions they dispatched 150 Junkers 88 and Heinkel 111 bombers, escorted by as many Messerschmitt ME-109 fighters, to wipe it off the map. In this the German Luftwaffe very nearly succeeded. The workshops and cookhouses were wrecked; the sergeants' mess, the WAAF quarters, and the airmen's barracks were all left uninhabitable. Ninety percent of the station's transport was damaged or destroyed; one hangar received a direct hit and two aircraft were burnt out; and all electricity, water, and gas mains were cut off. But Biggin Hill survived and went on to send fighters to do battle for many another day.

On May 15, 1943, five months before our arrival, René Mouchette, CO of the 344 Free French Squadron, and Jack Charles, the former armament officer at Aston Down who was now CO of 611 Squadron RAF, shared in the shooting down of the station's thousandth Hun, an FW-190 over Caen aerodrome in Normandy. The event was celebrated by the biggest party in Biggin Hill's history, a gala affair held at Grosvenor House in London to which 1000 guests were invited, including the heads of Fighter Command and Bomber Command, at a prodigious cost of £2500.

To some in our wing, such as Jeep Neal and Ian Ormston, the move to Biggin Hill was like coming home; 401 Squadron had been stationed there earlier, from October 20, 1941, to March 18, 1942. To the rest of us it was a welcome transition from sleeping, eating, and washing outdoors to enjoying the amenities and performing our ablutions indoors again.

The officers' mess was one of those imposing permanent force buildings like the one I had first seen and lived in at Watton, during my Advanced Flying Unit training back in the fall of 1942. It was separated from the rest of the station by a road that ran past the west end of the main runway. This mess boasted the added luxury of a swimming pool. Alas, all this comfort was not yet to be ours to savour. The powers that be were intent on making sure we earned our blood money—our hard-living allowance—by condemning us to abandoned barracks that had seen better days. It was our first experience with biscuit mattresses—three square pads on sagging bed springs that took some getting used to. Willy, De Bub, and I shared a room with Hayward's girlfriend's Irish setter, who insisted on sleeping on the foot of my bed, muddy paws and all.

The temporary officers' mess was a converted commanding officer's residence, a small two-storey building that served as a dining room downstairs and as a bar with a fireplace upstairs. The change for the better—much better—was the food. The Staplehurst messing sergeant must have got lost in transit, thank God. Nobody missed him. There was no more mush-with-the-cream-and-sugar-already-in-it. Now we had the real thing: porridge with the option of helping ourselves to the condiments. And the rest of the meals were excellent. Augmenting this improved cuisine was a tea house, on the same side of the road running past the permanent mess, at which eggs, so scarce in wartime Britain, were always in plentiful supply.

Social amenities abounded in the vicinity. In the immediate neighbourhood, along the road south of the station leading east off the main thoroughfare, was the pub that had served Biggin Hill pilots since way back when. One table was inscribed with the signatures of many Battle of Britain pilots.

The nearest town was Bromley, a London suburb several miles to the north that was 15 minutes or so by bus or taxi. It offered a variety of pubs and a good hotel, the Bromley Court, as well as the unforgettable Bromley Country Club dance hall (facetiously nicknamed the "gonorrhea race track"), with its fine selection of local young females. And, of course, London was within easy reach, a half-hour's train ride from the Bromley railway station.

Social activities were high on the agenda at Biggin Hill that winter. The days were short, so there was plenty of time for evening recreation, and the weather was "duff" a lot of the time, so on many days we stood down. The station was the scene of regular dances both for all ranks, in one of the hangars, and at the officers' mess, which hosted some of the most lavish wartime parties in the south of England. Being so close to the various headquarters in London, they also attracted many of the brass.

Our discomfort in the barracks block did not last long. Taking matters into his own hands, Jeep had us moved into the permanent mess, which was close to our dispersal, across the road on the west side of the field. This was to be shortlived, however. Keith Hodson, the field commander, and Buck McNair, the Malta ace who had taken over from Dal Russel as Wingco Flying, decided on a policy of rotation. Each squadron would have a month's stay in the permanent mess and spend the rest of the time in the barracks.

Our biggest cause for elation at this time was our conversion from the Spitfire V to the new Mark IXB, generally accepted as the finest version of that famous fighter. Powered by a 1650-horsepower Rolls-Royce Merlin engine, it had a maximum speed of 408 miles an hour at 25,000 feet. One of its most appealing features was the automatic supercharger that cut in at 20,000 feet, which could also be activated manually below that altitude. This put the aircraft at a great advantage over the FW-190 and the ME-109, which had hitherto counted on a flagging performance from the Spitfire at that altitude that they could easily outrun. The IXB also offered improved firepower: two 30-millimeter Hispano cannons and four .303 calibre Browning machine guns. And finally, in the words of our leading ace, Johnny Johnson, "It was such a delight to fly."

The new Spitfires were fitted with a 45-gallon drop tank that from underneath resembled a bomb or a cigar. However, it still did not give us enough range to escort the Flying Fortresses beyond the Dutch–German border when they flew their daylight missions into the heart of the Third Reich.

One late afternoon in October, two Forts landed at Biggin, which was the only field open in the entire south of England. They had been badly shot up after a raid on the Schweinfurt ball-bearing factory—a round trip of 800 miles that had taken them deep into Germany. One of the bombers had a hole in the starboard wing you could have driven a Jeep through. Two of the engines had been knocked out.

On alighting, the pilot signalled the blood wagon (ambulance) orderlies to bring out the body of one his crewmen. "The boy came forward to the flight deck," he explained, "to take a photograph over the target. He was standing there when a piece of shrapnel from the flak blew his arm right off. We were under such heavy attack from enemy fighters, no one could leave their station to help him, and he bled to death." Our MO, Doc Thorn, followed the medics into the aircraft. He emerged carrying something in a blanket. "What's that?" someone asked. "See for yourself," Doc said. It was the severed arm of the dead crewman. I nearly lost my lunch.

Following Doc out of the bomber was a short fellow wearing a baseball hat and a bright orange turtleneck sweater. When he alighted he got down on his hands and knees and kissed the ground. "I'm never going to leave you again," he promised. He was the rear gunner. "We were under attack for six solid hours. To hell with that noise," he grumbled. "That was my twenty-ninth trip. That leaves one to go to complete my tour. Well, they can make it without me."

That was a devastating mission for the U.S. 8th Air Force. Sixty Flying Fortresses were lost and some 600 crew members were reported missing. As the skipper of one of the bombers that landed at our field put it, "Airmageddon! You could have walked to Berlin on the parachutes!" Adding insult to injury was the fact that the raid had no decisive effect on the output of ball bearings which were so essential to the German war industry. It was a wasted effort at a terrible cost. It was becoming obvious that without long-range fighter escort, deep penetrations into the enemy heartland would have to be curtailed.

Our ground crews were busy modifying our new Spitfires, fresh from the factory, and synchronizing the guns to put them in operational condition. During that time, my cousin Jack Vaughan, whom I hadn't seen since January at the Savoy, visited the station at my invitation. He had been posted to Italy, which the Allies had invaded on September 3, beginning their methodical, slogging advance northward. His job as an army intelligence officer would be to interrogate enemy prisoners at the front line the moment they were captured.

We had been out on a fighter sweep when Jack arrived at the station. He was waiting for me in the anteroom when I reached the mess. We went upstairs, where I changed from battledress into my uniform before going downstairs to meet the others in the bar before dinner. Neither of us was prepared for what happened next.

As we entered the room, Jeep stepped forward, shook Jack's hand, and said, "We've all been waiting to meet that son of a bitch of a cousin Bishop's been complaining about all week." Hammy clapped him on the shoulder. "Welcome to 401," he greeted Jack, "despite what Bish has to say about you." It had been well rehearsed. The others all joined in in the same vein to try to make my "bloody" cousin feel at home. Jack took it all in good spirit and thoroughly enjoyed the "thrash" we had that night before turning in.

I'd wanted to take Jack up for a flight in our squadron Tiger Moth the next morning, but Jeep vetoed the notion on highly sensible grounds. "If he wants a flip, someone else can take him up. If you do it, you'll start showing off and probably have an accident." In any case, wet weather the next day scrubbed all flying. But Jeep's sage precept became a hard-and-fast unwritten rule that applied to all visitors from then on. When I said goodbye to Jack that afternoon and wished him luck, he radiated confidence, anxious to see some action. "Don't worry, he said. "The war will be over by Christmas." I made a small bet with him that victory was at least a year away.

Another visitor to Biggin Hill that fall was a former member of the squadron, Don Morrison. A year earlier, on November 8, 1942, when he was shot down by an FW-190 over France, he was the leading RCAF ace in the RAF Fighter Command, credited with six enemy aircraft destroyed, four probables, and four damaged. Don had managed to bail out—minus his left leg, which stayed in the Spitfire. In the fall of 1943, because he was an amputee he was repatriated in a prisoner-of-war exchange, and stayed with us for a couple of days before shipping home to Canada. The biggest drawbacks to being a POW, he told us, were sheer boredom and lack of food. "Most of the time is taken up planning how to escape," he said.

At that time we had two new flight commanders. Jack Sheppard took over A Flight and Deane MacDonald, DFC, who had served with 401 Squadron and then became a flight commander with 403 at Kenley, was made commander of B Flight. Another second-tour pilot, Lorne Cameron, also joined the squadron during this period.

During October, a delegation headed by De Bub Hayward and including Mac McRae, Norm Maybee, and Bill Morrisey entrained for Netheravon to take a brief course in glider towing. The "boffins" were military scientific geniuses constantly on the lookout for something new to fill our time. They had got the idea that for the coming invasion, in the event of a shortage of transport aircraft, ammunition and other supplies could be packed into small ply-wood General Aircraft Hotspur gliders and towed to the Continent by fighters. Having completed the course, our delegates returned to Biggin Hill to give us a demonstration.

I was paired with De Bub in the Hotspur with a full load of live ammunition. Grisle Klersy did the towing and Hayward drove the glider. We made a circuit, then Klersy released the glider and we were on our own. Hayward got the Hotspur down on the runway, but a crosswind blew us off the tarmac onto the grass at right angles to the direction we had landed in. We were headed for the perimeter. Hayward jettisoned the wheels, which slowed our speed somewhat, but not enough to prevent our skidding right into the barbed-wire fence at the edge of the field, tearing off part of the starboard wing in the process.

Luckily there was no other damage and the ammunition remained intact. Jeep, who had been watching this performance from dispersal, came rushing out in the squadron truck with Hamilton in the passenger seat. The four of us hitched the glider to the back of the truck with some rope. Hayward and I climbed into the back, and with Hammy in the cab, Jeep set off down the taxi strip to dispersal. We were just picking up speed when the Hotspur began swinging from side to side. Hayward banged his fist on the partition behind the driver's seat for Jeep to slow down. But Jeep took it as a signal to stop, and put on the brakes. The truck screeched to a halt and the glider banged into the back of it, knocking off the port wing.

Jeep climbed out and said, "Bishop, you're a jinx. Get the hell out of the truck and walk!"

"What about the glider?" Hayward beseeched.

"Blame it on your flying accident," was Jeep's curt reply, and he climbed back into the cab.

Some months later the glider/fighter experiments came to an end. The boffins had at last come to the realization that this means of transportation was impractical. Back to the drawing board.

At that stage in our operations, the 45-gallon drop tanks were giving us trouble. For safety's sake, the drill was to climb to 1000 feet over the field on takeoff, then switch from the main tank to the drop. If the transfer failed because of an airlock and you lost engine power, as was frequently the case, you could lower the undercart and land. The same problem occurred on actual sorties when pilots switched back to the main tank. We would fly to the limit of the range of the drop, the leader would signal "switch tanks," and we would make the transition, then pull the release to drop the "bomb." If the switch failed to take, you'd start priming the injection pump like mad to try and restart the engine.

On one fighter sweep we got the order to switch at 20,000 feet over Bruay. Mine didn't take, nor did Bob Hamilton's. We glided down in tandem, right over the Crecy Forest, pumping like mad, hoping to make it as far as the Channel before we'd have to bail out. We were losing height so fast I couldn't believe it. "Creaky" Forest was loaded with flak guns. Seeing our plight, the gunners opened up with everything they had, the ugly black puffs bursting all around us. You could hear the *phoofs* as they exploded—not a comforting situation.

Thankfully, over Étaples on the French coast, both our engines picked up almost simultaneously. By that time we were down to just under 3000 feet. We flew straight home. I was sweating, even though the temperature outside must have been well below freezing.*

Bob and I were lucky. On November 30, we lost two pilots, presumably—though there could be no proof—because of the same sort of airlock when they were switching tanks on a ramrod to Rotterdam, west of Vlaardingen on the Dutch coast. Both Al Studholme and Deane MacDonald experienced engine failure. Studholme bailed out and was immediately picked up by a German launch and taken prisoner.

Because he was at an altitude of 27,000 feet, MacDonald decided he had a chance to glide back to the English coast—a distance of about a hundred miles—a fateful decision, as it turned out. Lorne Cameron, his number two, faithfully stuck with him.

It wasn't easy. The air was bumpy and Cam had to throttle right back. They descended into the top of the cloud base at 10,000 feet. Now they were on instruments and the cumulus was thick and dark.

---

* We wore electric heating jackets, but they didn't wear well. They quickly became threadbare in some spots, exposing the wiring. After a few shocks from the wires, I discarded mine and opted instead for wearing an old hockey sweater under my battledress jacket and a white silk scarf around my neck.

All the while, Cam maintained R/T contact with control. They emerged from the cloud base at 2000 feet. It was snowing, and land was still not in sight. Cam knew they were in trouble. The shattered wingman described the episode's grim ending that night in the bar.

"When we were 1000 feet off the water, MacDonald decided to bail out. He pulled his hood back and started to push himself out of the cockpit. He was about halfway out, to his waist, when suddenly he lost control. The aircraft swung to the left—I was on his right—and went straight in, swallowed up by large waves. I was so low I skimmed them."

These incidents were far from the last of our experiences with the drop tanks. Meanwhile, Cam took over from MacDonald as commander of B Flight.

On September 1, 1943, RAF fighter pilot George Beurling, who had made his name as the leading Canadian ace in air battles over Malta, was sworn into the RCAF at Lincoln's Inn Fields HQ in London and posted to 403 Squadron at Kenley. He subsequently joined our wing as flight commander of A Flight, 412 Squadron.

George was a loner in every sense of the word. He put his CO George Keefer's back up when he refused to stand his flight on morning readiness. "The Battle of Britain's over," he reasoned, although not to Keefer's satisfaction. I got to know Beurling very well, though we never talked about air fighting—it was mostly about girls. He was an ace at that, too, and a lot of fun. When we'd go over to the Tea House for afternoon tea, while the rest of us were satisfied with ordering one egg, George would insist on three. "Puts lead in your pencil," he liked to say, a broad grin on his face.

He spent a lot of his time visiting the squadrons to discuss air fighting tactics and deflection shooting. (As mentioned earlier, his own guns were synchronized at 250 yards instead of the laid down standard of 350.) His lessons were far beyond both the comprehension and the ability of most of us. As Buck McNair put it at one of the briefings, "Don't bother with all that Beurling deflection crap. Just get right up the guy's jackson and let him have it."

That was providential advice. On the bright, sunny morning of December 20, we made a long-range fighter sweep, crossing into Holland at Flushing, flying as far as Eindhoven, then returning in the direction of Brussels. Our squadron was flying low echelon to port, with Cameron leading. I was flying number two to Sheppard in Yellow section, on the left of our squadron formation, with Bob Buckles behind me bringing up the third slot.

Over Brussels, a lone Dornier 217 bomber suddenly appeared to starboard, the crew apparently oblivious to the fact that a wing of 36 Spitfires had just joined them. "I'm lining him up," came Beurling's voice over the R/T. In other words, the rest of you stand by and I'll show you some deflection shooting. Doug Givens of 411 Squadron had other ideas. Spurred on by McNair's advice, he promptly pulled up sharply onto the Dornier's tail, so close he couldn't miss, and with a short burst of cannon and machine-gun fire sent the enemy bomber spiraling down in flames.

Five minutes later, northeast of Lille, I saw a large black twin-engine aircraft flying parallel to us about 200 yards to port. I immediately identified it as a Junkers 88 bomber with an extraordinarily large tail.* It was customary after having sighted an enemy plane to call up an alert on the R/T. In this case, "bogie at nine o'clock [at a right angle] straight and level." I didn't bother; it seemed unnecessary—surely everyone in the squadron had seen the 88, as it was so close.

But apparently I had been the only one to spot it. No one said a word as the enemy aircraft kept serenely cruising along, gradually outpacing us. When it was about 300 yards ahead, it abruptly changed direction, turning to starboard and flying on a course going the other way, directly beside us, closer than 100 yards to our

* We later established that it was a modified version, a JU-188 night fighter.

(*top*) Bishop's College School prep school soccer team, 1935. Author is third from the left.

(*bottom*) Author's father with Prime Minister Winston Churchill at the height of the Battle of Britain, 10 Downing Street, London, September 1940.

(*top*) Author with his father after just having received his pilot's wings from the latter, at No. 2 Service Flying Training School, Uplands, Ottawa, July 31, 1942.

(*bottom*) The Bishop family following the Wings Parade ceremony. Author's father, left, sister Jackie, the author and his mother.

(*opposite*) Bishop family with cast from movie, *Captain of the Clouds*, North Bay, Ontario, August 1941. Seated left to right: the author, his mother, film director Michael Curtiz, actor Jimmy Cagney, friend of the author's Margaret Johnston, and author's sister, Jackie. Behind the two, actor Alan Hale.

(*top*) Left to right: Willy Cummings, Don Orpen (401 Squadron adjutant), and the author wearing his Mae West life preserver at Catterick, Yorkshire, April 1943.

(*bottom*) 401 Squadron pilots at Staplehurst, Kent, summer 1943. Author is standing fifth from right. To his right, Bob Hayward and Bill Klersy. Extreme right Jeep Neal.

(*top*) Tex Davenport, left, with unidentified squadron mate. August 1943, Staple-hurst, Kent.

(*bottom*) Sawing wood to keep warm, Staplehurst, Kent, September 1943. Willy Cummings, left, Mac MacRae and the author sitting on the log.

(*top*) Author in his new uniform tailored by Anderson & Sheppard, Savile Row, London, two weeks before D-Day, at Tangmere.

(*bottom*) Tex Davenport, left, with the author after the former's escape from France. Tangmere, May 1944.

(*top*) Beny-sur-Mer, Normandy, July 1944. Right to left, Bill Klersy, Gerry Billing and the author.

(*bottom*) Left to right, Mac MacRae, Pamela Booth, the author, Cilla, at Standish Hall in Hull, Quebec, November 1944.

(*top*) The author with Cilla following their wedding at St. Andrew's Presbyterian Church, Ottawa, November 3, 1945.

(*bottom*) Author, left, then with Ronalds Advertising Agency Limited, Montreal, in charge of stage properties during coast-to-coast dealer meetings to introduce change of identification from the McColl-Frontenac Oil Red Indian insignia to the Texaco Star and T.

left. The whole scenario was unbelievable. The JU pilot and Shep must have seen each other at the same moment, suddenly creating one of the clumsiest aerial encounters of the war. They were within a few yards of each other when the Junkers abruptly skidded to starboard and dived. A goddamn good thing it did too, or they would have collided—and me along with them. Shep banked sharply to port and I followed so closely behind that the cartridge cases from his cannon shells were bouncing off my wings. I opened fire at the same time. But our attack was way too late—the bomber had had time to get out of the line of fire. All I could see in my ring sight was the tail of the enemy aircraft, but hell, at least I'd fired a shot in anger at last. Buckles, behind me, was in a better position to take solid aim than either Shep or I, but he was also in the most danger. The enemy rear gunner took dead aim at him.

A sloppy performance all around. It took Lorne Cameron, leading Red section, to rescue it. In his businesslike fashion he barked over the R/T, "Get the hell out of the way. I'm coming down." Cam wasted no time demonstrating his accuracy. Swooping down, he let off a brief burst that blew the Junkers' Perspex windscreen apart and sent the bomber diving to the ground on fire.

Meanwhile, Buckles reported, "My engine's been hit and I've lost it, so I'm bailing out."

"Merry Christmas, Buck," came his buddy Norm Maybee's cocky reply. A few minutes later he would come to rue that Yuletide greeting.

We were a few miles south of Gravelines when Maybee, the tail man in Red section, and Bill Morrisey, the number four in Blue section, collided. Both bailed out safely. Buckles, Maybee, and Morrisey all became prisoners of war.

So the squadron, by this time cut off from the rest of the wing, made its way home across the Channel three pilots short, but with a victory to add to its list of laurels. Shorthanded but unbowed and proud, we made our traditional "Prince of Wales feathers" salute—a 401 trademark on return from a sortie—the centre section climbing straight ahead and the other two sections fanning out and climbing to the left and right.

Our remaining complement of pilots and the groundcrew were agog when they saw that three aircraft were missing, and were all ears when we landed. Jeep said to me rather proudly, "I hear you got in a squirt. I'll tell that to Cilla when I see her." He had completed his second tour three days earlier and was scheduled to return to Canada. He could look back with pride on the closely-knit squadron he had formed. Now it was time to step down and hand over the reins to his successor.

I had a strong inkling, as some of the others probably did, as to just who that might be. The next evening, in the bar of the permanent officers' mess, Cam proclaimed, "I haven't had a good drunk since joining 401. The time has come." A harbinger? Well, we certainly made up for lost time that night. It was a good thing that the weather turned duff the next day; most of us were in no shape for anything serious—like flying!

That afternoon Keith Hodson paid a visit to our dispersal. The sudden appearance of the field commander augured something important in the wind and brought most of us to our feet. I even managed to snap off a salute. "Cameron is your new CO," he announced without fanfare. "I don't know your opinion, but as far as I'm concerned he's shit-hot, and he's taking over as of right now." And with that he was gone.

"No surprise to me," Tex Davenport said. I agreed; it had been a meteoric performance. A month earlier he had joined us as a flying officer, just another guy—but what a guy. A few days previously he had been made flight commander of B Flight with the rank of flight lieutenant. Now he was our "boss"—a squadron leader. And he wasted no time in establishing that he really *was* the boss, too.

An hour later, Cam showed up at dispersal. I was sitting nearest to the door, so I stood up, saluted, proffered my right hand, and offered my congratulations. He smiled and sat down. He asked if Jeep was around, still referring to him as the CO. Then he got down to brass tacks. Rising to his feet, Cam said, "I don't know what you think of this appointment and frankly I don't care. I'm the CO and we're going to do things my way, and you're going to have to accept it. If you don't like it, we'll find something else for you to do." That was it—simple, straightforward, and to the point. Meanwhile, it was business as usual.

We were still having trouble with the drop tanks. A day earlier Ian Ormston had become the third casualty of the airlock problem. He was leading the wing for a fighter sweep and had just switched over from the main tanks when his engine quit cold. Because the other two squadrons were still taxiing out and taking off, he was forced to try and put his Spitfire down on the grass. However, his approach fell short and he hit an obstacle at the edge of the field. The Spitfire crashed into a small hollow between the main runway and the taxi strip, where I was halfway to the takeoff point. I saw the aircraft strike the ground—it seemed to break in two. Ormy tumbled out, still strapped to his seat. The impact broke his back. He was hospitalized and invalided home, lucky to have survived.

On November 23, the day after Cam took over the squadron, I was flying number two to Bill McRae in Red section on a fighter sweep to Cambrai. We had just crossed the coast when, about four miles inland, heavy flak erupted all around us. Mac's Spit took a hit. He heard a loud bang and called up to say he thought he could smell rubber burning, and was turning back before his aircraft caught fire. I accompanied him. When we landed, we found a large, ragged hole in the left side of the fuselage, just behind the cockpit. A jagged piece of shrapnel had embedded itself in the undercarriage warning horn, right behind Mac's ear, and had burned out the rubberized connecting wires. When the horn was later taken out of all the Spitfires, Mac would say, "I had a strange feeling that they were removing my shield."

A week later I flew my last sortie of 1943, bringing my total operational outings to 34. Our job was close escort to Flying Fortresses, their mission the destruction of "no-ball" (non-ballistic) targets.

These were ski-shaped concrete structures, and we were completely in the dark about their purpose. We did know, from the attention paid to them by Allied Bomber Command, that no-balls must have some sinister significance. Indeed they had. They were built to launch the V-1 (*Vergeltungswaffe, or* vengeance weapon)—which would become familiarly known as the buzz bomb or doodlebug—a pilotless, jet-propelled flying bomb carrying 1870 pounds of explosives. Allied intelligence and aerial reconnaissance photographs revealed that the V-1 had a 17-foot wingspan and a fuselage 22 feet long. Other photos showed that by the middle of December 1943, 83 of the "ski sites" had been built in the Pas de Calais. All of them were pointed at London, the distance to which the V-1 was designed to fly before its engine cut out and the missile fell to earth and exploded.

For the second time in a week I had to return to base DNCO—duty not carried out. Two-thirds of the way across the Channel, the Spitfire of my number one, Sandy Halcrow, developed engine trouble. Under those circumstances, as had been the case with McRae a week earlier, it was the partner's duty to take the lead, riding shotgun, and in the event of a ditching, to fly cover and signal the Air-Sea Rescue Service.

Sandy was able to coax his engine across the Channel to the English coast, but our troubles were just beginning. The weather was solid down to 200 feet, and underneath the weather was drizzle. I led the way partly on instruments and partly on visuals. We made it to Biggin all right, but had to circle four times before we could land safely. Ironically, by the time the wing returned, the weather had cleared.

Next day, Christmas Eve, I accompanied Keith Hodson to Kenley for lunch with George Drew, leader of the Conservative Party of Ontario and a close friend of the family. At Kenley we joined two other RCAF pilots whose families were friends of Drew's. All of us, including Keith, were from Ontario. When Drew asked what we expected when we returned home, Keith spoke for the rest of us when he said, "After experiencing the civilized fashion in which the British serve drinks over here—anything from ale to vodka, even with wartime shortages—we'd like to see a change in the drinking laws when we get back." At the time, except for hotel dining rooms, where beer and wine were served, and an abundance of sleazy beer parlours—most of them lamentable, many of them disgraceful—Ontario was dry. Drew took the comment in stride. On the way home, Keith said, "Not a bad guy for a politician—give him something to think about." Think about it he did. Drew must have taken our words to heart, because eventually Ontario's liquor laws were completely revamped when Drew became provincial premier.

For the next week the weather was so bad there was no flying until New Year's Day, 1944. Around noon we had just begun getting into the spirit of the occasion (and recuperating from king-sized hangovers) when the call came to the bar to assemble for a briefing. Our ebullient wingco, Buck McNair, responded by announcing, "This is someone's idea of a piss-poor joke!"

In any case, the sweep was uneventful, and by the time we got as far inland as Poix, in France, clouds forced us to turn back, making our exit at Le Treport, on the coast. Halfway across the Channel, Buck gave the order to fire off all the guns to empty the ammunition drums. But I didn't hear him; my R/T had gone dead.

At the debriefing Buck summed up the outing with the terse comment, "Well, we got away with it," then asked if everyone had fired their guns. I got to my feet and admitted that I hadn't heard the order. "Why not?" Buck wanted to know. I told him that my R/T went dead. "Well," Buck asked, "did you report it U/S on the L-17?" (This was the maintenance work log.) I shook my head; I'd forgotten to.

"Bishop," Buck barked. "You great prick! Some day there'll be a Hun up your ass and I'll yell 'Break!' but you won't hear me and you'll be shot down. Then what's old man Bishop going to say?"

Happy New Year!

•   •   •

Before the old year was out the station commander, Keith Hodson, on instructions from on high, laid down the law on prangs. Accidents of any kind—taxiing, landing, taking off—anything—would be severely dealt with. In rapid succession, four pilots from our squadron were posted because of various incidents, none of them serious enough in my opinion (which I still hold) to warrant such harsh punishment as banishment. But those were the rules, and there was no exception.

One of these incidents unfortunately resulted in the pilot taking his life by shooting himself in the head. This was a personal tragedy for me as well. Don Kelly came from a wealthy New York family and was on his second tour. We had become very close friends. Though I never heard it from Don himself, Jeep Neal told me that Kelly, who had learned to fly when very young, had reportedly volunteered to fight in the Spanish Civil War for the Republican government forces against Franco's Fascist insurgents. He was a very gutsy guy. He flew as my number two on occasion and stuck to me like glue.

On the evening before his suicide, Don and I were having a drink in the bar of the permanent officers' mess. I was trying to console him when he suddenly took a handful of bullets from his pocket (you had to leave your service revolver at the door) and said to me, "Some son of a bitch is going to get his." I pleaded with him not to do anything foolish. That was my last conversation with him. His infraction was a simple taxiing accident. I realized later that he had taken his posting as an insult to his ability as a pilot and his integrity as an officer. It was very sad. There but for the grace of God . . .

Ironically, some time later, Lorne Cameron, who as CO had to sign off on the postings of the unfortunate recalcitrants, taxied into one of the signal vehicles at the runway takeoff point, damaging both it and his Spitfire. His immediate reaction was to tender his resignation to Hodson and McNair, as CO of the squadron, but instead he got a firm rebuke: "You're the person we want for that job. Now go back and do it!" And that was that—an early lesson in management.

By the beginning of 1944 the air war over Europe had changed dramatically. The introduction of the modified American Mustang (P-51) fighter with the high-altitude Merlin engine in late December 1943 marked a turning point in the air war over Hitler's Third Reich. Equipped with long-range drop tanks in addition to increased capacity in their wing tanks, the new American fighters could escort the Flying Fortresses and Liberators anywhere over Germany. Furthermore, the Mustangs could not only protect the bombers, but as hunters they could sweep the skies clear of enemy fighters in all directions.

Ironically, now that we had the aircraft—Spitfire IXBs—to tackle the FW-190s and ME-109s on our own terms, we rarely encountered the enemy, even though we deliberately flew diversionary sweeps to lure the German fighters away from the American bomber fleets and into battle. These sorties were necessarily confined to the limit of our range even with drop tanks: as far as east of Eindhoven, in Holland, to within 20 miles of the German border. But Generalleutnant Adolf Galland, General von der Jagdflieger (Luftwaffe Fighter Command), wasn't buying. He was judiciously husbanding his forces to strike at the daylight aerial invaders over his own turf.

Our diversionary sweeps were not only a bind, they were also torturous. Because of the winter weather over Europe, at times we would climb through as much as 22,000 feet of cloud on instruments. The only indication we had that we were over enemy-occupied territory was when the flak began bursting around us. The eeriest sensation of all was when it burst while we were still in cloud; it had a scary prismatic effect that made it look a lot closer than it really was.

Itching for action and a break in the monotony, some of the

more intrepid individuals volunteered for "rhubarbs"—two-man low-level attacks against enemy coastal ground targets. These pin-prick raids were Churchill's idea for keeping the Germans on the defensive during the days immediately following the evacuation of Dunkirk in 1940. They may have accomplished that objective to some degree, but for the most part they proved fruitless and hor-rendously costly. Some of our best fighter pilots were lost on these raids, including the Canadian Battle of Britain ace Willie McKnight, who had 16^1/$_2$ victories. By the winter of 1944 the raids had long outlived their usefulness and were frowned upon by our com-manders, including Tin Willy MacBrien and Keith Hodson. How-ever, a little persuasion went a long way, and they were occasionally condoned.

Not long after the turn of the year, a pilot from 412 Squadron led one such foray deep into France. On the way out, while crossing the coast, his aircraft was hit by flak and the back of his neck was peppered by shrapnel. Although he made it back to base, he had lost so much blood that he died on the way to the hospital.

When Grisle Klersy learned of this, he said to me, "Dead? Okay to come over here and have a few parties and all that. But dead? That's taking things too far." Nevertheless, it did not stop Grisle from joining forces with Tex Davenport a few days later. Under the protection of weather, right down on the deck where they could not be seen (but could be heard), the pair flew a rhubarb to attack a no-ball target inland from Le Touquet.

As Grisle and Tex crossed the French coast through drizzle and snow squalls, flak erupted all around them. The precipitation was so heavy that they lost visual contact with each other. Tex radioed that he'd lost his engine and was going to pancake. Klersy immediately reversed direction and headed back across the Channel, the weather still right down on the deck. He made it back home, incredibly with-out a single hole in his aircraft. But he was badly shaken up by the incident. We all missed Tex, Grisle and I particularly.

On the morning of January 17, the commander of A Flight, Jack

Sheppard, went for a swim. The mission was a ramrod escort to 54 Marauders attacking a no-ball target in the Le Treport–Poix–Amiens area. Halfway across the Channel, Shep's aircraft began a glide toward the water. His R/T had packed up, so we lost radio contact with him. At 28,000 feet he bailed out, landing on the surface safely, and inflated his dinghy. Hayward switched over to radio channel D for Dog and gave the mayday signal (from the French *m'aidez,* help me). He and Klersy covered until the latter, his fuel running low, was forced to head back. He landed at Hawkinge, on the coast, with only two gallons left. Hayward remained on the scene until Shep was picked up by an Air-Sea Rescue launch, the Channel being too rough for a Walrus seaplane. Padre Forbes, the wing cleric, called the performance an "act of Christianity." Hayward shrugged it off. "Shep would have done the same for me," he said.

Next day the weather was bright and clear for a change, and for once we actually sighted enemy fighters. But the operation was a washout. To begin with, the Marauders we were supposed to escort to bomb the German airfield at St. Omer inexplicably turned back just north of Dover. Across the Channel we could see condensation trails over Calais—enemy fighters. We quickly climbed to 27,000 feet, but by the time we reached altitude the enemy had turned tail and dived away out of sight.

The following morning back to bad weather—practically down on the deck—for a diversionary fighter sweep. When I started up my engine, the windscreen immediately oiled over. I zigzagged out onto the taxi strip, but it was hopeless; I had no forward visibility at all. I taxied back to dispersal, switched off, and asked my ground crew, Smitty and Hunt, to wipe the windshield clean. By this time the wing had taken off, but I told them I wanted to start up again. They were against it. "You'll never catch up," Smitty pleaded. "And look at all that shit you'll have to fly through," he added, with a doleful look at the low ceiling. I waved them off, started the engine, and hurriedly taxied out for takeoff. They were right and I was wrong.

I steered the heading we had been given at briefing and climbed into the overcast. But it quickly became obvious that I would never catch up—and if I did, my chances of sighting the others were virtually nil. I made a 180-degree turn, set a reverse heading back to Biggin, and began a slow descent. I soon found myself in a snowstorm, so I tried to get under it. I wasn't watching my altitude too carefully, and suddenly I was skimming the rooftops of a village. In the process I'd got lost, and the visibility was so poor there was no question of map reading. Finally I radioed control to give me a homing back to base. I wasn't breaching security, because by now the wing would be at least halfway across the Channel.

When I had landed, taxied in, switched off, and climbed out of my Spitfire, Hunt and Smitty were half grinning, as if to say "I told you so." But the expression was one of sympathy as well. We were very close to our ground crew and tried to live up to their expectations. My case was no exception, more so after this flight, I realized, after shedding my flying clothes in dispersal. Tacked to the wall was a recruiting advertisement for the RCAF from a Canadian magazine that featured a picture of my father in his air marshal's uniform. Handwritten in ink on the page were these thoughtful words: "To Bish from the Ground Crew of 401." I was deeply touched, and remain so to this day.

Because the diversionary sweeps proved unproductive, we were relegated to flying escort to Marauders that were bombing aerodromes. But we also continued to escort the Fortresses to no-ball installations. Occasionally these sorties drew German fighters, but only at a distance; and they were reluctant to tangle with the "beehive" cover that we provided around the bombers. However, it did indicate the importance the enemy attached to these targets, although at our level we were still in the dark as to what they were for. Ours was not to reason why.

But, on the brighter side, we did see some resolute action—the ranger free-for-alls and the baby blitz.

•   •   •

Back in August 1943, in the wake of the concentrated five-day-and-night "firestorm" bombing of Hamburg, in which 50,000 were killed and 800,000 rendered homeless, Hitler angrily avowed, "We must deal such mighty blows to our enemy in the West that he will never dare to risk another raid like Hamburg." Whereupon he appointed Generalmajor Dietrich Peltz in charge of Luftwaffe bomber forces as "assault leader against England." What ensued was a pitiful effort. Launching a series of night air raids against London with a ragtag fleet of JU-188s, FW-190s, and ME-110s and MW-210s, in the first week Peltz lost 57 bombers. Nevertheless, the night incursions persisted.

To prevent detection during daylight, the Germans held their bombers inland until dark before moving them to forward bases to take off on their missions. In an effort to destroy these raiders, RAF Tactical Fighter Command wings were assigned to four- and eight-aircraft forays called rangers. Crossing the Channel before dawn to stay under radar detection range, we would climb to 3000 feet and scour the countryside inland—with the primary purpose of finding the aircraft, but incidentally to knock out any trains we came across as well.

One night during the first week in February, Jerry "Ding Dong" Bell, Klersy, and I were returning from the gonorrhea racetrack (the Bromley Country Club) Saturday night dance in Hayward's car. Directly ahead of us we saw a shower of what looked like fireworks cascading down. De Bub pulled the vehicle off to the side of the road and we all got out. A series of explosions ensued as incendiary bombs struck the road and the fields around it. We all fell flat on our faces in the ditch. There were a few small fires, but no noticeable damage. However, we took a detour back to the station. Such was our introduction to the "baby blitz."

On February 14, 1944, Hayward exacted revenge for the four of us when, on our first ranger, he spotted an ME-210 taking off from Chartres, southwest of Paris. He dived down, opening fire, and the aircraft hit the ground and burst into flames. It was his first experience at this sort of operation, which was to become his trademark.

Next day I drew station orderly officer duty, a noon-to-noon assignment that was not overly arduous—more of a standby job than anything else. But I had earlier made a date in London for that evening, so Willy Cummings agreed to fill in for me.

The evening started off with a rendezvous at the Haymarket Club, then Mirabelle's for dinner, followed by dancing at the Bagatelle ("Bag of Nails") and ending at the Coconut Grove in the small hours of the morning. I did not get back to Biggin until after breakfast the following morning. I went to our room, picked up the OO (orderly officer) armband that Willy had left on my bed, put it on over my raincoat, then walked down to dispersal through the drizzle. My timing could not have been worse. When I arrived at the door, Keith Hodson was leaving with the Canadian High Commissioner, Vincent Massey, to whom he was giving a guided tour of the station. I saluted and Keith introduced me. After asking after my mother and father, Massey inquired of my duties as orderly officer. I explained that they were pretty routine, making the rounds of the messes, the control tower, and the guardhouse. Throughout our conversation the station commander looked noticeably perturbed. As they were leaving, he leaned over to me and said in a voice that could not be overheard, but with a message that came across loud and clear, "At least you might have shaved."

Mail call!

A letter from Jeep stating that he had dined at 5 Blackburn Avenue with my mother—my father was out of town—Cilla wasn't available—"had a date with an Aussie with a pair of gongs," according to Jeep.

A package from home containing a clipping from one of the New York tabloids speculating on who will be consort to the future Queen of England, Princess Elizabeth—yours truly one of the contestants very much in the running. I showed it to De Bub and swore him to secrecy; we buried it under my mattress.

A letter from my old man, who wrote, "If you follow what the papers are saying about you, please reserve a room for Mum and I in the east wing of Buckingham Palace complete with hot and cold running chambermaids."

On February 25, I flew my fiftieth sweep—withdrawal support for Marauders—an uneventful sortie with 10/10 cloud over the Channel and 5/10 over France. It was a good thing the trip was so lacklustre. I was feeling so cruddy that after we landed late that afternoon, I went straight to bed, waking up next morning with a severe case of flu. Doc Thorn consigned me to sick quarters, where I took 10 days to recover. I was still feeling a bit shaky when I returned to the squadron, so I was given a week's sick leave.

Through Canada House in London I arranged accommodation at a charming country hotel I had heard about at Crowborough, on the Sussex coast, where I stayed for a week. One night in the bar I met a Canadian Army captain whose regiment was quartered nearby. He invited me to his mess for cocktails the following evening. His companions were impatient to see some action; some of them had been in England for several years and had been put through an endless series of exercises and manoeuvres. When it came time to leave, the CO asked me if I was any relation to you-know-who. I denied it.

The next day I had regrets; I sensed I had been guilty of bad manners. But on such occasions—and they were not infrequent—denial was my gut reaction to the enquiry (accusation?) from people I did not know. In those cases my father's fame acted as an albatross around my neck, an encumbrance I'd rather be without; it made me feel uncomfortable. When I encountered the captain that evening, I asked him to apologize to his CO for my rudeness. "He'll understand, I'm sure," he assured me, then added, "I think I know how you feel. You have my sympathy."

March 1944, our last month at Biggin Hill, was by far the most productive and memorable for our squadron. During that period (mostly during my absence) the unit scored seven enemy aircraft destroyed and two damaged. The winners were Cam, with two destroyed and one damaged (he was awarded the DFC around this time), and Shep, with two destroyed. Grisle, De Bub, and Sandy "Duke" Halcrow each shot down an aircraft, while Willy Cummings scored one damaged.

On the downside, we lost two pilots one day after the other. They were forced to bail out over France when their engines developed airlocks while switching over from the drop tanks to the main tanks. On Monday, May 15, Ray Sherk, who had been with the squadron exactly a month, parachuted into a field at the edge of the Newfoundland Regiment cemetery at Beaumont-Hamel. The very next day Ken Woodhouse came down near the village of Remerangles, south of Amiens.

A moratorium was immediately imposed on the use of drop tanks until the airlock problem was solved, which eventually it was. Both Woody and Ray evaded capture—thanks to the French underground—to escape into Spain.*

To our complete surprise, on March 26, only 10 days after he had gone down, Woody walked into dispersal, large as life. We asked him a lot of questions ("Did you get wet, Woody?"), which for security reasons he was unable to answer. He did admit that he had to lie doggo for a while because he sprained his ankle when he landed, and that he had been in Paris, where the sight of the German troops made him shudder.

All three squadrons in the wing had vacated the permanent officers' mess to make way for one of the barrage groups from RAF Balloon Command. However, we still enjoyed its bar facilities. We had no idea what those guys were doing there, and they seemed none the wiser—though if they were, they weren't talking. Later we

* For the details, see Unsung Courage by Arthur Bishop: Chapter 1, "They Kept Coming Back."

would find out that they hoisted a barrage across the southern width of London as a defence against the flying bombs.

On March 23, we made our last sweep from Biggin Hill, a ramrod escorting Marauders to Creil. It brought us within eyeshot of Paris, which made me think of all those French in the city living under the German jackboot. We knew about the Gestapo and its reprisals against the French Underground. I wondered if our brief presence signalled to the citizens below a sign of hope that one day soon they would be free. The sight of the Eiffel Tower that morning was an inspiring one that I will never forget.

We were scheduled to leave Biggin Hill during the first week of April for Fairwood Common, in Wales, on the northern coast of the Bristol Channel. We were to go on a 10-day dive-bombing and air firing course. The bombing of the no-ball targets had so far been unsuccessful, according to intelligence reports. Air Command decided that dive-bombing would be more accurate and effective. This tactic did not take into account that the Spitfire had never been designed for that purpose.

Before we left Biggin we held a squadron farewell party at which I was elected—conscripted—into acting as emcee. The 401 diary recorded the event as follows:

Everyone packed up and dispersed to wash up to get into town to collect their girls for the Squadron party. The party started at 7.30 p.m. in the White Hart and after drinks dinner began at 8.15. This was probably one of the finest thrashes we have had for some time and novelty dances with inviting prizes gave it that extra touch. Most of the pilots had rooms for themselves and the girls in the Bromley Court. The next morning, drinking continued until past noon when F/O W.T. (Grisle) Klersy pulled off another performance when he captured a chicken in the backyard and climbed through the window, triumphantly carrying the squawking pullet through the lounge.

Chapter 15

Bombs Away!

Fairwood Common, Wales—April 8–18, 1944

> If we'd got two decent long-range tanks
> to hang under the wings, instead of those
> other things, we could go to Berlin with
> the Yanks and get stuck into some real
> fighting.
> —Wally McLeod, second-highest-scoring
> Canadian World War II ace (21 victories)

Initially our purpose in practising dive-bombing was to prepare us for attacking no-ball targets. But we were also training for the roles we would play in the softening up for the invasion of Europe—and eventual ground support for the army when and after that took place—dive-bombing and low-level bombing, as well as air-to-ground firing.

The Spitfire had been designed for none of those things—it was a fighter, not a fighter-bomber. It was designed for air-to-air combat, where it could more than hold its own. Dive-bombing and low-level bombing, as well as ground strafing, left it deplorably exposed to sustained and accurate ground fire. Unlike the Typhoon and the American Thunderbolt (P-47), which were built for dive-bombing as well as rocket firing and were powered with air-cooled engines, the Spitfire had a liquid-cooled in-line engine. The basic difference was that the former could sustain substantial damage, while in the case of the latter, a single bullet or a small piece of shrapnel slamming into the radiator or piercing one of the feed lines could put the Spitfire right out of business. Nevertheless, to invoke the idiom of the day, "We pressed on, rewardless!"

And why not? We were all looking forward to the "big show"— the invasion—the ultimate scuffle with the Luftwaffe in which we all might stand a chance of grabbing that brass ring. Our dread was that we would be taken off ops before it took place. Here's the way Mac McRae put it: "We all expected the invasion to be soon, and we all wanted to be in on it, so we cheated outrageously [in making out our monthly reports of numbers of trips and hours logged]. If we had flown, say, 10 trips in a period, we would report perhaps four or five."

The firing/bombing range at Fairwood Common was a beach and its perimeter on the Bristol Channel, only minutes' flying time from the airfield. The air-to-ground targets were on the beach, and we usually practised this tactic in pairs. Offshore was a 50-foot-square yellow raft on which we practised dive-bombing, using a 12-pound smoke bomb slung from a rack on the belly of the Spitfire—an exercise that we practised solo.

With practice I found that I could achieve a fair degree of accuracy. The procedure was to climb to 10,000 feet, then wing over in a half-roll into the dive. You took aim at the target through the ring-and-bead sight. At 5000 feet you released the bomb, then pulled out of the dive. Generally I blacked out, but not before I could get a glimpse of my bombing result. I found that by leading the target—aiming the dot almost ahead of the raft—I could hit it squarely each time.

Air-to-ground firing was another story. The targets were laid out along the water's edge and were fired at from inland. There were two posts some yards apart from which hung black balls, which were apparently all-clear signals, but Grisle Klersy, with whom I was paired for the exercise, and I were not aware of that. A team of two monitors who measured results was housed in a shelter buried in the sand, looking out to sea. The roof of the shelter was covered with sand over a layer of sandbags, and it was virtually invisible from the air, even at low levels.

On our run in, Grisle and I opened fire well ahead of the targets to gauge the path of our bullets. It was good shooting. Pleased as punch, we made a second run, this time choosing as targets those beautiful, juicy black balls hanging from the masts. Right on—no trouble at all; we blasted them to bits. Returning to the field, we felt very proud of ourselves—a real pair of sharpshooters.

Scotty Murray had returned to the squadron to take over our flight after Jack Sheppard was promoted to CO of 412 Squadron (George Keefer was made wingco in Buck McNair's place). He greeted us as we climbed out of our kites. "You guys!" he said, shaking his head. All hell had broken loose down on the firing range. Our bullets leading to the target had penetrated the roof of the monitor hut, and the poor guys were scrambling around trying to hide under tables and chairs to avoid them, scared out of their wits. They weren't at all pleased either that we'd shredded their precious signal balls. "You guys!" Scott repeated, to which De Bub Hayward added his two cents' worth: "Don't worry, Scotty. You'll get used to them."

A few days later, because flying had been rained out, we visited the firing range. Grisle and I kept our distance, particularly when Bob Hamilton reported with a grin, "They are very anxious to meet those guys who did all the shooting." Discretion being the better part of valour, we lay doggo.

This wasn't the only run-in with authority around that station, which was run by a bunch of snotty pukka types—with emphasis on *non-operational*. At tea one afternoon in the mess dining hall, when I reached for a third biscuit, the station adjutant, whom I had nicknamed "the CO's little bumboy," said to me, "Don't be so greedy. Don't you know there's a war on?"

"Damn right I know," I snapped back. "And why the hell aren't you in it?" He told me he was going to report me to the station commander, like running to mummy. All over a bloody biscuit!

Cam, who was sitting next to me, said to him, "Well, you can report me too," and picked up the whole plate, adding, "This is one of the lousiest messes we've ever had to put up with."

Our 10-day Fairwood Common interlude came to an end on April 18, 1944. After three unsuccessful attempts, thanks to cloudy weather, we finally arrived at our new home at Tangmere, near Chichester, on the Sussex Coast. Back to the real thing.

Chapter 16

Softening Up

Tangmere, Gloucester—April 19–June 5, 1944

> It is comforting to learn that Bill had so
> many nice friends & I'm sure in the lives
> you have been called to live, friendships
> you make living, working, fighting, yes
> dying, together are unequalled anywhere.
> —Willy Cummings' mother, in a letter

At Tangmere it was back to tents and "hard living," although we were given privileges to use the permanent officers' mess bar. Tangmere, a mainstay RAF fighter field during and since the Battle of Britain, was situated directly north of the Isle of Wight, facing the Baie de la Seine across the English Channel. Initially we concentrated on dive-bombing no-ball installations, but the targets soon extended to bridges and other targets. We were about to experience a lesson on the difference between practice and application.

Bomb hang-ups, for one thing. On the day after our arrival we flew our first dive-bombing mission on a no-ball target, 20 miles inland from Berck, on the Pas de Calais coast. But this time we weren't carrying little practice smoke bombs—we were armed with 500-pound high incendiaries. The bombing was accurate and there was no flak. But unbeknownst to him, Mac McRae's bomb had failed to come off in the dive. It was hanging halfway up on the rack. On the way back to the coast, it finally dropped, although he was unaware of that as well and nobody took the trouble to tell him.

He would later write, "I noticed several of the others banking and skidding around. I thought they were looking for something on the ground. . . . When we got back I was told that they were looking to see where my bomb hit."*

On the following afternoon, on a no-ball dive-bombing strike south of Abbeville, Scotty Murray had a similar experience, only somewhat worse. As he was coming out of the dive, his number two reported over the R/T that his bomb hadn't come off. I was flying the tail-end position as Scotty jinked, climbed, and dived on the way back across the English Channel, but the bomb stubbornly refused to drop. Finally, when we reached Beachy Head, on the English coast, he called up to say he was bailing out (you couldn't risk a landing under those circumstances). He set his aircraft out to sea, climbed out on the wing, and jumped. The rest of us in the section circled around as he parachuted down. Scotty hit the ground quite hard, and after unhitching his chute, lay down on his back and lifted one leg to indicate he'd injured it. Fortunately, it turned out to be only a sprain that kept him grounded for a few days. Meanwhile, as soon as he bailed out, Scotty's aircraft had reversed direction and crashed into a field. Ironically, the bomb did not explode.

But our business wasn't just no-balls, dive-bombing, and hang-ups. On the next evening our squadron, carrying 90-gallon drop tanks to give us maximum range, flew a ranger search for enemy aircraft and ground targets. South of Abbeville, I spotted a bogie ahead of us above, duly reported it, and put on full throttle. Then— it had to happen to me—I couldn't get my tank to drop off. I had to watch in frustration as the others gave chase while—with the extra weight of 90 gallons, or what was left of it—I couldn't even keep up. De Bub nailed the ME-110 with Cam's help and it crashed into

---

* We later learned that the earlier, high-level bombing had not been as ineffective as we had been led to believe. In response, with typical Teutonic ingenuity, the Germans had replaced the concrete structures with lightweight portable metal launch sites that could be hidden in the trees and, if discovered, easily moved elsewhere.

some trees. At least I got full marks for having spotted the Hun in the first place, but that didn't ease my dejection at not even being able to get a crack at it.

However, what cheered me up considerably when we repaired to the mess tent for drinks after the debriefing was the appearance of Tex Davenport. He had returned to the fold after being missing since January, when he was shot down during that rhubarb against a no-ball target. Tex had managed to escape through France into Spain. I chided him for pranging my precious YOK. "In the shape it was in when I climbed out of it, you wouldn't have wanted it back," was his reply.

On the morning of April 27, our dive-bombing target was a bridge near Carentan, on the Cherbourg peninsula. This was a squadron effort in which I flew number two to Cam, who was leading Red section. Hayward, who was flying Red Three behind me, was in radio liaison—on a separate channel from the rest of us— with an aerial reconnaissance Mustang flying above us to take pictures of the bombing results. By switching back and forth from channel to channel, I was in touch with Hayward and could keep the rest of the squadron informed of developments should the need arise.

The bombing was a piece of cake—or so it appeared at the time. There was no flak and enemy fighter interference was now getting to be a thing of the past. When we returned to Tangmere, Cam asked if I'd noticed whether or not all 12 aircraft had climbed up after the bombing. I hadn't really noticed; I was too busy playing follow-the-leader and conversing back and forth with Hayward to pay much attention. Hayward hadn't noticed either, he was so preoccupied. In any case, the three sections had become separated, making a count well-nigh impossible.

Klersy came into dispersal looking devastated. He reported that he had followed Willy Cummings in the dive when suddenly Willy's Spitfire passed the vertical and became inverted. Nor had his bomb come off. At the end, Klersy could no longer stay with him; he was forced to pull out or dive into the ground. That is obviously what happened to Willy, though no one saw it.

Hayward and I walked back to our tent feeling thoroughly dejected. "*C'est la guerre*," was all De Bub could find to say. Usually the CO wrote the letter of condolence to the next of kin, but because Hayward, Willy, and I had been roommates for over a year, De Bub and I also wrote letters to his parents. It was difficult to find the right words because we had no real proof of his fate, although we were sure he'd bought it. We had to consider the family's feelings, and we had no God-given right to tell the next of kin what we were certain had happened. That confirmation had to come from official sources. Meanwhile, Willy was listed as missing in action.* In replying to my letter, his mother wrote:

You will never realize how much Mr. Cummings and myself appreciate your recent letter and your very fine reference to our Bill . . . . now we have the sad news that Bill lost his life on April 27 . . . through the International Red Cross from German sources . . .

I am confident the squadron must have known Bill's fate at the time. Your letters all read that way to us now, but if you did there was not a word from yourself, Bob Hayward or S/L Cameron that would indicate such, so we kept on hoping.

It is comforting to learn that Bill had so many nice friends & I'm sure in the lives you have been called to live, friendships you make living, working, fighting, yes dying, together are unequalled anywhere.

This may not read like a very cheerful letter, when we are urged to keep up your morale, but I am sure you realize our feelings these days when so many will be coming home.

---

* When we later moved to France, after the Cherbourg peninsula had been liberated by the Americans, Bob Hayward, then the CO of 411 Squadron, took one of his pilots who was bilingual with him and found the wreckage of Willy's Spitfire. He also visited the grave where the French had buried him.

Three days after Cummings' demise our target was a no-ball site south of Dieppe. The flak was heavy. This was the first time I had experienced what it was like to dive straight into it, and it made me twitchy, to say the least. I reacted by returning the fire with my own cannon and machine guns, for all that might achieve. Meanwhile, Jerry Billing, a veteran of the Malta air battles and an OTU instructor between tours (where he met Lorne Cameron, who had arranged for his transfer to our squadron when he became CO), was beset with his own problems. As soon as he dropped his bomb, his controls reversed. When he pulled back on the stick to come out of the dive, the nose of the aircraft went forward instead of backward, pushing the aircraft beyond the vertical into an inverted position. In desperation, he rolled the aileron trim wheel back and forth. No response. He then did the same with the rudder trim wheel. That did the trick. The Spitfire skidded out of the dive, banking over on its side in a steep turn through our bomb bursts, mere feet off the ground.

The cause of this phenomenon was open to conjecture. I wrote in my log book, "The answer to Cummings, I guess." One theory was that, beyond a certain speed—say 450 to 500 miles an hour—there was a danger that the ailerons might tear off. But this had not happened in either Cummings' or Billing's case. However, that was the rumour circulating at the time. As a precautionary measure, white and yellow lines were painted on the inboard cords of the ailerons so that when the control column was centred in a dive, the white line would show. If the yellow line appeared, it was a signal to reduce speed. How fatuous could you get? As Mac McRae put it, "At the same time, you were supposed to keep on target and make sure you didn't fly into the ground!"

My own belief is that both pilots were diving at close to the speed of sound. A year earlier, the Aerodynamics Flight of the Royal Aircraft Establishment (RAE) at Farnborough conducted a series of diving tests to determine why many fighter pilots were experiencing loss of control of their aircraft at high speed, a condition called compressibility. A PR Spitfire Mark II was chosen for the exercises, one that could reach a speed of 620 miles an hour, or about Mach 0.9, a fraction under the sound barrier. Until the advent of the rocket-powered Bell X-1, which broke the sound barrier over the Mojave Desert on October 14, 1947, no other propeller-driven aircraft had achieved such speed. After the war, in speed tests by De Havilland, it was discovered that when aircraft approached the speed of sound, the controls reversed themselves. We knew that had happened in Jerry's instance, and it must have occurred in Willy's. All this, even at this late date, is still perhaps an issue. But I rest my case.

Tangmere was becoming crowded both on the field and in the air, as well as at the bar of the permanent officers' mess. At this time 127 Wing (formerly the Kenley Wing) welcomed 403, 416, and 421 Squadrons. It was commanded by Wing Commander Lloyd Chadburn, bringing the total field establishment to six squadrons, and making the circuit a busy place at times. Our old friend Tin Willie MacBrien was the 127 field commander.

A few days afterward we welcomed another stray back to the fold—Ray Sherk, who had bailed out over France back in March after his engine failed because of an airlock. He had managed to evade capture and, like Tex Davenport, had escaped across the Pyrenees into Spain.

During the month of May, I flew 12 sorties. Five of them were dive-bombing attacks on no-ball targets. We still had not learned, apparently, that the Germans had abandoned these concrete launching emplacements in favour of the portable steel variety. Nevertheless, they were well defended. On one occasion the entire wing was assigned to one of these targets, led by 411 Squadron. The leader of the section, the CO, Norm Fowlow, was just winging over into the dive when flak exploded the bomb under his Spitfire, blasting him and his aircraft into smithereens. For the rest of us waiting our turn, it was a grisly, chilling sight to watch the bits and pieces fluttering down through the anti-aircraft fire. After the Cummings and Billing incidents, I had made it a practice to release my bomb almost the moment I went into the dive—to hell with dropping down to 5000 feet. And this recent calamity only served to intensify my trepidation and determination to get rid of the goddamn thing as soon as I could. I found out later that some others were doing the same thing.

We lost two of our best pilots during that month. On May 7, while he was flying a ranger, Tommy Dowbiggin's engine failed to restart when his drop tank went dry. Tommy bellied into a field, jumped out of the aircraft, and ran for it. Our policy was to destroy our own aircraft under such circumstances. Tommy obviously didn't want to waste time lighting the flare provided for that purpose. Cam took the matter in his own hands and destroyed the Spitfire with gunfire. Ironically, several days later when Air Marshal Sir Arthur Coningham, Air Officer Commanding (AOC) 83 Group, visited our airfield, he told us in a pep talk not to bother destroying our own shot-down aircraft, because "once we get moving we'll go so fast the enemy won't have time to do anything with them"—an omen that D-Day couldn't be far off. In the meantime, he urged us to "shoot the feathers off anything and everything."

As if on cue, a few evenings afterward, Cam and I destroyed two trains east of Caen. On the first attack Cam took out the engine, while I crippled the three end cars, including the caboose. On a second assault we reversed roles. When we landed, I didn't bother making out a report (it wasn't mandatory in any case) and forgot all about the escapade, although I did make a laconic entry in my log book: "CO and I destroyed two trains." But Cam must have passed on the word.

Next morning Smitty, my rigger, and Hunt, my fitter, accosted me and said, "We heard that you got two trains last night." I nodded. "Well, you should tell us. We like to know these things." They were right; I had been delinquent. The ground crew had a right to know. They were proud of what I had done—after all, they were the ones who kept me flying. However, I managed to dissuade them from painting two trains on my kite, YOK, which would have caused me no end of embarrassment among my confreres.

Our second casualty of the month was Bob Hamilton. On the morning of May 19, I was still in bed—it was my morning off—when Scotty Murray entered the tent and announced, "Hammy's in France" (actually, it was Belgium). Whoa! Wait a minute. He shouldn't have been flying in the first place—it was his morning off, too. But at the last minute an extra pilot was needed in a hurry and Hammy's tent was closest to dispersal; therefore he was the handiest to recruit. He hadn't even had time to dress properly and had hastily pulled on his pants, flying boots, and battledress jacket over his pajamas.

The squadron had been flying over a German airfield near Tournai when Hammy spotted an aircraft about to take off—or so he thought. Too late he discovered that it was a decoy being winched across the field to sucker fighters into a flak-trap of flak. He flew into a wall of fire, the bullets riddling his aircraft with a clatter. Although he had very little altitude, he managed to bail out, but his chute opened only just before he hit the ground.

He was immediately picked up by an aging home guard whose hands trembled as he pointed a rifle at him. "*Invasion?*" he asked and, slinging his rifle over his shoulder, marched Hammy in front of him off toward the nearest army post. But not for long. Hammy suddenly turned around and slugged him, took his rifle, and ran toward a farmhouse, entered through the kitchen door—to the astonishment of the family eating their breakfast—threw the rifle on the floor, and ran out the front door into an orchard, where he climbed a tree and waited.

It didn't take long for the search dogs to track him down. He climbed out of the tree and surrendered and was taken to a jail in a nearby village. His captors were nonplussed that this pilot who claimed to be an officer—Hammy never wore rank insignia or wings on his battledress—was still in his pajamas. However, his dog tags correctly identified him to the Germans.

After being interrogated, Hammy was eventually sent to Stalag III prisoner-of-war camp at Sagan, where he was immediately consigned to the cooler (solitary confinement) and charged with assaulting a German soldier and stealing his rifle. When he asked a fellow P O W in the next cell if he thought that was a serious offence and what sort of disciplinary action he might expect, the reply was, "Well, I don't want to alarm you, but they shot 50 guys here the other day for trying to escape."

All this we learned later—after the war. At the time Cam was furious. "That's the last goddamn time anyone is going down on those bloody airfields. I've just lost one of my best pilots."

Add this to that ironic scenario: That evening, while Hammy was cooling his heels in a French village jail, the lady he was to meet for dinner in London was tapping her foot at Victoria Station in anger at being stood up.

Around this time, one of the photographic section NCOs went around taking pictures of the pilots and handing out eight-by-ten copies of the result. One of them was a picture of Tex and me, which I mailed home, noting that Tex had just escaped from France. But Tex had other plans for his copy. He had it blown up and framed, with a caption identifying us as having just taken on 40 Focke-Wulf 190s while a downed pilot was being rescued from the English Channel. He then rented window space to display it in a store near where his girlfriend worked.

One day he skillfully walked her by the store, stopped abruptly, turned around, and stared into the window. "My, my, what is that?" he asked. According to Tex, she was absolutely captivated. Grinning from ear to ear, he said, "She told me, 'My, you are such a brave man.'"

•   •   •

Midway through the month the squadron was given 72 hours' leave—a kind of Last Supper before the invasion. Most of us made our way to London. Klersy and I telephoned ahead to reserve a suite in the Savoy Hotel, identifying ourselves as squadron leaders. For old times' sake we stopped at Biggin Hill en route, spending the night at the Bromley Court. Next morning, when we checked into the Savoy, a grim-faced, snotty little registration desk clerk eyed us warily and said, "I hope you boys aren't planning on a lot of parties." On the way up in the elevator, Grisle said, "What the hell does that stupid son of a bitch think we're going to do? Hold a church service?"

For the next two days we lived it up, doing all the rounds. Our suite became a squadron headquarters—to hell with the desk clerk. On the last night we started out at Cracker's Club, dined at Mirabelle's, then taxied over to the Coconut Grove, where we were met with a long lineup. Being a paid-up member in good standing and well lubricated at the time, I ignored the lineup, threw my weight around by giving my name to the doorman, and demanded a table for my friends and me. It worked. We were promptly ushered in ahead of everyone else.

Next day, the bad news. When we checked out of the Savoy, in addition to the room rate, we were charged an extra £14* damages to the mattresses, on which copious drink had been spilled, and for one of the telephones, which had been pulled from the wall. Didn't they know there was a war on?

On the evening of May 20, returning from a squadron dive-bombing attack on a railroad junction in the Laon–Chievres–Cambrai area, we flew over the Vimy memorial, the setting sun casting a

* equivalent to $70 Canadian at the time—a pretty hefty price for a couple of flying officers to pay.

glow on this magnificent monument. It is a sight that branded itself on my memory—it seemed to blaze like a shining symbol of hope for the oppressed French who were suffering under the yoke of the German conqueror. Fittingly, when we returned from our sortie, we became part of a massive invasion deception plan.

During this period the Germans were engaged in photographing the south of England from the air to try to piece together Allied intentions from our troop and transport concentrations. This became more and more difficult for the Germans, because of our overwhelming air supremacy. But some planes were deliberately allowed to get through so that they could see massive ground concentrations, with ships and landing craft filling almost every English harbour and creek.

That was exactly what Supreme Headquarters Allied Expeditionary Force (SHAEF) wanted them to see—an Allied buildup in southeast England. Dummy landing craft known as Big Bobs had been grouped in the Thames estuary and the Channel ports. Squadrons of wooden tanks had been gathered in Kent and Sussex fields. Landing craft moved ostentatiously down the east coast of England.

To add to the deception, a mass aerial buildup also appeared to be taking place. Our role was to return from France into the southeast area and pretend we were going in to land. After announcing our intentions over the R/T, we would lose height right down to the deck and then, preserving radio silence, fly back to Tangmere at zero altitude.

All this illusion paid early dividends. The Germans were convinced the landings would take place across the Straits of Dover. On May 21, Field Marshal Erwin Rommel issued a bulletin stating that "the fixing of Montgomery's headquarters south of London confirms that the main strength of the enemy's forces is centred on south and southeast England."

On that very date, Doc Jones, our medical officer, held a mass stabbing that involved most of us who had managed to avoid our regular (once yearly) TABT shots. Jerry Billing and I immediately suffered from reactions to this hated inoculation. We armed ourselves with a bottle of whiskey each and holed up in a room in the permanent officers' mess, right next to the station soccer field, until the effects wore off—at least a day later. We were nauseated, had no appetite, and suffered from aches and chills all at the same time. We couldn't relax, couldn't sleep. We consoled ourselves with our mutual misery and regular helpings of Scotch.

Around two o'clock in the morning we were easing off a bit, when suddenly there was a tremendous explosion that made everything in the room shake and nearly knocked us out of our beds; it was soon followed by a second one. The airfield was being bombed—or at least the soccer field was. For the moment our ague was forgotten as we dove for shelter under the beds. A fat lot of good that would have done if the air raid had been a serious one. It appears that it was merely a hit-and-miss or drop-and-run affair, but it did leave two gaping holes in the soccer field.

Random raids like this were to be expected; the mass buildup meant that the troops and equipment in our area were practically wall to wall. With the amount of fighter power we had, German raiders couldn't dare risk forays in daylight. They had to rely on individual night raids, taking potluck by dropping their loads anywhere, sure that with the density of troop concentrations below they would be almost certain to make a score.

Rod Smith was another veteran of the Malta air battles. He was with our squadron a short while before being posted as a flight commander to 412 Squadron. Rod and I spent an afternoon in nearby Chichester on a pub crawl. In one establishment two American soldiers joined us. That was probably the last chance they would have to join in a drinking session for some time. Carrying their rifles and wearing helmets and backpacks, they were ready to board one of the invasion ships. Seeing them brought home the fact that the invasion was getting closer by the minute.

Early in June we had a visit from General Dwight D. "Ike" Eisenhower, who addressed both our wings in the station auditorium. I had first seen him almost two years earlier, in September 1942, at the cocktail party given by my father in Claridge's Hotel. Now he was Supreme Commander of the Allied Expeditionary Force. But he struck me as more of a politician, a goodwill ambassador rather than a general commanding the largest invasion force in history. His speech was strictly a public relations job and to me, totally uninspiring. I will never forget his closing remarks to us. With that wide grin of his, for which he was to become world famous (not to mention its getting him elected U.S. president), he said, "I'm inviting you all to a party I'm giving. That party's going to be in Berlin." No RSVP required!

In my own isolated world, things were changing. Bob Hayward had been posted to 411 Squadron as a flight commander. My new tentmates were Babe Fenwick, who had been with the Desert Air Force, and Tony Williams, a married Englishman whose parents lived in New York. We weren't roommates for very long. Early in June our ground crew left to board the invasion ships, taking with them our tents to set up at an airfield we'd move to in France. Our aircraft were being serviced by RAF ground crews, and we now moved into the luxury of the permanent officers' mess.

Ironically, the public relations people at Lincoln's Inn Fields, RCAF Headquarters London, saw fit at this period to send us one of their masterpieces: phonograph records of a pepper-upper by Air Marshal Gus Edwards, who had stepped down earlier in the year as AOC of the RCAF overseas. It began, "What have I done this day to win the war—" That was enough; we didn't bother to play the rest. We took the boxful of discs outside and played skip-them-off-the-tarmac, which fittingly shattered them to bits.

On June 3, we suffered our last squadron casualty before D-Day. That afternoon we flew a fighter sweep at 20,000 feet over the invasion area. At the time we had no idea that in a few days we would be flying over that same territory at 1000 feet—as fighter cover for the British and Canadian armies fighting their way inland from the beaches. I flew number two to Klersy, who was leading Yellow section. Behind me McRae filled the number-three spot, with Cy Cohen as his number two in the fourth spot. By a quixotic quirk of fate, Mac, who had been waiting for an aircraft replacement, was assigned a Spitfire normally flown by Cohen. At the last minute Cy asked Mac if he would mind swapping planes, to which the latter agreed. A fortunate turn of events—for Mac, anyway.

The sky was absolutely cloudless as we crossed the French coast at Grandcamp, swept west, then turned north across the Cherbourg Peninsula, where the U.S. Airborne troops would land two nights hence. We were starting home across the Channel, east of the peninsula, when Cohen started losing height and radioed that he'd lost his engine. The three of us in the section throttled back and lost altitude along with him. When we were down to 2000 feet, I called him and said, "Cy—time to jump. Get out!" But there was no answer.

Down to 1000 feet and Cy had still made no effort to bail out. I called Klersy. "Bill, I think you better give a mayday."

Grisle reacted immediately: "Going over to D for Dog."

I switched channels also and heard Grisle giving the distress signal. Unhappily it was to no avail. At just under 500 feet Cy finally climbed out on the port wing and jumped backward. I was closest to him and I watched. Strangely, he seemed to make no effort to pull the ripcord of his parachute. He simply dropped, belly first, his arms extended before him like a sky diver. He hit the water after what seemed to me an eternity, but in reality it was only a matter of seconds. It just gobbled him up.

I had been so intent on watching Cy that I did not see his aircraft strike the water. But it, too, simply disappeared. Klersy reported over the Dog channel that the pilot's 'chute had failed to open, but that we would make a search. The controller advised that we were three miles north of where we had given the mayday.

The three of us—Gristle, Mac, and I—flew right down to the deck and made a square search around the spot where I had seen Cy go in. I remember being surprised at how choppy, cruel, and dirty grey the water looked, because at altitude it had seemed so serene, blue, and friendly. Our efforts were futile, of course. But squadron camaraderie made it our duty not to abandon a buddy if there was even a ghost of a chance that he had survived. However, there was no sign of life. The squadron log and Mac reported that the only trace left was the green marker dye on the surface from his Mae West life jacket, but I never saw it. We broke off the search when our fuel got so low we had to give up.

The next two days were confined to convoy patrols just off the south coast between Brighton and Bournemouth, over the invasion fleet assembly points in the Solent, and at Spithead, north of the Isle of Wight. I noted in my log book, "Nuttin' doin'."

Looking back, I realize that month leading up to the invasion was one of the most enjoyable of my life. Oh, to be in England now that spring is here! They were exciting days, some of them romantic and fun, albeit not without their tragic moments of comrades lost. But that was all part of the game. History was being made and we were very much a part of it. In my youthful eyes all seemed right with the world. I found it very thrilling.

Late in the afternoon of June 5, 1944, I phoned "Snack Bar," the sector controller, to ask permission to air test my Spitfire, which had just gone through a regular inspection. A female voice answered my request in no uncertain terms: "You know you can't go up there with all those ships in the Channel!" I was dumbstruck. What had happened to military security? Over the phone, no less. I hung up, shattered. But to hell with Miss Snack Bar—I carried out my A/T anyway. She was right, though. The Channel was crowded with ships in all directions around the Isle of Wight, over which I put YOK through its paces. The sight left little doubt that *that* time had come.

That evening all the pilots in our wing were assembled in the mess tent to receive the word. Tin Willie MacBrien, now group commander of the Canadian fighter wings, announced that tomorrow was D-Day. No surprise—but where? Dramatically he uncovered a large blow-up of a map, and then with a pointer indicated where the invasion would take place: along the Normandy coast between Cabourg in the east and Quineville, on the Cherbourg Peninsula, to the west. The role of the three Canadian Spitfire wings, our own 126, Lloyd Chadburn's 127, and Johnnie Johnson's 144, would be to fly fighter cover for the British and Canadians landing on Gold, Juno, and Sword beaches in the east. The Americans would land at Utah and Omaha beaches in the west and would be covered by their own fighters. Our patrols would be limited to an hour and would be rotated among the three wings.

When we stepped outside in the dark, the invasion was already getting under way. We could hear the drone of engines and see the exhausts and navigation lights of aircraft overhead, on their way to France, to drop paratroops and tow gliders carrying other airborne infantry.

We retired with great expectations of a real donnybrook the next day—something right out of *Hell's Angels*. Before turning in, Cam gathered us together. "When we mix it up with the Huns tomorrow, forget all that formation stuff. Everyone for himself." His words were greeted with a hearty hurrah.

Chapter 17

The Real Thing

Tangmere, Sussex—June 6–20, 1944

> You are about to embark on a great cru-
> sade. The eyes of the world are upon you
> and the hopes and prayers of all liberty-
> loving peoples go with you. . . . We will
> accept nothing less than full victory.
> —General Dwight D. Eisenhower,
> Supreme Commander, SHAEF

Tuesday, June 6, 1944. D as in D-Day. D as in disappointment, too.

I wasn't scheduled to fly until the second patrol, so I took my time over breakfast, arriving at dispersal to hear Babe Fenwick, who had been on the first sweep, making a radio broadcast for the CBC. It didn't sound very exciting. "There was no enemy interference whatsoever," he said. "It was rather peaceful, in fact. But it was a bit cloudy."

It seemed that the choice of Normandy as the invasion site had caught the Germans off guard. But we figured that the Luftwaffe wouldn't waste much time getting its act together and would soon make an appearance—or so all of us getting ready for the second patrol hoped. It seemed a reasonable enough assumption to make. The German air force had lots of airfields in the vicinity and, being a highly flexible organization, it wouldn't take them long to reinforce their depleted fighter strength in France with squadrons from

Germany. But we were to be badly disappointed. That big air battle we'd been waiting for was not about to materialize.

Incredibly, the Germans had been completely taken by surprise. Despite all the training and preparation to defend against an assault on *Festung Europa*—Rommel's plan was to contain any attack on the beaches long enough to launch a swift and crushing counterattack from his armoured reserves—they had not been expecting an invasion on the day it took place. Rommel was not even in France; he had left the day before for his home in Ulm on the Danube to celebrate his birthday with his wife. Before leaving, he wrote a note to his naval advisor, Admiral Ruge: "It eases my mind to know that while I'm away the tides will not be suitable for landings. Besides, air reconnaissance gives no reason for thinking they are imminent." The Germans had miscalculated in expecting the invasion at high tide—the landings took place between low and high water.

Moreover, they had been totally deceived by the bogus army in the southeast of England, and were expecting the main assault to take place in the Pas de Calais. But early on, Field Marshal Gerd von Runstedt, the Commander-in-Chief West, soon realized that the Normandy landings were no feint, and he wanted to rush his two Panzer reserves there. However, he was unable to do so without permission from *der Führer*—and Hitler slept in until 10 o'clock—he had not learned of the invasion. By the time Hitler granted permission to move the Panzers, it was too late; the Allies had too strong a toehold. And when the tanks did get rolling, they were subjected to relentless Allied aerial attacks. So heavy, in fact, that the enemy called the main road from Vire to Beny-Bocage *ein Jabo Rennstrecke*—a fighter-bomber racecourse.

Overnight our aircraft had been painted with black and white invasion stripes for instant friend-from-foe recognition. Shortly after 1100 hours, we took off as a wing. During the 20-minute flight across the Channel we flew over an endless stream of vessels steaming south towards the Baie de la Seine, each ship flying a barrage balloon at about 300 feet to ward off low-level aerial attacks.

We patrolled at 1000 feet offshore from the beachhead to avoid enemy flak inland, which we had learned from earlier patrols was "hot and heavy." Our operations were controlled by a fighter-direction ship lying offshore among the countless other vessels. It was a strange sensation to be flying at this altitude over the coast of France. We were accustomed to maintaining a height of 20,000 feet to avoid enemy anti-aircraft fire. Now here we were at low altitude over what was to us in the air, at least, friendly territory. Four things stand out in my memory: the crowds of landing craft and the troop and supply ships with cable balloons rising above them, the broken gliders strewn across the fields like smashed wooden matchboxes, the smoke rising from small fires here and there, and the lack of Luftwaffe interference.

Our biggest danger that morning was collision with other Allied aircraft. Bombers, fighter-bombers, reconnaissance aircraft, and artillery and navy planes were all crammed into that crowded airspace below the clouds hovering above us at 2000 feet. Small wonder the Luftwaffe never showed up. (There was a single exception: Jack Godfrey, the 128 Reconnaissance Wing wingco, lost the number four in his section when a lone FW-190 shot him down.) In my log book I noted, "ALLIES INVADE FRANCE!!! Patrolled Caen area. Nothing doing at all. Weather 5/10 cloud." So much for my look at D-Day.

But next morning—June 7, D-Day plus one—our luck changed. D as in dramatically. I was on the first patrol, flying number two to Scotty Murray, who was leading Yellow section. There was broken cloud around 1000 feet, and because the British and Canadian armies had advanced well inland, we now patrolled back and forth over the expanded bridgehead, roughly between St. Aubin-sur-Mer and Arromanches—a distance of some 12 miles—just above the clouds. The ground below was colourfully littered with gliders and large red, blue, green, white, and yellow supply parachutes from the previous night's reinforcement operation.

Our hour was just about up when McRae reported a Junkers 88 breaking out of the clouds. I saw it diving on the ships off the beach. But the enemy bomber hit a balloon cable and disappeared in a burst of white smoke.

Another JU-88 appeared directly in front of our section, flying away from us. With a well-aimed deflection shot, Scotty Murray set the enemy's port engine on fire as the pilot broke to the left. Now we played hide-and-seek, darting in and out of the clouds. I wove steadily from side to side to throw the air gunner off his aim. It was tricky trying to keep the JU in sight, avoid getting hit, and at the same time prevent a collision with my leader.

Then, as the German bomber gradually lost height, we were suddenly out of the clouds. When I gauged my range to be about 400 yards, I took aim and let go a 10-second burst with my two cannon and four machine guns. The volley knocked the bomber's tail off. We were now right down on the deck. The Junkers hit a fence and exploded in a ball of flame. I hollered, "Yahoo!" like I'd just roped a steer. Fortunately nobody heard me—I hadn't flicked on the R/T lever.

It had been a banner morning for 401 Squadron. In addition to Scotty's kill and my JU-88, Cam had accounted for two enemy bombers, while Dick Cull, Jerry Billing, and Doug Husbands had each destroyed one. Sandy Halcrow was credited with a probable; the JU-88 he was chasing was on fire before it got away from him. In the process, a cannon shell from the bomber's air gunner had pierced his Perspex hood. When last seen, the 88 was being chased by an American P-47 Thunderbolt.

The Duke wasn't the only one to experience a chance encounter with a Thunderbolt. McRae found himself directly behind a German four-engine Heinkel 177. He had it squarely in his sights and had just pressed his gun button when a Thunderbolt cut right in front of him. Mac was furious that he'd been robbed of a score by an American who had no business being in our airspace.

In addition to our own bag, the wingco, George Keefer, also destroyed an 88, and his old squadron, 412, shot down two others. And there was still more glory to come for 401 that day.

At the time of going to press I learned that our efforts has massacred a JU-88 fighter-bomber unit that had been operating over the Bay of Biscay. On D-Day plus one it had been hastily reassigned to the Normandy area.*

After lunch, on the second patrol, the squadron ran into half a dozen Focke-Wulf 190s, which dropped their bombs on the bridgehead, then broke up to try and get away. One of them wasn't fast enough, and Grisle Klersy nailed him. That brought the list of victories for the day to seven destroyed and one probable. The downer was that we suffered our first casualty since the invasion had begun—Shorty Marshall, believed shot down by enemy flak, was posted missing.

That evening I flew my second patrol of the day, paired up with Grisle Klersy. All of us were feeling pretty cocky and confident— too much so. It was getting dusk when Grisle and I ventured over the ancient Norman capital of Caen (which we deliberately mispronounced "kay-en"), about 12 miles south of Juno beach, where the Canadians had landed. But the flashes from the flak guns quickly scared us off; the Germans weren't likely to give up that strategic point without stiff resistance. We flew home across the Channel in darkness—the end of a very exciting day.

Every morning now, we would check into the briefing tent for the

---

* Letter to the author from Squadron Leader Christopher Goss of the Royal Air Force, August 15, 2002. ". . . the unit you attacked was I or III Gruppe/Zerstörergeschwader 1—they were a long-range fighter unit equipped with a day version of the Ju 88 night fighter. When the Allies invaded, they were withdrawn from operations over the Bay of Biscay and were ordered to carry bombs. Understandably, they were slaughtered, losing 4 on 6 Jun and 6 with another 2 badly damaged on 7 Jun 44; as a result, the unit was disbanded early August 44."

up-to-date "gen" on the Allies' progress in Normandy, which was illustrated by maps mounted on easels. The bridgehead was being steadily consolidated and expanded. Bayeux, five miles south of Gold beach, had fallen to the British army the day before, the first French city to be liberated by the Allies. The British and Canadians were continuing their advance on Caen. In the American sector, U.S. forces had begun an advance toward the port of Cherbourg, at the top of the peninsula. An RAF bulletin reported that captured Russian "volunteer" troops were being shipped by the Germans from Guernsey, in the Channel Islands, to Brest. The bulletin's sardonic comment: "But they will all die."

Compared to the excitement of the day before, June 8 was a disappointment—there was absolutely nothing doing. I flew one patrol that day, but after the JU-88 fiasco of the day before, the Luftwaffe failed to make an appearance. I noticed that a lot of fires were burning on the bridgehead, the smoke from one blaze towering to 4000 feet.

At the end of the patrol, showery weather proved a bit of a bind as I returned to Tangmere to land. Those inclement conditions proved to be a precursor of a storm that struck the next day, which we spent on readiness. But heavy winds and rain made it impossible to take off. The weather also didn't make it any easier for the naval ships towing prefabricated artificial Mulberry harbours across the Channel. The harbours had to be set up as quickly as possible to allow Allied ships to bring in supplies, as the French port of Cherbourg had yet to be liberated.

Next morning, June 10, our assignment was to escort Halifax and Sterling four-engine bombers that were dropping supplies to the British and Canadian troops. En route, off the port of Le Havre, we saw a flotilla of German E-boats (torpedo boats), which, together with the U-boats, were menacing the convoys sailing from the British coastal ports to Normandy. De Bub Hayward, leading his flight in 411 Squadron, took it upon himself to give the controller a blow-by-blow description that rambled on and on. Later

Klersy would say to me, "Our pal De Bub is a great guy, but he talks too much." Nevertheless, his efforts brought results. Rocket-firing Typhoons were soon on the way to sink the enemy torpedo boats.

Over the next few days our patrols were pretty routine, and although the controller on three different occasions reported Huns in the Le Havre area at 20,000 feet, we were unable to make contact. Answering one call, Klersy and I ended up chasing a pair of Mustang reconnaissance planes.

On June 13 I reached the ripe old age of 21 ("What an old man you're getting to be," my mother wrote). To celebrate, Cam took me with him in the squadron Auster touring plane to Brighton, where his girlfriend was staying on leave with a fellow WAAF. That evening, when we were on the way to a dance, a flying bomb was exploded by anti-aircraft fire close to where we were walking. Instead of taking cover, the crowds on the boardwalk clapped and cheered. This was the launch of *Operation Rumpelkammer*, the bombardment of London by the V-1s.

On that particular night, only one of the doodlebugs reached London. But on the nights of June 15 and 16, 144 crossed the coast, 73 of them landing on the British capital. One fell near Chichester on June 16, resulting in our field being subjected to three night alerts during that period.

On the morning of June 14, an emergency meeting was held by the Chiefs of Staff Committee (CSC) to decide what action should be taken by the air forces. Forty-two V-1 launch sites ("no-balls") had been identified in the Pas de Calais and in the neighbourhood of the Somme. It was estimated that it would take some 3000 sorties by Flying Fortresses to destroy them. This would create a serious diversion of bombers from the invasion front. It was agreed that nothing should interfere with the battle being waged in France, which was now only nine days old. Consequently, only two of the suspected V-1 supply sites—at Domleger and Beauvoir—were bombed.

On June 14 our squadron landed in France for the second time (I had missed out on the earlier visit), at an airstrip at Beny-sur-Mer, three miles inland from the coast. The site had been bulldozed earlier and metal mesh matting had been laid down. Our purpose was to refuel from jerry tanks and to have long-range tanks fitted to our aircraft for an armed reconnaissance ("recce") well beyond the front line.

We were greeted by a flight sergeant in full regalia armed with a holstered revolver. Speaking with a thick South American accent, he was all business. I never learned what his capacity or designation was, but he must have enjoyed some sort of official status. He told me he had spent the morning supervising the disposal of dead Germans. "I want my men to be heartless and cold-blooded," he said. "I had them pour gasoline on the corpses and set fire to them." He then pointed to a skull—what was left of a cow. "Boche," he sneered, and marched smartly away.

Our armed recce took us over Caen—where we encountered intense ground fire—east to Évreux, northwest to Le Havre, and finally back to Tangmere. Klersy and I took out a truck headed in the direction of Normandy. We must have hit the fuel tank, because there was a big explosion and we left the vehicle in flames.

A telegram was waiting for me when I walked into the mess that evening. It read: CONGRATULATIONS ON YOUR RECENT SUCCESS STOP DAD AWARDED THE CB STOP LOVE MUM. When I showed it to Klersy, he laughed and said, "Well, you got the Hun, but your old man got the medal."

Three days later I received a letter from her, the start of which, in the light of what happened that evening, was somewhat prophetic. "You must be having a very exciting time," she wrote. "I have been praying you would be finished your ops tour before the invasion started, but now I realize you would have hated not being in it. We are all keyed up over it but there is nothing we can do about it. I feel terribly useless."

Exciting time! Well, yes, you might call it that. On the evening of June 17, flying the tail position in my section on a bridgehead patrol, I found myself over the mouth of the Seine River between Le Havre to the north and Honfleur, on the south bank. It was getting dark and I could barely make out the aircraft directly in front of me. Suddenly I was caught in vicious crossfire, with a series of fiery red balls coming at me from both sides. I was scared shitless, and just wanted to get the hell out of there as a fast as I could. I put on full throttle and began jinking up and down and weaving from side to side. But those gunners knew their stuff and kept right on firing. Finally I got right down on the deck, mere feet above the water. Risky in the dark, but I had no choice. Then all of a sudden I was out of range and on my way north. I couldn't see the rest of the squadron, and at that point I couldn't have cared less. I simply wanted to get home. I was still sweating by the time I landed. Exciting time? I guess so.

Later that evening we were alerted that the squadron would be moving to France in the next few days.

Chapter 18

On the Continent

Beny-sur-Mer, Normandy—June 20–July 25, 1944

> An Above Average Fighter Pilot.
>
> —Hap Kennedy,
> 40 Squadron Commanding Officer

The squadron moved to Beny-sur-Mer, officially designated B-4 Airfield, on June 19, but I didn't go until the next day, because my aircraft needed some maintenance. When I arrived, late the following afternoon, the boys were already well dug in. Our tents were set up in a row that ran along the north side of a field that we shared with the other two squadrons in the wing. On the west side a large officers' mess tent had been set up, behind which was a water bowser (tanker). A path leading from the entrance to the mess ran to the edge of the road, which ran through the village of Beny to Bernières-sur-Mer, where the Queen's Own Rifles had landed on Nam beach (part of Juno) on D-Day.

To the north of the field was a stone wall. Behind it, a military cemetery for Canadians had been established. There were already three graves marked with small wooden crosses. One of them read "Cpl. J. Bishop." No relation, but rather chilling.

At dinner time there was another "pleasant" surprise. In the officers' dining mess tent I came face to face with the messing sergeant from Staplehurst days, good old Cream-and-sugar-is-in-the-mush-sir himself. He hadn't lost his touch, either—the food was worse than ever.

Except for the CO, who had his own accommodation, the rest of us were assigned three to a tent. I shared mine, which was right behind the mess tent, with Doc Jones, our medical officer, and Tony Williams. According to most of the guys, the problem during sleeping hours wasn't the German bombers prowling around at night—their target was the shipping offshore—or the noise from the "oyster" mines they dropped going off. Nor was it the constant barking of the ack-ack guns, which was bad enough. The problem was pieces of burning shrapnel raining down from the exploding anti-aircraft shells.

Most of the pilots solved this problem by digging trenches large enough to accommodate their canvas camp cots; they then covered the trenches with planking or other material. But Doc Jones refused to go to ground. He found some corrugated metal to cover his bed and made a special shelter with part of it for his dog, Dinghy, who slept at the foot of his bed. Tony Williams' response was blunt—"To hell with it"—and he slept quite soundly above ground without any sort of protection. I wanted to dig a trench, but Doc Jones, who outranked me by one ring (he was a flight lieutenant and I a flying officer), would have none it. However, he did offer to dig a dugout for me, roof and all, behind the water bowser. For the time being, like Tony, I too would have to sleep above ground.

Scotty Murray told me that in the interim I might want to take advantage of one of the slit trenches the army had left behind. They were bedded with straw, and with a blanket and a pillow could be quite livable. However, that first night, after a few Scotches—which were rationed—and several glasses of Sauternes as chasers (there wasn't any beer), I was sufficiently relaxed to simply crawl between the blankets and doze off. But not for long.

When the ack-ack guns began barking, my liquefied false courage deserted me. Tin helmet, pillow, and blanket in hand, I made for the nearest slit trench, in which I bedded down for the rest of the night. By the end of the third day after my arrival at

Beny, Doc had completed the promised dugout, into which I moved cot and gear.

Once we got settled, our main purpose in life was to paralyze all enemy movement, from first light to dusk, by road or rail—especially by road. This meant that the Germans had to reinforce their positions chiefly at night, and to prevent this, night fighters were dispatched during the hours of darkness.

On June 21, the day after I arrived, the squadron experienced its first casualty since moving to France. My former tentmate, Babe Fenwick, was chasing a Hun south of Bayeux when our gunners opened up on the Focke-Wulf. Their shells hit Babe instead. His remains were recovered and an impromptu military funeral was held in the cemetery the following evening. Doug Husbands and I and two others acted as pallbearers, while Cam led the cortège. During the march, Monty Berger, the wing intelligence officer, hustled up to Cam and announced that the squadron had been alerted to scramble. This earned a sharp rebuke from the CO, who snapped, "We're attending a funeral," and the procession proceeded. When Berger reported this to the wingco, George Keefer, another squadron was scrambled in our place. Our padre, Ron Forbes, conducted the service. Then our section returned to readiness until dusk. Business as usual—war leaves little time for mourning.

The next afternoon, I flew my first mission since arriving. Our objective was to dive-bomb a pair of bridges over the Orne River, just north of Caen, that the Germans were holding. Following the bombing, which was successful—both bridges were knocked out— we went in search of transport south of the Normandy capital. Scotty Murray, with whom I was flying, blasted a German staff car off the road. But we had to cut short the sortie when the weather started to close in after only an hour and a half.

In Normandy we had to cope with either gumbo-like mud or thick limestone dust that choked the Merlin engines' induction system. As a result, the engines had to be fitted with special filters, and the airstrips had to be watered at night to keep the dust down—when it wasn't raining, that is.

On June 26 we again went hunting for transport. I flew two patrols that day in atrocious weather, with the ceiling down to 400 feet. However, our efforts did pay off; we shot up half a dozen trucks. I saw a small open troop carrier; the soldiers were seated facing each other, their rifles between their knees. The truck was inching along a winding road in my direction. It would have to pass by two buildings about 30 feet apart on my approach side of the road. I aimed my gun on the gap between the buildings. The moment the carrier appeared in the gap, I let off a three-second burst of cannon and machine-gun fire from a range of only 100 yards. As I flew over it, the truck literally bounced off the road and tumbled into a ravine on the far side.

That night we learned that the port of Cherbourg had been liberated by the Americans. But the enemy had made sure that the Allies were denied use of the harbour. The German defenders had carried out to the letter Hitler's directive to leave the port a "field of ruins"; they had reduced it to a shambles. This was a serious blow to the Allies, who had counted on Cherbourg as a means of bringing men and equipment ashore. An additional concern was a gale that had lasted three days, from June 19 to 22, the like of which had not been seen in the Channel for 80 years. It had wrecked the Mulberry harbours, reducing the number of troops and equipment landed sharply, by two-thirds.

Nevertheless, the buildup was growing steadily. By the last week in June, 875,000 men had been landed in Normandy, as well as 100,000 vehicles and 200 tons of stores—all crowded into a bridgehead 50 miles wide and varying in depth from 8 to 12 miles. And 31 Allied squadrons were operating from beachhead airstrips. It was probably the most compressed staging platform in military history.

On June 27 our squadron scored its biggest strike against German transport. That morning, in rare clear weather, we set off south to Argentan, then swept northeast to south of Rouen. We came across a large convoy of open troop-carrying trucks—there must have been 50 or more—moving down a road with open fields on either side. We could hardly believe our eyes.

In pairs we dived at the vehicles, spraying them with our fire, then turned about and made another run. Spitfires were flying all about, going in every direction—it's a wonder there weren't any collisions. And there was no return fire, although some of the soldiers doubtless took potshots at us with their rifles. Most of them, however, were fleeing the vehicles and trying to take cover in the ditches. It was a total slaughter.

After comparing notes when we landed, we figured the tally to be approximately 27 trucks, half "flamers" and half "smokers." It was impossible to estimate the number of casualties we'd inflicted. I still find it hard to fathom why the Germans, knowing we had complete air superiority, would risk such a large convoy over that open route in broad daylight. But then one wonders what our fate would have been, had any of us been unlucky enough to be forced down amid all that chaos. I shudder at the thought. Those guys on the ground would have been decidedly hostile, to put it mildly.

That evening we very nearly lost our CO. Through an unfortunate set of circumstances Cam found himself all alone near Beauvais amid a gaggle of 15 Messerschmitt 109s. He had no alternative but to fight it out. If he had tried to run for it, they'd have clobbered him for certain. He dropped down to tree-top height and began turning madly, as tightly as he could, a manoeuvre in which the Spitfire always held the advantage. Each of the 109s took shots at him, then finally all but three of them ran out of either ammunition or fuel, or both, because they broke off and landed at a field not far from Beauvais.

Cam managed to elude the others by twisting and turning and flying under two of the Seine bridges that still remained intact, an exercise the Hun pilots showed no interest in trying to match. Cam was a shattered man when he landed, but this response was superseded by anger that his number two had deserted him. That individual soon found himself on a landing craft back to England, with Cam's best wishes that it would be one helluva seasick voyage.

One afternoon a familiar figure appeared at the field behind the wheel of a Jeep, decked out in army battledress and helmet and sporting the Military Cross. Sydney Radley-Walters, an old boarding-school friend from BCS days, was now a major in command of the 27th Canadian Armoured Regiment. Through the grapevine he had learned of my whereabouts and decided to look me up on his afternoon off. Rad took me on a tour of the beaches, which were crowded with men and equipment as well as with German prisoners. He pointed to a church that looked forlorn and lonely, which he said "stood out like a phantom and a guide on D-Day. Despite all the shelling, it still stood there."

Rad also told me that he was pretty sure that Ian Maclean had probably been taken prisoner. Ian was a former schoolmate of ours whom I hadn't seen since over a year ago, at the Dewars' Dutton Homestall estate. His tank had been hit in one of the battles with the Panzers, but the crew had been able to jump out, some of them badly burned. I relayed this information in a letter to my parents, who passed it on to Ian's mother. They told me she was very grateful, because up to that point she had had no official word.

After supper on June 28, on a bright, clear summer's evening, we were flying east of Domford, south of Caen, at 14,000 feet. Suddenly we were bounced by a dozen Focke-Wulf 190s from out of the sun in the west. Cam, who was leading the squadron, and I, as his number two, broke into the attack in a tight climbing turn to port. These enemy pilots were obviously singling out the section leaders. I heard Cliff Wyman, flying number two to Scotty Murray, who was leading Yellow section, call the break. But it wasn't soon enough. One of the 190s shot up Scotty's engine, forcing him to bail out.

Cam and I levelled out behind our two Focke-Wulfs, but even at full throttle we couldn't catch them. They had too much zoom coming out of their dive. However, we managed to wipe out a small column of trucks on our way back to base. In the meantime, Klersy shot down two of the enemy aircraft, while Hap Kennedy accounted for another. In addition to the loss of Murray, who bailed out safely and later managed to evade capture, we also lost the services of Bob Davidson, who was posted as missing and later presumed to have been killed.

On the following morning after breakfast, as several of us were walking around the south end of the airstrip, we heard a *tack-tick-tack-tick*. We looked up to see a Spitfire firing at an ME-109 not more than 500 feet above us. It didn't last long—about a minute more and the German pilot bailed out, landing right in the middle of the Crepon airstrip (B-2 Airfield), home of 127 Wing. Andy Mackenzie, a flight commander with 403 Squadron, ran over to the enemy pilot just as he was shedding his parachute, and pointed his service revolver at his head. Another one of the pilots dashed out with his camera and took a picture. It was all in jest, but the downed German wasn't amused. He took off his flying helmet and spat on the ground, then calmly began combing his hair.

Later, Dal Russel, then CO of 442 Squadron, flying out of St. Croix-sur-Mer (B-3 Airfield), was present at the interrogation of the captured flyer. Noting the fine, highly polished, bright-red-fleece-lined flying boots he was wearing, Dal offered to give the pilot an hour's head start to get away—if he would exchange them for the standard-issue boots Russel was wearing. The German didn't think that was very funny, either.

The following day it was my turn to take a fall. At noon I was at the bar enjoying my third glass of Sauternes before going in to lunch, when Dick "Dad" Stayner,* commander of B Flight, asked me if I would fill in as a sub–section leader. He wanted a fast okay, because the squadron was due to take off in 15 minutes. I said, "Sure," and finished my drink. We then hustled over to dispersal. My position was number three in Blue section.

"Ding Dong" Bell was my number two. "Dad" was leading the section. Cam was leading Red section, and Hap Kennedy, who had replaced Scotty Murray as commander of A Flight, was leading Yellow section, with Jerry Billing as his number three. The squadron formation called for Blue section to fly on the right, Red in the centre, and Yellow on the left.

We flew south, then east. We were somewhere south of Villers-Bocage at 300 feet when all hell broke loose. Ground fire zeroed in on us from every direction, red tracers all over the place. Suddenly I heard an ominous clank underneath me, just to the right. Jerry called up, "Blue Three, you're pissing glycol." I looked out the right side to see engine coolant streaming from the starboard radiator in a fine white mist, marking me as a lame duck for every gunner in the vicinity. And focus on me they did.

I turned north to get out of the gunfire as fast as I could. But I wasn't sure what to do next. I was too low to bail out. All I could see below me were trees, and I knew my engine would soon pack up. Jerry was right beside me, which was some comfort. I considered pancaking on my belly on the treetops when, miracle of miracles, an airstrip suddenly opened up before me. Just in time! Flames were licking the top of the engine cowling around the fuel-tank cap. I throttled back, cut the ignition, and pushed the nose down, banging wheels-up into the ground, which fortunately was muddy, allowing the aircraft to slide gently to a stop. I unstrapped myself, got out of the plane, and made a dash to the edge of the field in case the aircraft caught fire and blew up.

I felt a bit nauseated by it all—Sauternes on an empty stomach

---

* Stayner was the only married pilot in the squadron, with three children.

and the lack of lunch were beginning to tell. I took out my escape kit and emptied out the chocolate bar and Horlicks malted milk tablets—which were supposed to sustain you for at least two weeks if you were evading capture—and gobbled them all down. My Spitfire presented a sad sight sitting there, nose down, the propeller bent. But the flames had burned themselves out. I knew that Jerry would report where I was, so I sat back on the grass and waited.

Half an hour later, Willy "No Neck" Worrell, our maintenance crew chief, arrived in the squadron Auster. We had a brief argument because he felt I hadn't made a proper landing. I told him that any time he would like to fly with me into all that flak, I would welcome the chance to show him what it felt like. But I realized I shouldn't have lost my temper. I climbed in the Auster and was flown to Beny-sur-Mer, where Cam congratulated me on getting back.

But the news wasn't all good. When I was hit, at least I was close enough to our lines to get back. Jerry Billing wasn't so lucky. He was on the German side of the front when his Spitfire was hit by flak and he lost his engine. He managed to belly-land in a field and make a run for it, hiding in some bulrushes to evade capture.

Two days later came July 1, 1944, Dominion Day, and one I would not soon forget. East of the Orne River, returning from an armed recce, our section of four Spitfires was bounced by half a dozen ME-109s. As each of us broke around and upwards into the attack, we were split up, and it was every man for himself.

My evasive manoeuvre lifted me right into the cloud layer above us. Facing in the opposite direction, I tried to get my bearings from the instruments. Then a quick look at my fuel gauge told me I was flying on empty. I had to get home—fast!

I dropped down out of the cloud and made a sharp 180-degree turn to starboard. Taking a quick look around, I could see none of the rest of the section—nor the Huns, thank God! But my worries were far from over. The Merlin engine started to sputter. If it quit on me now, I'd come down east of the Orne, where the Germans could take me prisoner. I was sweating—in a funk—priming the fuel pump for all I was worth. Over the bloody Caen canal at last, engine still spitting like a son of a bitch. Then, finally, mercifully, the airstrip came in sight on my left. If only I could keep the engine going, I'd be home free.

As I lined up on the north-to-south runway, the engine started coughing intermittently. I jammed the undercarriage lever into place and heard the wheel come down with a reassuring clunk. Then it happened. The Merlin conked right out on me. Another problem: I had too much height. That's when I should have pulled the undercarriage back up and pancaked on the ground. But I didn't. I panicked. I shoved the stick forward to put the nose down, the propeller windmilling in front of me, and conveniently forgot to put the flaps down to induce drag and slow my speed.

I hit the ground around 100 miles an hour, too fast for normal landing. The Spit bounced once, then hit the ground again. The port wheel root broke right off. The aircraft spun at right angles, bending the propeller blades and the left wingtip. And as if that wasn't bad enough, I noticed I'd failed to take the normal precaution of turning off the gun button on the control column. Luckily my prang failed to trigger either the machine guns or the cannons, which could have added murder of innocent bystanders to my clumsy performance.

I quickly redressed that oversight, flicked off the engine switches, unfastened my safety and parachute harnesses, and climbed out of the aircraft, feeling like an absolute idiot. A piss-poor show. After a year and a half on ops, I should have been capable of a lot better. But perhaps, after all, that was the problem. Everyone has his limits of tolerance, and perhaps I was overstepping mine. I'd been at it too long. I thought I knew it all and had become a complacent smartass. I was tired too, maybe. But at least the only bit of me that hurt was my bruised ego.

Having watched the whole sorry spectacle from the operations trailer across the strip, the tall, impressive figure of the airfield commander, Keith Hodson, came bounding over. A paternal pat on the shoulder and then, "Are you okay?"

I nodded.

"You have a knack of picking up flak, don't you?" he grinned, referring to the incident two days earlier when I got hit by ground fire.

I shook my head. "No, sir," I replied, "this time it was finger trouble, loud and clear."

I knew I was in trouble, and because I felt downcast, I pretty well kept to myself for the rest of the day. My biggest fear was that I would get kicked off the squadron, the fate of so many others last winter during the crackdown on accidents. I worried how the disgrace of that would sit with my old man. By evening I was absolutely despondent.

Cam summoned me to his tent. He lectured me that there was no use brooding over the incident, and recited his experience of running into the signal trailer at Biggin Hill shortly after taking over as our CO. "You just have to forget it and get on with the job." He then promised he would go to bat for me with the wingco, George Keefer, and Keith Hodson, who would decide my fate. He told me he didn't want to lose me to one of the OTUs as an instructor—the standard assignment once your tour ended—because I was one of his best pilots, even though my record showed five accidents. "But none of them since I've been CO. I'll tell you, it's no life being an OTU instructor after you've been on ops—and I speak from experience." He told me to meet him in the mess later for a drink. "Give me an hour to square things up," he said, "and for God's sake, cheer up!"

The "prisoner" entered the mess tent "courtroom" right on time. As I timorously made my way to the bar, I was surprised—and relieved—to see that the jury of George Keefer, Keith Hodson, and Buck McNair was all smiles. Cam seemed in particularly high spirits. There was no need to ask what the verdict was.

Keefer handed me a drink, and in his usual quiet way said, "We hate to lose that aircraft, Bish, but you're off the hook. Carry on." Cam cut in ebulliently, "See, Bish, I told you not to worry. It's okay." Keefer had the last word: "Your problem, Bish, is that your CO doesn't like you."

Next morning, on the way to breakfast, I stopped by Cam's tent and said, "Thanks, Boss, thanks for everything." Cam waved me off with a grin: "Get going, Bishop, and don't be late."

As if to atone for the previous day's blunder, on July 2 I flew two sorties, both of them in the afternoon. The first took place right after lunch, a dive-bombing mission to take out a pair of bridges south of Caen. We followed our usual procedure to avoid flak west of the city by "going through the gate," crossing the northern Orne River going east, then flying south. After the bombing the squadron became separated, each section heading south at 11,000 feet, looking for trouble. Three from our section—Hap Kennedy, Grisle Klersy, and I—soon found it: 30 Messerschmitt 109s about 4000 feet above us. Almost immediately we found ourselves on the edge of a melee involving what appeared to be a hundred aircraft embroiled in a series of turning, diving, climbing dogfights, like a scene out of *Hell's Angels*—a real spectacular, this one live and in Technicolor. One incident will always live in my memory. An FW-190 suddenly came diving down, twisting as it lost height. When it came out of the dive, it was so close I could make out the markings on his wings. On one was the German black cross, on the other an RAF roundel—and our black and white invasion stripes, too!

We climbed above the tumult, chasing after the 109s, which somehow got split up, probably becoming embroiled in the turmoil. Kennedy went off on his own somewhere while Klersy and I ended up climbing behind two of the enemy aircraft. As we drew closer, we could make them out to be an FW-190 (Grisle's) and an ME-109 (mine)—an odd couple.

Both our superchargers kicked in at around 19,000 feet; we soon had the height and speed advantage and began to close in. Klersy opened fire, too far out of range, I thought, but nevertheless his bullets and cannon shells found the mark. The 190 flopped over onto its back and went into a dive, flames streaming from it.

I took aim on the 109, but just as I was about to open fire, the enemy pilot pushed the aircraft into a 60- to 70-degree dive. I tried to follow, but even with my throttle wide open he had too much speed for me, quickly widening the range. Finally, in frustration I let go a few exasperated bursts, but the German, recognizing my dilemma, defiantly waggled his wings as if to thumb his nose at me—the son of a bitch.

When we landed, Hap Kennedy related his own experience. He had got behind a section of five 109s, and from 150 yards he fired a burst at the nearest one. The 109 climbed to 13,000 feet, but the Spitfire's rate of climb was superior. Hap got in a couple more good squirts, noticing strikes on the fuselage. The Messerschmitt was obviously in trouble; the prop was windmilling but the pilot had slowed to a glide. In hopes of getting him to land on our side of the line and take him prisoner, Hap reduced his speed down to 120 miles an hour and closed in on the 109.

The pilot looked at him, and Hap gestured, pointing back north. The enemy pilot slowly banked his aircraft to the left, turned around to the north, and straightened out, continuing to glide at 120 miles an hour.

"He looked at me a number of times while I glided along beside him," Hap told me. "I watched him carefully, but was not afraid of him doing a kamikaze on me. I was sure he was injured, probably in the legs. Otherwise, why wouldn't he bail out, or at least wave to me? But a lethargic turn of his head was all I could get out of him. Quite a few times I had been in close formation with 109s for a minute or so while lining up on them, but never before had I got into tight formation with the enemy."

It became obvious that the German was not going to be able to make it as far as the front. He made a wheels-up landing near

Bernay. Hap did a quick run over the aircraft with his cine-gun camera before leaving, but the German pilot didn't get out of his aircraft.

We had been having problems with confirmation of our victories by 83 Group Headquarters. The AOC, Air Marshal Harry Broadhurst (who didn't like Canadians), was rejecting our combat claim reports out of hand, demanding to see proof from our cine-gun camera films. While Klersy's film on this occasion showed strikes on the enemy aircraft, there was no filmed record of its having caught fire, although both of us saw it when it dived out of the way. I was busy chasing the 109, so I only saw it go into the dive, but Grisle was certain from the way it was burning that it must have crashed. Group HQ rejected his claim and my confirmation of an aircraft destroyed. Grisle ended up with a probable. Angrily, he told Monty Berger, the IO, to "take the bloody thing off the board." However, thanks to pressure from George Keefer, the matter was eventually resolved—Grisle got his "destroyed."

After supper I made a second sortie, once again south of Caen, where we beat up some transport in the face of fierce ground fire. After my experience with that same kind of flak a few days earlier, it made me very, very twitchy.

Next morning we were off the deck before dawn, to try and catch German overnight transport before it got light. Just as dawn broke we caught a line of trucks near Falaise. Cam, who led the attack, had to belly-land in a muddy field when his engine was damaged by flak. Hap called up, "Are you okay, Red One?" Back came the curt reply, "Get the hell away from here!" so we wouldn't draw attention to him.

We thus lost one of the finest squadron commanders in the business, both on the ground and in the air. Fortunately, Cam was never made a prisoner of war. He lived with the French resistance for a month or so before a collaborator turned him over to the Gestapo, who put him in chains and threw him into a jail in Bordeaux. While

en route to a POW camp in Germany, he escaped and made his way
back to the squadron, then based at Poix in France.*

That day Tex Davenport and I had the afternoon off—part of the
rotation system of 24 hours on duty, 24 hours off. We hopped a
ride into Bayeux, the first French town to have been liberated. The
place was packed to the gills. Flags hung from windows; flowers
filled the window boxes and decorated doorways. Cafés were so
filled to overflowing you'd think it was New Year's Eve. Even the
local whorehouse was doing a land-office business, a long lineup of
British soldiers outside awaiting their turn—assembly-line fornica-
tion—under the watchful eyes of several military policemen.

We turned our attention first to a meat store, even though it was
strictly against military regulations to deprive the "half-starved"
French population of their food—official orders from Field Marshal Bernard Montgomery, no less. Well, the local population
didn't look very half-starved to us, and they didn't have to put up
with the meals our favourite messing sergeant doled out. Nor was
there any shortage of meat or poultry in the store. So we bought
ourselves a solid supply of steaks. We next repaired to a sidewalk
café. There was no shortage of wine, either—after all, this was Cal-
vados country.

After saturating ourselves with quantities of Sauternes, we went
in search of transport back to the airstrip. Night had begun to fall.
Luckily we found an ambulance driver who was agreeable because
he was heading back to our vicinity, but he might have to make
some stops first. We climbed into the back and promptly passed
out on two stretchers.

Some time later, we were awakened when the driver and his

* For details of Cameron's escape, see *Unsung Courage* by Arthur Bishop,
Chapter 1: "They Kept Coming Back."

medical orderly opened the back door of the truck and told us to get out. We figured we'd arrived. Then we heard gunfire. Two wounded soldiers were helped onto the stretchers in our place and we sat on the floor. Tex asked, "Where are we?"

One of the soldiers replied, "This is as close to the war as you can get. The Krauts are over a hill out there."

"Shit," Tex said. "Let's get the hell out of here or we'll end up flying for the Luftwaffe."

When we finally reached Beny-sur-Mer, the driver let us out and we thanked him. Then the ambulance continued on to the beach, where the wounded would be put aboard ship to take them back to England. We gathered up Hap, Klersy, and a few others, then went over to the dining tent, made for the kitchen, and cooked up the steaks. It was a real feast. I hadn't felt so well-fed since leaving England. As Bob Hyndman put it, "I've been so hungry I could have eaten one of the tent poles." It was lucky our favourite messing sergeant didn't show up for our impromptu banquet, or we would have shoved some steak up both his nostrils.

Next morning, at the crack of dawn, Tex and Klersy, who had been given command of A Flight—Hap Kennedy had been made squadron CO—took off on their usual Hun hunt, searching for high-flying reconnaissance Junkers 88s. ("This guy's getting to be a second Beurling," Tex said of Klersy, an admiration I shared. "He's already got seven and a half planes to his credit.")

Dawn flights had not exactly been my liking recently. I had a hard time getting myself out of bed in the mornings. I felt tired and was having minor chest palpitations that disappeared once I got up and got busy. On top of that, I had a toothache, and I knew the tooth would have to be pulled. But I had to wait until "Toothy," our dental officer, received a fresh supply of novocaine. Meanwhile, I learned to live with it. Strangely, once I got into my kite and turned up the oxygen, my weariness would disappear and my toothache subside. But it was only temporary.

On July 5, I returned from an evening patrol in which we had

escorted rocket-firing Typhoons that were attacking a large formation of tanks assembled in the trees near Dreux. I was so exhausted
that I headed straight for the mess, downed several Sauternes, then
stretched out on Williams' cot and fell asleep. When I awoke an
hour later it was dark. Tony told me that George Keefer had paid a
call; they had talked for the entire hour, but I hadn't even stirred.

I was getting careless, too. Next day I flew two patrols, both of
them uneventful. Taxiing out for the second "do," I came so close
to Walter Johnson's Spitfire that if he hadn't cut his engine, his
prop would have chewed away my port wingtip. I didn't need that
kind of hassle. It would have been goodbye ops tour, hello OTU,
that's for doggone sure.

On the morning of July 7, I was flying the rear position of a four-
man section behind Tony Williams, patrolling between Bayeux and
Cabourg. After an hour we began the return to Beny at 5,000 feet,
underneath a solid layer of cloud. Suddenly, what looked like a gaggle of Mustangs dropped out of the overcast, headed in the opposite direction on our right. It quickly became evident that they were
ME-109s. Mac McRae, who was leading the section, had a gut feeling that we were being set up, that the ME-109s were simply bait
for another section of Huns above them. As he wheeled the section
around in behind the Germans, he called the controller for a section of reinforcements. At that very moment, an FW-190 popped
out of the cloud and dived straight past me. Afraid that others
might follow him, I broke around in a climbing turn, right into the
overcast—shades of a similar experience six days earlier. When I
dropped down into the clear, my section and the Huns were
nowhere to be seen. I decided to made it back to base pronto, but
was determined not to repeat my Dominion Day performance. I
didn't; I brought good old YOK down all in one piece.

Mac was the only one who scored, bringing down one of the ME-
109s in flames. He was pretty happy; it was his first victory in three
years of operational flying. His hunch about a Hun backup above
the overcast had been right. When the reinforcement section was

scrambled, it ran into a formation of 20 ME-109s and FW-190s and managed to shoot down two of the enemy aircraft.

That evening George Keefer and Dal Russel, who had taken over command of our wing on the previous day, invited Tex Davenport and me to join them in watching the scheduled bombing of Caen—a prelude, after 31 days of bitter resistance, to the capture of the city. All day long, Sherman tanks rumbled along the road past our field, raising dust on their way to take up positions along the river Orne. We set off in a Jeep and drove to a knoll that overlooked the target area. For a solid hour, covered by an umbrella of 10 squadrons of Spitfires, two waves totalling 475 Lancaster bombers dropped 2363 tons of explosives from 8000 feet on selected targets north of the Normandy capital.

As the first wave flew overhead, we experienced a series of deafening booms, and wondered whether the bombs were falling short of the target. It turned out to be artillery cannon—Bofors guns in the field next to us—opening up on enemy anti-aircraft positions. They certainly did little to douse the heavy anti-aircraft fire that erupted. At first we could see the bomb bursts, but eventually there was nothing but a miasma of smoke.

In the second wave, one of the bombers was hit and set on fire. It began a slow spiral downward, but there was no let-up in the torrent of flak that poured toward it following its descent all the way. Tex shouted, "For Christ's sake, leave the poor bastard alone. He's had it!" There were no parachutes, and soon the bomber disappeared in the smoke and debris thrown up by the bombs.

Many of the Lancasters must have been hit by flak that evening, and doubtless there were casualties among the crews. We never found out. But I do remember a picture in one of the papers a day or two later, showing a Lancaster that had belly-landed in Normandy, not far from us. None of the crew, the paper reported, was injured.

That evening marked the start of the turning point in the crucial Battle of Normandy. To this day I am glad that I was a witness to it.

Two days later, on July 9—33 days since the landings and after sus-taining 5000 casualties—the British and Canadians seized the ruins of half of Caen, and at last captured the airfield at Carpiquet that had been a D-Day objective.

By the following morning, the pain from my toothache had become unbearable, even though Doc Jones had dosed me with painkillers. And the promised delivery of novocaine still hadn't arrived. Toothy got on the blower to one of the advanced field hos-pitals south of Bayeux to arrange for a dental unit there to make the extraction the next day.

I had a hard time sleeping that night because the pain had become so intense, but at least I had the consolation that, by the same time tomorrow night, my troubles would be over. Little did I know. Next morning I set off in a Jeep with a driver. The conges-tion on the road, now that the offensive in our sector had begun—artillery, armoured cars, Bren gun and troop carriers, trucks, tanks, and an assortment of other vehicles—made modern highway rush-hour traffic look like the Indianapolis Speedway by comparison. It took us three and a half hours to make the 12-mile journey.

When we arrived at our destination, I was informed that because of the heavy casualties suffered at Caen and Carpiquet, novocaine was in short supply, and if I still wanted to have my tooth pulled, it would have to be without benefit of anesthesia. I knew it wouldn't be pleasant, but anything would be better than the agony I was enduring. So I had no choice, and the sooner the better. The dentist and his orderly went to work. The latter put his arms under mine and took a firm grip on my chest to hold me steady, while the den-tist put the clamp around my tooth. My back teeth are long and deeply rooted, which didn't make the dentist's job any easier. He had to struggle for 10 minutes to pry the molar loose. The pain was so excruciating it left me in a state of shock.

I was sweating and trembling so badly, it took two heaping shots of straight rum to calm me down, but I was still in a sort of daze. I don't remember much about the trip back to Beny, but as soon as I got there I stumbled over to my dugout and lay down. Although the dental types had supplied me with small squares of gauze to arrest the bleeding, I couldn't get it to stop. However, I did manage to doze off and on for two hours or so. I was still feeling groggy, so I got up and walked over to the mess and had a couple of drinks. They didn't do much good. In fact I felt quite dizzy, so I went outside to where some of the others were gathered, in the hope that the fresh air might revive me.

As I was trying to collect myself, who should come over but our old friend Tin Willie MacBrien. Loudly he barked at me, "Arthur! What's this I hear about you smashing up another of our aircraft?" I must have presented a pathetic sight, with blood drooling down my chin.

Before I could answer, Klersy stepped between us and angrily confronted the group captain: "When you've flown as many operational hours as he has," he almost growled, "you might get away with that. But not before. And I don't like you talking to one of the pilots in my flight like that." That ended the sorry scene. I stumbled back to my dugout and lay down, with no thought of supper; I had no appetite for food. I finally dozed off into a fretful sleep.

When I got up next morning, my cot was covered in blood. My mouth was still bleeding, and so sore I couldn't face the idea of trying to chew anything. I decided to forget about breakfast. Doc Jones took one look at me and said, "You're going to sick bay." He escorted me some distance from the living-tent area, to where there were two tents for patients, in which trenches had been dug about three and a half feet deep, extending to all four sides. There was even matting on the floor. Very comfortable compared to what we'd been accustomed to, but I was in no shape to enjoy it. I was in one of the tents and Doug "Hubby" Husbands, who had to be isolated because he had mumps, was in the other. At least it was someone to talk to, but at that point I was in no mood for conversation.

After a few days of lying in bed, the bleeding had stopped and I began to feel a bit better, but eating was still a problem and I was starting to get hungry. The right side of my jaw had become swollen and turned grey, as if it had been bruised. It hurt, and I couldn't get my teeth apart. It was like having lockjaw; I couldn't take in any solid food. One of the MOs solved this problem by cooking some canned porridge, which was like a purée. I was able to wash this down—the gap left by the extracted tooth helped. I tried all kinds of things to try and get my teeth apart, like forcing them open with my fingers and putting a piece of wood between them. At least I could take a drink—water and tea, that is. The porridge wasn't all that nourishing, but at least I didn't feel so hungry. I whiled away the time reading old magazines that the orderlies brought me and wrote a few letters, one to my parents and another to Cilla. When I'd get up to walk to the latrine, I felt terribly weak.

I must have been in bed for about four days when, one morning, Hap Kennedy and Grisle Klersy arrived. It was the first I'd seen of anyone from the squadron and I was ready to assure them that give me another week and I'd be good as new. Then they broke the news. "Your tour's finished, Bish," Hap said. "You need a rest. We're sending you home."

I was stunned. And I was hurt. It brought tears to my eyes. My initial reaction was that it was a dismissal. I'd been making too many mistakes and perhaps they were catching up with me. Or blame my childish sensitivity on a sickly physical condition. (Many years later, when I introduced Hap to my wife as "the guy who kicked me off ops," Hap said, "Bish, you were *ill*.")

Both Hap and Grisle assured me that I would be missed, but that six months back home, probably with a stint as an OTU instructor (perish the thought), would be a welcome respite. I would still be welcome to return to the squadron.

After they left my mood changed. At first I was lonely. The squadron had been family to me for nearly two years. Being posted from 401 was like cutting an umbilical cord. I would no longer be part of the team I had flown and fought with, a team made up of the greatest guys I would ever come to know, brave and loyal, men who would give you the shirts off their backs. It was comradeship that would never fade, a friendship that those who had not shared in our experiences together could never understand. Then my mood began to change to one of relief. I was never one to deny that I was afraid, even at times scared out of my wits—who wasn't? That was only human. I was proud that somehow I had been able to live with that, even if I was not entirely able to overcome it.

Even though I now felt left out of it all, my mood was rapidly changing from despondency to joy and gratification. I had a lot to be thankful for. I was alive and in one piece—and I was going home! Already the tension was beginning to drain away and, relatively speaking, my health started to improve.

I shared this good fortune with my parents and Cilla in my letters home. The responses were memorable, though completely different. Cilla enclosed a picture of herself and a friend seated by the swimming pool of the Ottawa Country Club. It was in sharp contrast to Beny-sur-Mer—there were no lovely girls in bathing suits on our dust-ridden field, especially girls like Cilla in particular, with a flower in her hair—an image that stayed with me.

The other reply was from my father, which read in part:

Tonight on my arrival here [Ottawa] I had a letter telling me that you had your tooth out and had finished your first tour. We have been most anxious to hear when that tour would be over as you have been on active service for a very prolonged period.

You have had a long session of it and from everywhere I hear you have done a very gallant job and, although words of praise are hard to express, we are very proud of everything you have done.

I imagine that, when you are back here and after a bit of a rest you will be longing for the excitement of war. But I also know from my own and other people's experiences in the last war and this, that you must be badly in need of a rest, and by rest I don't necessarily mean playing golf and sitting around but there are other things to be found in Canada still such as the Standish Hall, the Normandy Roof and lots of lovelies.

I cannot tell you what a relief it is to feel that, for the time being at least, you will get some respite and, my God will I be glad to see you!

Good luck, old boy.

—Pop

When he wasn't flying, Bob Hyndman was busy sketching portraits of the pilots. When he finished mine I was flabbergasted at how gaunt and haggard I looked; I could hardly recognize myself. I had lost a lot of weight, and although my appetite had returned, the diet to which we were subjected was hardly designed for bodybuilding.

The wheels of progress turn slowly, and this was certainly true of the air force. It took two weeks to process my posting. Meanwhile, I slept in the comfort of the sick bay, where Husbands was also recuperating from mumps. One night there was a tremendous explosion. One of the nightly German raiders had mistakenly dropped an oyster mine in a field close by, instead of offshore, but at the time it seemed that the airstrip might be the target. Absolute silence followed, then Hubby, almost in a whisper, asked, "Mind if I come over and join you?" I welcomed the company.

While waiting around, I joined several others in a drive to Caen. The countryside was littered with dead farm horses and cattle, part of the ravages of the battle, and the stench was frightful. The streets of the city were clogged with rubble. Perched on the steps in front of a church was a dead German soldier, slumped over, still holding onto his rifle—he must have been killed by concussion. We didn't stay around that scene too long; it was too grotesque, too macabre. No one seemed to pay any attention. The soldiers were too busy clearing the streets. Civilians strolled by here and there, looking somewhat stunned by it all. At least they had been liberated, but there was none of the joie de vivre we'd witnessed at Bayeux. Still, the people were now out of danger; by this time the battle had moved south toward Falaise.

On July 25, 1944, the date of the American breakthrough in the west at St. Lô, I said my goodbyes to 401 Squadron. I gave YOK a final pat and then said farewell, first to my ground crew, then to the pilots. Hap Kennedy made a final endorsement in my log book:

Good luck "Bish." An Above Average Fighter Pilot.

—IFK

Chapter 19

Homeward Bound

July 25–August 14, 1944

> My God wil I be glad to see you.
>
> —Father,
>
> in a letter to the author

Just before lunch I was driven to a nearby airstrip, where a twin-engine Anson transport would take me to Northolt aerodrome, northwest of London. From there I was to proceed by rail from London to Warrington, where the RCAF Repatriation Centre was located, halfway between Liverpool and Manchester, in Lancashire. But before I left France, I was to experience some typical Royal Air Force bureaucracy. I went into the mess tent and sat down to have some lunch. An RAF wing commander—a "wingless wonder" (non-aircrew)—sneered at me, "What unit are you with?" I replied that I had just been posted off my squadron and was taking a flight back to England. "You don't belong in here," he harrumphed. "Out! OUT!" I slammed my knife and fork down on the table, got up, and left.

I had no sooner sat down on a chair outside when a friendly New Zealand pilot came out of the tent and said to me, "Don't listen to that old bastard. Come on back in."

I shook my head. "It doesn't matter," I said.

"Alright," the Newzie replied. "Wait here." A few minutes later he appeared with a plate of food, complete with knife and fork.

An hour later we took off. We flew northwest to the Contentin

Peninsula just under a cloud layer, at about 2000 feet. About halfway up the west coast we could see what looked liked two fairly lengthy concrete ramps—like extended no-ball launch pads, except these were absolutely straight. They were pointed directly west. I often wondered whether they were rocket sites aimed at New York.

My second encounter with RAF red tape came at Bognor Regis, on the British south coast, where we landed to refuel. I went straight to the adjutant's office and asked for some clothing coupons. I had left France with what I was wearing—my battle-dress jacket with the hockey sweater underneath, although I did have a uniform tunic in my bag. The adjutant was another auto-cratic wingless wonder who'd never seen a shot fired. He told me that I'd have to make proper application and needed authorization. Shit! I'd just come from the battlefield, so to speak. And where had this little asshole been all that time? I said, "I'll show you authoriza-tion," and pointed to my flying boots with the soles practically worn right through, and then to my hockey sweater. "There's your authorization." Then I added, "For your edification, because you wouldn't know it sitting behind that desk, they don't sell shoes and shirts in France where I was, and I'm going to look pretty scruffy reporting to headquarters in London looking like this. I'll tell them you wouldn't help me." After this salvo he relented, and I got my coupons.

When we arrived at Northolt, the officers' mess quarters were filled to capacity. I was resigned to either sleeping in a chair some-where or going into town to find a room. However, I struck up a conversation at the bar with two RAF pilots, and when they learned I had just left France, they were full of questions and eager to get over there and have a look. They managed to wangle a trip in the Anson in which I had landed, which was returning to Normandy that evening. Meanwhile, I could have their room. I wished them good luck and said, "Give the back of my hand to that little prick of a wing commander."

The first thing I did was take a bath, a luxury I hadn't enjoyed for over a month. I'd forgotten what warm water felt like. I changed into my uniform and cut the tops off my flying boots with the knife provided for that purpose; this was to make them look like ordinary shoes if you were evading capture. I now looked fairly presentable.

I had the best meal I'd enjoyed since leaving England, and there was no shortage of Scotch. After I went to bed, I could hear faint sounds of explosions in the distance, from the flying bombs landing in London.

Next morning I went into the city to shop for some shoes, then visited the Eaton's office to say goodbye to the resident director, Percy Portlock. He told me that the flying bombs were terrifying the city much more than the Blitz had. He said one had exploded on the street below, and he'd been thrown from one side of his office to the other. Fortunately, we were not disturbed that morning. I delved into my trunk that I kept in the office for some shirts, socks, and underwear, which I packed into my zippered travelling bag. Then we went to the Carleton Club for lunch. Percy said he had wired my parents that I was on my way. He had been told by RCAF HQ, with whom he'd been in touch, that I would probably be setting sail in about two weeks.

After lunch I took a taxi to Anderson & Shepherds, the Savile Row tailors, to pay the bill for a uniform they had made for me earlier. While I was en route, the air raid sirens went off. When we reached the tailors, I got out and asked the driver to wait. The cabbie said, "Not bloody likely, mate," and drove off without even waiting for the fare. I could hear the grinding sound of a buzz bomb, when suddenly it stopped. That meant it was about to drop. I had no sooner entered the store than one of the clerks said, "Downstairs, please, sir." But by that time the doodlebug had already exploded, a short distance down the street. We went outside and could see smoke rising. Someone mused, "I wonder what poor devil got it this time?" It was symptomatic of the low morale of Londoners at the time. They were having a rough time of it. I didn't envy them—France seemed a safe place by comparison.

When I got back to Percy's office he was fit to be tied, so worried was he about what might have happened to me. Bombs had been bursting all over the place. He wanted me to hurry to Euston Station and get out of London. I picked up my bag and got to the station without incident. On the way to Warrington, I shared a compartment with Wing Commander John "Jack" Godfrey,* who was also being repatriated. He had commanded 128 RCAF Reconnaissance Wing, flying Mustangs. Our journey was a very pleasant one, but it might not have turned out that way. We learned later that the platform from which we had boarded was blasted by a flying bomb—half an hour after our departure.

Several old friends were already at Warrington, among them Buck McNair and George Keefer, as well as two ex–401 Squadron buddies, Ray Lawson and Don Wilson. Next day I received an order to report to the CO's house that evening to have cocktails with Wing Commander Denton Massey, brother of Canadian High Commissioner Vincent Massey. He told me it would be about two weeks before the next draft would be sent home.

There was very little to do at Warrington except attend two daily parades, one in the morning and another after lunch. They were strictly a formality; we lined up and were instantly dismissed. In the afternoon, most of us took a train into Manchester. The main hangout was the hotel in the centre of town. Nearby was what claimed to be the longest bar in England. It extended through a chain of pubs next door to each other, right around the four sides of a complete block. These establishments and the hotel itself abounded with female companionship.

For variety one evening, three of us—Mac MacDonald, Army Armstrong, and I—attended the motorcycle races at the edge of town.

---

* See also *Courage in the Air*, by Arthur Bishop. In 1973 Godfrey was appointed to the Canadian Senate.

We got ourselves pretty well oiled at the stadium bar. When we went outside to get a taxi, Mac got into an argument with the driver over the fare, and slapped him. A constable on duty quickly intervened before the situation got further out of hand. Since that was the only taxi in the vicinity, we were compelled to take the tram. However, we didn't realize it only went a certain distance, then turned around and went back to the outskirts. We were now faced with walking back into town, and at that late hour we would miss the last train to Warrington.

A woman standing in the doorway of one of the row houses that lined the street came to our rescue, offering us bed and breakfast for two pounds each. The catch was that there was only one bed, but, hell, that was better than nothing. We were too sloshed to be choosy, anyway. But our problems were only beginning. After we got into the room, we had to relieve ourselves and we couldn't find the bathroom—because there wasn't one! (We learned later that the toilet was out back of the house.) So we opened the window and let fly in turns. Someone who happened to be walking by nearly got sprayed, and let out a yell. We told him to bugger off, and shut the window.

Now our dilemma was how to douse the light, which was a bulb hanging from the ceiling. We tried to find the switch, in our search pulling some wallpaper off one of the walls. Army finally solved our predicament when he discovered the chamber pot under the bed. He picked it up and threw it at the light bulb. That put out the light all right, but it also sprayed pieces of glass all over the place, mostly on the bed, so we took off the blanket in the dark and thoroughly shook it. In the end we did manage to get some sleep, all three of us sharing the bed—although passing out would be a fairer description.

We were woken in the morning by the master of the house, who opened the door, had a look at the paper coming off the wall and the pieces of glass on the floor, and demanded, "What the hell's been going on here?" Mac answered him: "Don't worry, Pop. We'll be down for breakfast right away." We assembled in the kitchen and sat down to a repast of fried ham and powdered eggs. Having missed dinner the night before, I was hungry enough to eat anything. Not Mac. He took one look at the greasy spread and barely made it through the door before he threw up.

I put up one more black (made a *faux pas*) before we received our sailing orders for home. That was in the Shakespearean Club, a very exclusive Manchester establishment. Somehow Don Wilson had befriended an elderly member, who put him up as a temporary member during our stay at Warrington. Don invited me to meet him there one evening. Skipping the afternoon parade, I went into Manchester before lunch and managed to work the long bar, shifting from one pub to the next. Then I decided that what I needed to sober me up before meeting Don was to take a Turkish bath. But the heat and steam served only to exacerbate my condition and I was in rollicking shape when I arrived at the Shakespearean.

Don introduced me to his sponsor, a mild-mannered old gent sitting in a leather armchair in the club lounge. I replied by mumbling, "To be or not to be, that is the question!" and flopped into one of the chairs. I was past the point where I could follow a conversation, but whenever there was a lull in the discussion, I rose to my feet and came right to the point with, "To be or not to be, that is the question!" Finally, a highly embarrassed Don Wilson said that we had to be leaving to catch our train. He told me after we left that it was a good thing we'd probably be leaving in a few days, because he didn't think he'd be too welcome in that club anymore. Certainly I would never be proposed for membership.

On the morning of August 5, we were paraded and told that we were confined to the station, and that we would be boarding a train that evening to take us to a ship sailing for home. We were given no further details, and spent the day restlessly waiting to be taken to the station.

When we boarded the train at dusk, we had still not been told what our destination was. We knew, however, that we were heading north, and spent an uncomfortable night sitting up in the dark, shivering—most of us didn't have outer coats. By morning the train had slowed as it made its way slowly through the suburbs of Glasgow to the docks on the south side of the River Clyde. Tired and hungry, we took a ferry across the river to board the *Queen Mary*, the large luxury-liner-turned-troopship. (The name of the ship had been removed; we learned its identity only after we had got under way.) Sixteen of us shared upper and lower bunks in a cabin that in peacetime would have served as twin accommodation.

Having dumped our luggage, such as it was, we hastily made our way to the dining room—which was large and sumptuous—for breakfast. We learned that we would be setting sail that night. We were also told that, because the ship was manned by an American crew, it was dry. And none of us had had the foresight to stock up on liquor before we left.

That trip across the Atlantic was quite a different experience from the one two years earlier. This time around, there was no convoy, or even an escort. The *QM* relied on her speed to get us home safely. As an added precaution against U-boats—which were still about, although no longer anywhere near the menace they were in 1942—the huge liner zigzagged part of the way across. It took only five days to make the journey from Glasgow to New York City, a distance of 5000 miles. It was a pleasant trip; most days were bright and clear and we spent them on deck sunbathing.

During the voyage we were kept abreast of the war news via the ship's radio and the daily bulletins that were issued to us. In Normandy, the Americans, who had broken out in the west at St. Lô on the day I left France, were now driving east. They planned to turn north to join up with the Canadians advancing south, to trap the Germans at Falaise.

One morning, halfway across the ocean, we were eating breakfast when my tongue caught on something sharp in my right jaw, where my tooth had been pulled out almost a month earlier. I pried it loose with my fingers. It was a jagged filling about one-eighth of an inch long, which had been dislodged from an adjacent tooth during the extraction and had fallen into the cavity—the cause of my mysterious and uncomfortable "lockjaw" problem.

On the evening of August 11, we docked outside New York. After the blackouts in England and France, it was a sight I shall never forget—after two years, my first view of a city all lit up. Most of us stayed up on deck for a long time that evening to savour this wondrous splendour. One person next to me said, rather mournfully, "Think of all those guys who'll never see this."

Next morning we sailed into the harbour past the Statue of Liberty—another memorable sight—so close it seemed that we could almost reach out and touch her. People on tugs in the harbour shouted to us, asking where we'd been, and blew their whistles in salute. When we docked, we were greeted by one of Glenn Miller's bands. "On the Sunny Side of the Street" was one of the tunes, and it remains locked in my memory.

In the evening we went ashore to board a train to take us to Ottawa. I'd forgotten what it was like to travel by rail in such luxury. The trip from Manchester to Glasgow had been like journeying by covered wagon in comparison. Steak for dinner, comfortable Pullman coach berths, bacon and eggs for breakfast. We spent the evening oohing and aahing, gazing out the windows at the bright lights.

We arrived in Ottawa's Union Station on the morning of Sunday, August 13. As soon as we got off the train we were lined up on the platform to be marched into the station itself. Some people resented this return to military discipline after the relaxed overseas atmosphere we'd grown accustomed to. A few dissenters even offered caustic shouts of "Welcome home to good old Canadian bullshit!" Then a band struck up and we marched into the rotunda as the large crowd on hand clapped and cheered. We were a little taken aback by it all—and somewhat embarrassed. A fellow behind me said, "Look at that old babe over there—she's crying."

It took me a few seconds to orient myself to what was going on. To my surprise, though I should have expected it all along, my father was on the speaker's podium to welcome us home. I can't remember a word he said; I wasn't paying the slightest attention, I was so overwhelmed by what had happened over the past few days.

The drill was to report to the Repatriation Depot at Rockcliffe Air Station for clearance to go on 30 days' disembarkation leave. But after I said hello to my parents, my father assured me I could report later. Meanwhile Leth, our chauffeur, drove us home to 5 Blackburn Avenue. Nothing had changed. As I sat in the living room, it all seemed so tranquil after the hectic, noisy days in Normandy that I felt like a stranger in my own house. I couldn't help but comment on it. However, Margaret, our cook, welcomed me with a tray of bacon and eggs—the second such serving that morning, but this time with champagne—and I gradually began to relax and feel at home.

I was a little apprehensive about comparisons with my old man—the rows of decorations on his chest versus to my two lowly ribbons, the 1939–43 Star and the Canadian Volunteer Service Medal and Maple Leaf, in addition to my operational wings. However, I soon learned there was no reason to be. He showed a genuine, I might say operational, interest in my tour. For example, he wanted to know all about the Spitfire. I told him and my mother that I had been shot down only a few weeks ago. That sparked not only interest but sympathy as well. My father pressed me for details. I said, "It's not something I'm particularly proud of, but I did get away with it. Anyway, I like to say that, at least between us, we got seventy-three."

As the day went on, family friends dropped in to say hello and welcome me home. I began to realize that my father no longer regarded me as simply his son, but as a fellow fighter pilot, too. That naturally made me feel somewhat proud.

The first person I telephoned was Cilla, but her father told me she was staying with a friend at Lake McGregor in the Gatineau Hills. She returned to town that afternoon and we were reunited that evening. She looked lovely, glowing with summer tan, and even more beautiful than I remembered. So nice to come home to.

Chapter 20

Photographic Wing

Rockcliffe, Ontario—September 18, 1944–March 1, 1945

> . . . a pilot of a Spitfire displaying bad
> manners in the air by crowding a Service
> heavy transport machine in the vicinity of
> Rockcliffe Airport . . .
> —*Record of Logging*, 14 November 1944

What to do with an ex-operational orphan? My original posting was to Bagotville Operational Training Unit in Quebec as an instructor. But events moved rapidly after I got home.

In France on August 19, the Canadians, Polish, and Americans had closed the Falaise Gap, trapping German forces. Two days later, the Allies had crossed the Seine in pursuit of what was left of the German army, and on August 24 the Americans entered Paris. Though the war had some months to run, there was an aura of victory in the air. This had a profound effect on the RCAF.

At Bournemouth in England there was a plethora of aircrews waiting to be posted to squadrons; some would never be needed. As a result, the British Commonwealth Air Training Plan was wound down. Training schools were closing left and right, including the OTU at Bagotville. It would not be long before large numbers of personnel would be discharged. Instructors had become unneeded baggage. There was certainly no room for a potential OTU instructor on this side of the ocean. And if the RAF had wanted me, I would have been kept in England.

My father had always thought I would make a lousy instructor anyway. He promised to go job hunting for me while I was enjoying my leave at Ravenscrag in Muskoka. An inveterate opportunist, he took the direct route.

His old World War I comrade Air Commodore Geoffrey O'Brian, whom I had last seen in Bournemouth when I arrived overseas in September 1942, was now the CO at Rockcliffe. Under his command fell the Repatriation Depot, 12 Transport Squadron, and 13 Photographic Reconnaissance Squadron. Geoff suggested that, because there was a pair of Spitfires attached to the unit that nobody wanted to fly, it might be a good spot for me. During the second week of September I reported to Geoff, who gave me the gen on how to conduct myself.

"This is a permanent force [PF] outfit," he explained. "They are gearing up for a peacetime role: mapping northern Canada through aerial photography." (This objective had its genesis when the RCAF was founded in 1924, but the program was temporarily curtailed with the outbreak of war in 1939. Up until that time, only 868,000 square miles of Canada's four million had been surveyed by aerial camera.) O'Brian continued, "So give the impression that you're interested in staying in the air force—which I'm sure you're not." (He got that right!)

In addition to this posting, my father advised me that he had arranged for an extracurricular assignment for me: temporary attachment to his staff as his ex officio aide-de-camp. With the reduction in BCATP, activities his permanent ADC, Paul Rodier, had been assigned to staff duties in Montreal. Nothing too onerous, my pseudo-role as Paul's replacement would be chiefly on weekends, and for the most part would not interfere with my new flying duties. What my father had in mind was a little training in administrative procedures in preparation for civilian life. The position did have its monetary benefits; while serving out of the country (e.g., in the U.S.), I would receive an additional $50 a day in pay.

On September 16, 1944, I reported to 13 PRU Squadron headquarters at Rockcliffe. The wing commander in charge escorted me to the flight room in the hangar that housed the unit's aircraft, and introduced me to the deputy squadron leader, Flight Lieutenant Sheraton,* a PF type who had been with the photographic service since the 1920s. He made it clear to me that if I wasn't interested in an RCAF career in aerial photography, then "you're not our man." I gave him no indication that I had any other intentions.

The aircrews were a mixture of wartime operational types and those who had served their time in Canada: instructors from BCATP schools and pilots and navigators from Bomber and Coastal commands, as well as from Photographic Reconnaissance Command. I was one of only two ex–fighter pilots in the group; the other was Don "Bunty" McClarty. He had distinguished himself in the desert air-fighting in North Africa and had been shot down and captured, eventually, with my old squadron buddy Ray Sherk, escaping from a prisoner-of-war camp in Italy.

The squadron's principal activity was conversion from twin-engine Anson trainers to Mitchell medium bombers that had been modified for aerial photography surveying work. But there were other businesses at hand, as well. Training photographers was one of them. Norseman float planes and Lysanders, as well as Ansons, were used for this purpose. The two Spitfires and a lone Hurricane were used only sporadically, for exposure tests—photographing a variously toned white, grey, and black target at the east end of the runway, and occasionally—very occasionally—for a weather check.

My first flight with 13 PRU, in a Harvard, was a pilot check by Charlie Donaldson, a former instructor. I'd forgotten what a treat the Harvard was to fly, even though it seemed like—to paraphrase that earlier newspaper report—slow stuff compared to the swift Spit son Billy used to fly. We flew straight over Ottawa, and when we reached 1000 feet, I announced to Charlie, "I think I'll do a roll." "Not at a thousand feet over Ottawa you don't," came back the

* Not his real name.

caustic reply. So we flew east, away from the capital, climbing to 2000 feet, where I put the aircraft through the standard aerobatic training manoeuvres: roll, loop, roll off the top, and a spin recovery. Having passed muster as a pilot to Charlie's satisfaction, I was now ready for my first lesson on twins.

Though I had never been at the controls of a twin-engine aircraft before, I adapted quite easily to the takeoff—by far the most critical procedure—coordinating the throttles to maintain consistent power output from both engines. Once airborne, I found that the Anson, though slow and mildly lumbering, responded comfortably and smoothly, and landing was a piece of cake. After a second flip, Sheraton put me through an acceptance check, which I passed with no trouble at all.

Several practice flights later, up and down the Ottawa River— which I found so tame and boring I almost missed being fired at by heavy flak—I decided the time had come to indulge in something more exciting. "How about we play tag?" I suggested to Bunty McClarty. He agreed, and together we conspired to conduct a tail chase à la Spitfire. It was a cloudy day when he and I took off in sep- arate Ansons and headed south, flying in loose formation about 200 yards apart. My companion in the co-pilot's seat was a Czecho- slovakian navigator who wore the DFC and bar. He had served two tours with the Pathfinders, those intrepid crews of Mosquitoes who would precede the main night-bomber force at low level and drop flares on the target for the bombardiers to aim at—a risky business. Josef told me he had been over Berlin six times.

In the vicinity of Uplands, the overcast was down to about 300 feet. Time to start the chase. Bunty banked to the left, away from me. I followed close behind him, even though he was doing a lot of erratic jinking from one direction to another, throwing the Anson around like a Tiger Moth. It took some persistence to stay on his tail. Because it was beginning to drizzle, we were right down on the deck, making the exercise all the more difficult and exacting. A hell of a lot of fun, just the same. But Josef certainly didn't think so; he looked frightened to death. Six times over Berlin, sure—but this, with a reckless madcap at the controls? Finally I lost Bunty in the mist, broke off, and returned to the field, much to the relief of the veteran navigator. He might well have reported me as irresponsible, but he didn't. However, word must have got around, because I found it hard to conscript partners from then on.

I had been with 13 PRU for little more than a month when my promotion to flight lieutenant came through. This was a standard elevation in rank accorded to all RCAF aircrew a year and a half to two years after having been commissioned—it had nothing to do with merit. Nevertheless, Sheraton took umbrage. "How come you get such a fast promotion when I had to wait 15 years for mine?" he asked. Someone piped up rather unkindly, "Well, Sherry, we joined the air force when the air force needed men—not when the men needed the air force." But there was a marked difference in our F/L standings. His was permanent; our kind were wartime temporary reserve.

I was now, apart from Sheraton, who was deputy commanding officer, one of only two with F/L rank in the unit. This made me one of two flight commanders with authorization to book flights and other minor responsibilities. I took the opportunity to fly all the other types of aircraft on strength with the squadron, with the exception of the Mitchell, for which I would need a lot more Anson practice and dual instruction, and which I never wanted to fly anyway.

My first choice, of course, was the Spitfire. The two photographic reconnaissance planes were Mark VIIIs that had been kept in mint condition, thanks to the efforts of the ground-crew chief. He was thrilled that at last someone was going to fly them. I did—and they handled beautifully.

One evening, at the Standish Hall in Hull, I asked Cilla if she had ever seen a Spitfire in flight. Of course, she hadn't. I told her that next morning, weather permitting, I would fly one low over the Lisgar Building. The RCAF Headquarters was on Lisgar Street off Elgin Street, about halfway between her family's house and mine.

She worked there as secretary to the head of the New Zealand Air Commission, Group Captain "Tiny" White. She said, "You'll be taking an awful chance, you know. Someone's sure to get your number and report you. And over headquarters—you're crazy!" I assured her that I had it all worked out.

Vectoring straight east over air force HQ also pointed me straight in the direction of 5 Blackburn Avenue. At breakfast next morning before I left, I told my mother that I was going to give her another "thrill of your lifetime," and described my plans. She nodded somewhat dismally, as if to say "not again," and I was on my way.

At 1000 hours I telephoned Cilla from the flight room, told her that my watch showed 10:15, and asked her to phone my mother. Then I took off. Fifteen minutes or so later, as I was crossing Bank Street, which runs north to Parliament Hill, I cut the engine and glided down. By the time I was on the south side of the Lisgar Building, I was down to 100 feet. I banked to the left, looked down at the entrance, where Cilla and several others were standing, and waved. Then I straightened out, gunned the engine, and made for 5 Blackburn. Glancing up and behind me, I saw a Hurricane diving onto my tail. It could only be one guy—Bunty McClarty. I pushed the plane into a climbing turn as he flashed by, then flattened out and flew over the house at about 300 feet. I didn't bother to look down to see whether my mother was there; I figured I was pressing my luck. Enough fun and games; I made for the airport.

When I landed I sought out the crew chief. "Chiefy," I said, "I had a bit of engine trouble when I was over Ottawa. It almost died on me, but I got it going again."

He winked at me. "Probably the throttle quadrant slipped on you," my crew chief laughed. "No trouble at all. I'll tighten it up. Forget about it." The brass at HQ must have been too busy enjoying their coffee breaks to look out the window. There was nary a word.

That evening Cilla said to me, "I saw you—my hero!" I asked her to keep her voice down, mindful of the wartime slogan, "The walls have ears." My mother made no comment.

There were three aircraft on strength that I had never flown, and I was anxious to try my hand at them: the Hurricane, the Norseman, and the Lysander. The Hurricane was the slower, though no less worthy, forerunner of the Spitfire, and the cockpit arrangement was identical. It also had the same characteristics—tight turning agility and rapid climbing ability—an absolute delight to fly. The main difference from its successor was in landing the plane. Instead of having to curve in, you could make a straight approach. Unlike in the Spitfire, whose nose blocked out forward vision, you could look right over the Hurricane's engine hood.

The Norseman offered the chance to learn how to fly a float plane and at the same time engage in some recreation. On the takeoff run, the weight of the single Pratt and Whitney engine made it feel as if you would never get off the water. It seemed like a struggle, and then suddenly you were airborne, and by contrast the aircraft seemed light as a feather. On occasion, our flights provided us with an opportunity to land on one of the Rideau Lakes and indulge in a little fishing. When we landed, one of us would be relegated to concealing the catch (provided there was one to hide) until it could be disposed of. Chiefy knew full well what we'd been up to; he only needed to check the fuel gauge and make a quick calculation of the gas-consumption-to-time-airborne ratio to figure it out. We rewarded his silence with a gift of the catch—whenever we were lucky enough.

The Lysander, originally designed for army cooperation work at the beginning of the war, had later been superseded with the introduction of the Mustang and relegated to flying espionage agents in and out of France at night. Slots and slats fitted to the wing reduced stalling speed, to make short takeoffs and landings possible. How short I could never have imagined until I made my first flight. It seemed as if I'd just opened the throttle when suddenly I was airborne. It was unbelievable. The same was true on landing. The aircraft came to an abrupt stop, leaving me with most of the runway in front of me.

On my second flight I took along one of the ground crew, who were always willing to go for a ride. Leading Aircraftsman Holmes tucked himself comfortably into the back seat with full confidence in the pilot. Little did he realize. After my familiarization flight, I had decided to see what the Lumbering Lizzie was capable of. After reaching an altitude of 5000 feet, I dived the Lysander, then pulled up in a loop. At the top of the manoeuvre, with the aircraft right on its back, there was a fearful clatter and rattle as the slats and slots opened, and a ragged collection of maps, papers, keys, coins, ciga-rette butts, dirt and debris, and all kinds of other crap fluttered downward from the floor. Because I never wore my goggles when airborne—only on takeoff and landing, in case of fire—my eyes were filled with dust. And at that point the Lysander started to stall. I opened the throttle, pulled back on the stick, and went into a verti-cal dive, averting a spin. It was all rather unnerving, to say the least, but when I looked back, LAC Holmes was beaming, happy as a clam, as if everything had gone according to plan.

My next flight with the Lysander was far less adventurous, but with a highly interesting sequel. With one of the ground crew again as passenger in the rear seat, I had been stooging about enjoying the clear autumn day, but after some 45 minutes I got bored and decided to go back to the airport and land. Following the usual touchdown, which left an endless expanse of runway facing me after I had rolled to a stop, I pulled back the hood and took my time taxiing back in. When I reached the hangar, I waved to Art, the other flight commander, who was standing on the tarmac. He motioned to me to cut the engine by frantically crossing his hands, which I took to mean "quit fooling around." I quickly complied and climbed out, pulling off my flying helmet, and said, "She's quite a crate, Art." Without a word he took my parachute and hustled me inside the hangar, where he handed me my uniform tunic, almost pulling the battledress off my back. Then, pointing to a parked twin-engine transport, he said in a worried tone, "You're to fly to New York with your old man in the Lockheed Hudson. He's been waiting for you to come down for over half an hour, and he's getting madder than hell. So get cracking!"

When I climbed aboard, I was greeted by one very irate air marshal. His staff sergeant, Ken, and the plane's pilot and co-pilot didn't seem too happy either. I should have known better than to try and laugh it off in an armed camp. "It's a good thing I got bored," I said rather cavalierly, "or I would have stayed up a half-hour longer." This attempt at humour was lost on the angry parent. "They couldn't reach you by radio," he snarled. (None of the PRU aircraft except the Mitchells at Rockcliffe were equipped with R/T.) "I wanted them to send the Spitfires after you, but nobody around here knew how to fly them."

I should have known enough to quit, but I didn't. "It wouldn't have done any good, anyway," I replied. "I'd have dogfought them." With that the old man waved his hand in dismissal. End of discussion. I think he was concerned that I was not taking seriously my duties as ADC, into which I had just been suddenly propelled. Half an hour later, he told Ken to supply me with a pencil and notepad. He then instructed me, "I want you to write down the takeoff and landing times and make a note of the weather at each end. Then, when we land, you are to carry my attaché case for me." This was to be my indoctrination as an aide. But knowing my old man, I think he was also concerned that my dilly-dallying with the Lysander might upset his schedule. He had phoned ahead from the house that I was to be ready to take off when he arrived at the airport, which sent Art and the others into a tizzy because I was already on the runway. He was afraid that we would be late for lunch in New York, where he had already reserved the corner table in the Colony Restaurant dining room.

When we arrived at La Guardia Airport, Ken was given the assignment of conveying our bags (at home, Lethbridge had hurriedly packed my clothes in my absence) to the Ritz-Carlton Hotel, where we would be staying. We wasted no time in hurrying to the Colony by taxi, where we had lunch with Clayton Knight, who had headed up the committee to enlist Americans into the RCAF at the beginning of the war, and some others.

For dinner that evening, the venue switched to another perennial NYC standby—the 21 Club. This was strictly business—double entendre business in fact, for which my father wore two hats. The occasion was a meeting with the renowned Howard Hughes, aviator and aircraft builder and designer. In 1935 he had set a speed record of 352.388 miles an hour, and in 1938 had flown around the world in 3 days, 19 hours, and 17 minutes, in a Lockheed of his own design.

In dealing with the Hughes aviation interests, my father had a dual role to play. He represented both the McColl-Frontenac Oil Company Limited (which had paid his full salary as vice-president throughout the war) and the RCAF. And, although I cannot substantiate it, I suspect he was acting for the Canadian government as well.

Two tables had been reserved for us in a corner of the dining room. One was for Hughes and one of his executives, my father, with Clayton Knight acting as his liaison officer, and me. The other table, with telephones and papers spread out on it, was for four or five of Hughes' aides. Only my father and I were in uniform, but that didn't seem out of place.

I had no business experience or knowledge at that stage in my life, nor had I been briefed as to what to expect. But it seemed to me that the conversation during the meal was of a very general nature. Certainly it appeared that no great decisions were being made. Hughes, a tall, handsome, very debonair man, struck me as serious, abrupt, and totally devoid of humour. He made no attempt to disguise the fact that he was partially deaf in one ear, apparently the result of a plane crash. He had a preoccupied air about him, almost to the point of rudeness. He would suddenly turn his attention away from our discussion, collar one of his aides at the next table, and in a loud voice instruct him, "Wire so-

and-so and tell him etc., etc.," and "Telephone so-and-so in Burbank and have him cancel that contract for such-and-such." This
went on during the meal and over liqueurs afterwards. I noticed
that Hughes did not partake in the brandy, and whether he
indulged in alcohol during dinner was difficult to tell. I put his
entire performance down to conceit—as in showing off. However,
I still admire him to this day for his contributions, often at personal risk, to aviation.

Next evening, same place, same time—slightly different scenario, with just my father and I dining. Seated at the next table was
an army colonel and his female companion. The man had a loud
voice that drowned out any attempt we made at carrying on a conversation. My father turned around in his seat with the obvious
intention of asking him to lower his voice. The colonel grinned at
him and said, without dropping his tone a single decibel, "I've
heard my father talk about you!"

Nonplussed, my old man replied, "Oh, yes. How *is* your father?"
without the slightest idea of whom he was talking to. The colonel
saved the situation by immediately identifying himself—"Elliot
Roosevelt"—and proffered his hand. The upshot was that he
invited us to join him and his lady friend at their table for dinner.
An extremely pleasant evening was enjoyed by all, including stints
at the Monkey Bar, Spivy's Rooftop, and the Stork Club, followed
by a nightcap in my father's suite at the Ritz-Carlton Hotel.

Back to Rockcliffe and reality—the photographic wing. I was
becoming increasingly bored with the routine practice flights,
mostly in the Anson. I almost missed being fired at—almost!
Worse still, we were now being subjected to ground school to study
mapping from aerial photographs. These sessions were held in the
Lisgar Building, RCAF Headquarters, where Cilla also worked at
the New Zealand Air Commission. During breaks in the lectures,
there was at least the redeeming feature of being able to go upstairs
to her office for a chat. My boredom with all this business was in no

way assuaged when she told me she had learned that we were in for more and more ground school and less and less flying.

I got so fed up with it all that, on one chilly morning in mid-November, I signed myself out for Procedure 22, a Spitfire camera-exposure test on the black-white-and-grey target at the east end of the runway. I advised the control tower for clearance. Normally these tests were conducted at altitudes of between 200 and 500 feet. I had decided to go a little lower—down to 20 feet.

Chiefy must have had some inkling of what I was up to. After strapping me in the cockpit, he slapped me on the shoulder and said, "See you in jail!" I taxied out, took off, climbed to 500 feet, and flew east along the Ottawa River. Two miles downstream I made a steep turn to the right and reversed direction, gradually losing height in a shallow dive until I was down to within 10 to 20 feet, dead over the test target, at a speed of approximately 350 miles an hour.

I snapped off a picture and slowly began to regain height, flying parallel to the east–west runway. Over the Royal Canadian Mounted Police barracks at the west end of the field, I pulled up in a climbing turn to the right and once again flew east along the Ottawa River.

I repeated the procedure three times to complete the exercise, using three different lens exposures. On the last run, I could see people gathered along the ridge on the south side of the station, watching with—what? amazement? excitement? "What's that idiot up to?" Who knows? Anyway, I'd made my point. I'd thumbed my nose at KRAIR (the King's Regulations for the Air) and was ready to take my medicine. I landed and went straight into the pilots' room. No one said a word.

Just before lunch, I was standing in the bar of the officers' mess when the station CO, Geoff O'Brian, came into the room. I tried to make myself scarce, but that was impossible. He looked at me in a friendly, sympathetic way and said, "You know, for a moment there I thought you were trying to beat up the field." His remark was greeted with discreet silence, particularly on my part.* But a week later the Air Commodore could not afford to be so generous.

Meanwhile, a flight to Windsor, Ontario, was the springboard that, metaphorically speaking, for better or for worse launched me on my civilian flight path. As one who doesn't like being pushed into anything, I got conned into it, a not entirely uncharacteristic event where my old man was concerned. Typically, it all began innocently enough.

A few days after my Procedure 22 caper, I received word around mid-morning to get ready to accompany my father as ADC on a flight to Windsor. I wandered over to the transport flight tarmac next door and asked the pilot, Red Rogers, what the flight was all about. He didn't know.

My father arrived and we boarded the Hudson and took off. Once we were in the air, I asked him to brief me on the purpose of our trip. He simply replied, "We're having lunch with Mrs. Herman, who owns the *Windsor Daily Star*." I traded places with George Summer, the co-pilot, and Red let me fly the Hudson most of the way, until we were within reach of our destination.

On arrival we were greeted by a big, well-built man with a ready smile, who introduced himself as Lum Clark. A photographer from the paper rushed forward and took a picture of my father and me in front of the aircraft. Fortuitously we were both looking left and upward at precisely the same moment, watching another plane coming in to land. (I would later get ticked off for being derelict in my duties as ADC, for not having straightened my old man's tunic belt and leaving one of the pocket buttons on his tunic undone.) We then proceeded by limousine, with Lum Clark at the wheel, to Mrs. Herman's estate on Riverside Drive. Inside the mansion, we met Mrs. Adie Knox Herman, a very quiet, gracious lady whose warm, benign manner masked a will of iron.

---

* I learned later that there had been a strong complaint from the RCMP. One of their horses had reared and thrown the rider, who injured his leg. Nothing was ever officially said to me about it.

Before we sat down to lunch, Clark showed us about the grounds of the magnificent property, which overlooked the Detroit River to the north. At the east end there was a row of tall, handsome oak trees, which, we were told, had been transplanted from Windsor Castle park in England.

When we sat down to lunch (no drinks were served beforehand), I was placed at one end of the table, with Mrs. Herman at the other. My father sat on our hostess's right, Lum Clark on the left. My old man opened up the conversation by thanking Mrs. Herman for the support her paper had given to RCAF recruiting (which at this time had been curtailed). Mrs. Herman modestly answered that the paper had been pleased to make whatever contribution it could. (This ostensibly was the reason for my father's visit, but in fact it had a much more ulterior purpose, as we'll see.) The conversation then became a discussion about the upcoming Ontario provincial election, in which Premier Mitchell Hepburn was up against Conservative Opposition leader Colonel George Drew. I did not follow the argument too closely nor did I join in. Fortunately, I was not asked for an opinion. I had not been following politics, except in a very general manner, and certainly not at the provincial level.

Clark asked me what I was doing now that I had returned from overseas, and I furnished him with a brief rundown. He asked me about the German air force. Were they still a threat? I told him in a general way that I thought they would make one last all-out effort. My answer was about all I could muster in reply and still sound somewhat knowledgeable.*

We parted company after lunch, but that was not by any means the end of my association with Mrs. Herman and Lum Clark. Though I had no way of knowing it at the time, my father was set-

* My remark turned out to be highly prescient. At dawn on New Year's Day, 1945, the Luftwaffe Fighter Command launched *Operation Bodenplatte*, a surprise all-out low-level attack on Allied fighter fields in Holland, Belgium, and France. It broke the back of the German air force, which lost 500 planes. See also *Destruction at Dawn* by Arthur Bishop.

ting me up for a job with the *Windsor Daily Star* as a newspaper reporter. It wasn't even his idea—it was Leonard Brockington's. I had met the former head of the CBC at my father's reception at Claridge's Hotel in September 1942; at the time he was still wartime advisor to Prime Minister Mackenzie King. Brockington had suggested that a career in journalism might be just the ticket for me. He picked the *Windsor Daily Star*, for which he had the highest regard, and with good reason. It was one of the most versatile and respected newspapers in the country, its credo to "put public service first rather than be operated essentially as a commercial venture."

The paper had its genesis on September 3, 1918, as the *Border Cities Star*, a 16-page sheet that hit the street for two cents a copy. When the owner, her husband, died in 1938, Mrs. Herman took over the reins as chairman of the board, with Hugh Graybiel as publisher and Lum Clark, her adopted son, as operating vice-president. At the time of our visit, the paper was the most widely quoted in Canada, and was distinctive for it red front-page headlines.

November 14, 1944—a date that will live on *en famille*. The Allied armies were slowly advancing against the German Werhmacht in Europe and the Russians were closing in on Budapest in Hungary. U.S. navy aircraft were battering Luzon in the Philippines and the Norwegian government-in-exile was announcing that its troops were fighting alongside the Soviets in the far north. That day, my father suddenly arrived at the transportation squadron next door. He was going to take the daily morning milk-run flight to Montreal and return later in the day.

Too good an opportunity to miss! I booked myself out in the Spitfire, took off, and gave chase, but stayed out of sight some 2000 feet above and astern of the Hudson transport plane. Midway between Ottawa and Montreal, over Hawkesbury, right on the Ottawa River, I dived straight down toward the aircraft, pulling up on the right-hand side about 30 yards away, and executed a barrel roll around it. I then closed the gap to pull in closer to the transport, so my father could have a good look from the window. In the chance that he might not to be seated on the starboard side, I pulled up and rolled over the Hudson upside down, pulling out level along its port side and edging in close enough to make sure he could see me.

I then broke off, rolled to the left and down, and straightened out, right underneath the transport by some 100 feet. Then I pushed the nose down and put on extra throttle. When I was about 100 yards in front of the aircraft, I pulled up in a vertical climb, ending my aerobatic display with a roll off the top that put me in the opposite direction to my "quarry," and flew back to Rockcliffe.

On alighting from the Spitfire, I was greeted by a reception committee of not one, not two, but three squadron leaders. I was ordered to put on my tunic and cap, and was promptly escorted to the administration building and informed by the station adjutant that I was under open arrest. I was to proceed to the officers' mess and await further orders.

I had lunch and waited for the worst. Late in the afternoon I was summoned to the office of the station commanding officer (SCO), to which I was escorted by a squadron leader. Air Commodore Geoff O'Brian sat behind his desk, the station adjutant seated on his right. The squadron commander of the PR Wing, "Squirt" Wiseman, stood to one side. I was in the middle facing the air commodore. The pilot of the Hudson, whose name I do not recall, stood to my right. The SCO addressed him first, asking for a report on the incident. Apparently the pilot had become quite panicky over my performance, particularly because my father was a passenger, and that was why he had reported my actions over the R/T. He said, almost apologetically, that he had not known that I was the pilot flying the Spitfire, implying that he might not have reported if he had.

My turn came next. I reported what I had done as matter-of-factly as I could. Time for sentencing. O'Brian prefaced his remarks by commenting that, despite a favourable overseas record, in this case I had displayed bad manners in the air and therefore had to face the consequences. I was assigned to two weeks as duty flight lieutenant, which, of course, confined me to the station. A report was also duly "logged," a copy of which was signed by the SCO and then myself. It read:

REASONS FOR LOGGING: When pilot of a Spitfire displayed bad manners in the air by crowding a Service heavy transport machine in the vicinity of Rockcliffe Airport, on November 14, 1944.
    I certify that I have today reproved the individual concerned for the above reasons and have informed him that this report is being placed on record according to regulations.
                                            —G.S. O'Brian, A/C

The irony of this episode is that the logging never did go into my record. Mistakenly it was made out to Flight Lieutenant A.W. Bishop, J5121, a pilot on the same station and a good friend of mine from SFTS Uplands days. A further ironic twist to the incident is that my father—for whom I had gone to such pains to perform and was willing to pay the penalty—missed my performance. While I was pushing my aerobatic abilities to their outer limits, he was having a nap!

About this time a bulletin was circulated from RCAF HQ advising that the air force would be sharply reducing its aircrew strength. Anyone wishing for a discharge was to contact the respective commanding officer for speedy processing (a matter of a month from date of request). Almost simultaneously, all aircrew of the photographic wing at Rockcliffe were assembled to hear two "important" announcements. They related to the fact that pretty soon the war would be over and we would be assuming a peacetime role, requiring us to conduct ourselves according to certain constraints.

First off, we were told by Sheraton, the deputy CO, to get rid of all extra accoutrements and accessories, such as Maltese crosses, Caterpillar Club pins (which signified having bailed out over water), and other such paraphernalia. I said, "Sherry, if you want me to take off my ops wing [the winged golden O officially awarded at completion of a tour of operations], you'll have to come and take it off me yourself." He ignored me.

The second announcement was that, when the wing took up station in the north the next spring to carry out the photographic missions for which we were being trained, no compassionate leave would be granted. "There were plenty of wives who had babies whose fathers were overseas, and who were not given leave." Brave words coming from someone who had no overseas or operational service. That particularly upset Larry Philpott, who had earned a DFC with one of the RAF PRU squadrons and whose wife was pregnant.

Those announcements had a strong bearing on my subsequent decision, but what followed certainly clinched it. When my term as Duty F/L ended, I was immediately assigned as investigative officer regarding a theft of revenues from the officers' mess. A Service Police (SP) warrant officer, who had been a police detective, was given the job of helping me. His experience was invaluable in our search for the perpetrator(s), and we got along like a house on fire. The same could not be said for the legal officer in charge of the investigation, a wingless wonder little twerp of a flight lieutenant whose first name was Max.

After a number of interviews, the SP and I prepared an interim report on what we had learned—or not learned—which I duly dictated to one of the Woman's Division (WD) stenographers in Max's office and left it for him. After perusing it, he ordered—yes, ordered—me to report to his office the following morning. When I arrived, he proceeded to light into me in no uncertain terms. He may have had a point; I am sure that, by his academic standards, my report was no masterpiece, and unprofessional to boot. But it was his attitude I resented. I pointed out that he was not dealing with an AC2, that I held the same rank he did and didn't have to take any abuse from him. I agreed I would consult with the SP and prepare a fresh report. But he was still red in the face when I left.

On December 15, 1944, I was among a few hundred aircrew officers on the station who were granted two weeks' Christmas leave. Before I left, I revised the theft report with the help of my warrant officer friend and sent it over to Max's office. I couldn't resist adding a handwritten note at the bottom that read, "Merry Christmas! May Joyous Thoughts Be Yours!" I had already made up my mind that it was time to bring my air force career to an end.

This was the first Christmas our family—father, mother, sister, and I—had celebrated together in three years. During that yuletide season, as honorary chairman of the Salvation Army, my father had to sign copies of a certificate that numbered in the thousands. To ease the task, he had rubber stamps made of his signature, and we all took turns "autographing" the documents. While conducting this chore, my sister and I formulated a scheme that we thought would be good for a few laughs—a sadly mistaken presumption.

We tore two cheques from my father's cheque book in the desk in his den, wrote out one each to our respective selves in the sum of $30,000—not an infinitesimal amount in 1944—and duly stamped them with the rubber signature. We then put them in envelopes addressed to ourselves and placed them under the Christmas tree in the living room. On Christmas morning we went through our usual after-breakfast ritual of opening our presents. When they had all been opened Babes and I retrieved the envelopes and presented them to each other, trying to keep straight faces. We opened them up simultaneously, and then, with immature peals of glee, shouted, "Thank you! Thank you, Daddy!"

The old man was completely bewildered. When we showed him the "thirty thou" cheques, his perplexity quickly changed to annoyance. My mother simply couldn't stifle her laughter, but "Daddy" was furious. However, it *was* Christmas. To mollify him and keep peace in the family at this time of "peace on earth, goodwill towards men," Babes and I tore up the cheques and threw the pieces in the fireplace. Then the old man finally saw the humour in it—after all, we had just saved him $60,000!

When I returned to the photo squadron after my leave, Squirt Wiseman called me into his office to tell me that Max was not happy with the revised report, and wanted to see me about it. It wasn't an admonishment—he wasn't like that—it was simply a statement of fact. I told him that Max could get someone else to do it, that I was applying for my discharge. Squirt asked me in a very friendly way what my father thought about that. "I haven't discussed it with him," I replied. "It's my decision, not his. Anyway, he's already applied for his own discharge." Squirt respected my attitude. He promised to put my application in right away, saying it would take about a month to go through.

I now faced having nothing to do until my month's discharge leave, after which I would report to the Rockcliffe Repatriation Depot for a medical and the clearance process. As it turned out, altogether it would eat up about three months, which meant that after nearly four years I would become a civilian again around the beginning of April. Meanwhile, while waiting for the discharge to go through, I busied myself doing nothing. Each weekday I would take a taxi to the station and have drinks and lunch at the officers' mess. In the evening, Cilla and I, who were practically engaged, would go out or spend the evening at her family's house or mine.

One day, right out of the blue, my father asked me—challenged would be a more precise description—what I planned to do once I was out of the air force. I hadn't given it the slightest thought, and I had to confess that I didn't have the foggiest idea. He reminded me of the trip to Windsor and meeting Mrs. Herman and Lum Clark of the *Windsor Star*. "How would you like a job as a reporter?" he asked. More to get him off my back than anything else, I told him

I'd consider it. Then, in his own unabashed, forceful, but cunning way, he said, "What do you say I call Clark and ask him if he'll take you on?" He had backed me into a corner when I least expected it, and I was in no position to protest, so he went right ahead and picked up the phone—just like that. Clark told him they would be glad to have me and to let him know, once I had left the air force, when I could start.

I knew what cub reporters were paid—$25 a week for starters, quite a come-down from my tax-free $375 a month as a flight lieutenant—and I couldn't work up much enthusiasm. I knew very little about journalism, and what I did know didn't interest me much. I was totally ambivalent about the idea. (That would change over the next three months, but at this point I looked upon it somewhat disdainfully.)

Cilla recalls, "His father was rushing him into things at a time when he needed to relax. He was still a bundle of nerves. After what he'd been through, he could hardly have been expected to be ambitious about the future. After all, he was still only 21 years old."

Shortly after that incident, my mother and father left for Miami, Florida, to stay with Colonel Frank Clarke, a prominent member of the Canadian Army General Staff and a close acquaintance of Winston Churchill. In civilian life he was head of the family pulp and paper business, which also operated its own steamship line. I put l'affaire Windsor Star temporarily out of my mind—but not for long.

About two weeks later, my mother telephoned to tell me that the colonel would be glad to have me as his guest in Miami as soon as my leave came up. I went to ask Geoff O'Brian if he knew when I would get word of my release. He told me that it was a bureaucratic process and always took longer than we were led to believe, and that I would just have to be patient and wait and see. I wired my parents what Geoff had told me and said that I would let them know the moment I received notification. I received notice of my discharge toward the beginning of February and then left for

Miami. That holiday would be an important turning point in my life. It would completely reverse my attitude toward journalism— and to working for the *Windsor Star* in particular.

Colonel Clarke had a two-bedroom suite in a small apartment complex right on the beach, next door to the exclusive Surf Club. He had a bed set up for me in the living room because the guest bedroom was occupied by his other guest. This was Cornelius "Neil" Vanderbilt Jr., descendant of "the old commodore," Cornelius Vanderbilt, the railroad and shipping magnate whose fortune made him the richest man in the world. When I met Neil he was 47 years old and had been married and divorced five times. He was a gregarious, fun-loving fellow, whose ready smile and twinkling eyes with the ladies belied incredible experiences that he talked very little about. What I learned about him was mostly from other sources.

Neil was the family renegade; his father never forgave him for choosing the life of a roving reporter over the world of finance, which Neil found boring and repugnant. Instead, after his military discharge at the end of World War I, Neil became a freelance journalist for magazines and newspapers, eventually publishing three newspapers of his own. A dedicated Democrat in a family of staunch Republicans, he campaigned for Franklin Roosevelt, who eventually appointed him Presidential Agent (PA)—"a sort of private eye or public ear for the President." As such he roamed the world interviewing various heads of state, including Hitler, Mussolini, and Stalin and reported his impressions to FDR, who trusted his judgment implicitly.

One of his experiences that he did tell me about was his effort to bring to the American people the true horrors of the Nazi regime. Together with two French photographers, he bluffed his way into the notorious Dachau concentration camp, where the trio began filming prisoners—not only Jews but dissidents opposed to Hitler and Nazism—being whipped while tied to stakes. Their films and cameras were confiscated by guards and

Neil and his cohorts fled the camp—but they had achieved their aim. Other cameras had been concealed in the headlights of their car, and these films were intact.

When the pictures were shown at the Mayfair Theatre in New York, there were such angry protests from German-Americans that police reserves had to be called out. "After two weeks," Neil told me with a grin, "we were ordered to stop showing the movie by the secretary of state, Cordell Hull, on the grounds that it bred contempt for a friendly nation. Underline 'friendly'! There was nothing friendly about it as far as I was concerned. Hitler had ordered me expelled from the Third Reich because of some of the things I'd written."

At the time Neil was staying with Frank Clarke, he was recovering from a heart attack (his second), a cracked knee, and a broken ankle. His heart condition had been diagnosed as a result of tension and overwork. One of the first things he said to me when I met him was, "I hear you're going into the newspaper business." Well, well! Now where would that have come from? My old man was jumping the gun again, pushing me into something I had not agreed to.

But when I heard of some of the incredible adventures that Neil experienced as a reporter, I began to look at the possibility of becoming one myself in a much less jaundiced frame of mind—indeed, with some degree of enthusiasm. If all journalists were like Neil, it must be a lot of fun and, above all, exciting. These were qualities I found seriously lacking in the other directions that civvy street might lead me. I would find no excitement—and certainly no fun—in going back to school to study law or engineering, for example, or in selling cars or stocks and bonds or insurance. Or running a gas station or a bowling alley. Or getting a job in a bank. These were possibilities that those of us awaiting our discharge at Rockcliffe had discussed, none of which I had given serious consideration to. But Neil, in his laid-back way, quite subtly—unlike my old man—was gradually steering me in the direction of the newspaper business. In the end he completely won me over, my father notwithstanding.

Besides being a lot of fun, Neil was one of the most fascinating men I have ever met. He had become a true friend to me. Before I left Miami, he counselled me with this advice: "After the action you've seen as a fighter pilot, you're restless, like I always was. I think a reporter's job is just right for you and will give you the outlet you need. You'll love it. But don't kid yourself. It's hard work."

Roger! Thanks, Neil! *Windsor Star*—here I come!

Chapter 21

"Art Bishop
of the *Windsor Star*"

Windsor, Ontario—June 1945–September 1946

> During the time he was with us
> he developed steadily.
> —Adie Knox Herman,
> Chairman of the Board, *The Windsor
> Daily Star*, in a letter to my father

In the summer of 1945, when I joined the *Star*, it held the reputation of being the best journalistic training ground in Canada. The only school of journalism then in existence was at Columbia University in New York; most newsmen in those days had to learn their trade on the job. The *Windsor Star* was certainly well equipped to teach them. Taking it from the top, there was Mrs. Herman's own manifesto: "Our theory is to throw young fellows at the job and, if they have it in them they will do all right. We also encourage them to use their own initiative."

From a general instructional point of view, the managing editor, Harold "Pappy" Vaughan, one of the *Border Cities* originals, called the shots. He preached the importance of improving your writing by reading: "Read. Read everything you can lay your hands on. And study. Keep studying." It is a credo that I have never forgotten and have lived by to this day. He also urged us to keep copy tight and not to waste words, showing us stories from the New York tabloids that had to be kept short and terse because of limited space. He might well have had the words of the noted Hearst columnist Arthur Brisbane in mind. Brisbane once said, "No one reads words that have more than seven or eight letters, so if you want to continue journalism, try to learn to say things in under eight letters. Certainly no word should have more than ten letters."

For us cub reporters, our direct mentor was the paper's favourite son, who had worked his way up from newspaper boy to reporter to city editor—Norm Hull. He put us through the same learning processes that he had had to work out pretty well for himself. He taught us the basic "five Ws"—who, what, where, when, and why— and laid down the importance of getting names right. The *Star* had a hard-and-fast rule of use on first names, too. No initials, only proper names. William Harold Smith, never W.H. Smith. To put these lessons into practice, we were assigned to writing obituaries. Norm was popular with us; he had the knack of relating to us and earned our respect.

The *Windsor Star* had three columnists. Tom Brophy reported the goings-on at city hall. Dick Harrison, one of the finest newspapermen in Canada (he had turned down offers from two New York papers at a substantially higher salary), wrote the "Now" column, for which he was given carte blanche. His writing was classic; it obeyed Pappy Vaughan's rules for tight copy and was well worth daily study for its crisp, poignant style alone. The third columnist was Lum Clark, vice-president of the paper, who wrote a daily "As We See It" column, which was less aggressive and more low-key than the "Now" column, but no less influential and highly respected.

Lum's benign, mild demeanour belied an inner courage and strength. Serving as an infantry officer in the trenches during World War I, he was awarded the Military Cross for bravery under fire. In the 1920s prohibition era as a *Windsor Star* reporter, he holed up in a loft of one of the shipping sheds along the Detroit River to keep watch and report on the comings and goings of the notorious Purple Gang, which ran liquor from Canada to the U.S. across the river.

My first assignment, only two days after I joined the paper, was covering, along with the other reporters, the return of members of the Essex Scottish Regiment who had been taken prisoners of war during the Dieppe raid. Norm Hull posted a bulletin on the notice board that read, "We want to go all out with this one." Windsor was very much (and for that matter still is) the "Home of the Essex Scottish." And all out we went. Publisher Hugh Graybiel's daughter-in-law drove a small group of us to Chatham, where we boarded the train bound for Windsor, giving us a chance to interview the returning veterans before they arrived home.

The biggest reception of all was for Major Fred Tilston, who had been awarded the Victoria Cross for his action in the battle of the Hochwald Forest, in which he lost both legs.* He was driven through the city as tickertape fluttered down from the buildings. It seemed as if all Windsor had turned out to fete its number-one war hero that day.

Later, after I had gained some experience, among the beats to which I was assigned was the military, and the Essex Scottish was one of my stops. The other was HMCS *Hunter*, the Royal Canadian Naval Reserve division in the city. There was no RCAF representation, although the airport had served as an elementary flying training school during the war.

A group of us, led by Wing Commander Mark Davis, an ex-padre, put together an air force club that eventually became RCAF Branch 364 of the Royal Canadian Legion. Other calls on my beat were the existing local branch of the Legion and the office of the Department of Veterans Affairs. In combination, all these outlets gave me enough ammunition to write a weekly column, "Chatty Bits about the Veterans."

---

* For Tilston's story, see *Our Bravest and Our Best, The Stories of Canada's Victoria Cross Winners*, by Arthur Bishop.

When Cilla and I became engaged, in August 1945, we set the date to get married on Saturday, November 3. That fall, Clarice Tappson, the *Star*'s jovial society editor—Hollywood's Hedda Hopper and Louella Parsons all rolled into one—gave our wedding announcement a big spread, in which she didn't spare the horses. It drooled with name-dropping. My Eaton ancestry for one, and the guest list, among them the Duke and Duchess of Sutherland and, of course, Cornelius Vanderbilt Jr. While Cilla and her family were making the wedding arrangements, I was busy trying to find a place for us to live within my means (my salary had escalated from $25 a week to $30). At the same time, I had to move from my room in the house I was renting because the owners' son was returning from overseas. With only a month to go before our marriage, I checked into the downtown Norton Palmer Hotel.

My search for accommodation in the low price range, which was hard to find everywhere right after the war, proved unsuccessful. I was getting frustrated and discouraged, and didn't relish the prospect or the expense of having to live in a hotel. But Pappy Vaughan, the managing editor, who had found me the room in which I had been living (the family were friends of him and his wife), came to my rescue. Through a lawyer friend of his, Harold Larkin, they turned up a single-room apartment on Pitt Street, three blocks west of the *Windsor Star* building.

It wasn't fancy and it wasn't large, but it would meet our needs. And the rent was right—$25 a month. When you opened the door after climbing three flights of stairs, you walked straight into the narrow but fully equipped kitchen, beyond which was the bathroom, though there wasn't any bath, only a shower. On the right was the bedroom/living room, with a breathtaking view of some warehouses on the south side of Pitt Street, facing the river. It was furnished with a chesterfield, an armchair, and a kitchen table and two matching chairs. For sleeping, there was a pair of Murphy beds that folded up into a wall cavity; sliding panels on either side hid them from view.

On the Sunday before the wedding, the staff threw a stag party for me at the home of our chief photographer, Bert Johnson, on the beach at Amherstburg, south of Windsor on Lake Erie. Festivities got off to an early start and continued throughout the day, ending with a barbecue, after which most of the guests drove home. A hard core that included me, Norm Hull, and Red Lockwood, one of our reporters and a good buddy of mine, stayed on to continue the celebration of my last days as a bachelor. The party climaxed with an empty-beer-bottle duel between Red and me. I was the loser, stepping into the bottom of a Cincinnati Cream bottle, which slit open a gash under my right eye. I'd had enough refreshment all day to be too numbed to feel any pain. But the others were rushing about with towels as the cut spewed blood like a geyser.

With some alarm, Bert Johnson said, "We've got to get you patched up. You've got to be on deck on Saturday, and that's only five days away."

Norm Hull butted in, "Yeah, what the hell are the Duke and Duchess and Cornelius going to think?"

There was no doctor in the vicinity, but Bert rushed me to a veterinarian who lived down the street. He stitched up the gash, effectively stopping the bleeding, and applied a heavy gauze bandage that would have done Lassie proud. Next morning when I looked in the mirror, there was no sign of any bleeding, but the skin around my eye was beginning to turn a nice deep purple shade. Nothing like a shiner at the altar. Well, there wasn't anything I could do about it except hope for the best and concoct a story that might be acceptable and possibly even believed. By Wednesday, the day I was leaving for Ottawa, the purple colour was turning to a yellowish-grey and with any luck might just pass muster. But I was still wearing the bandage, which made me look like a hockey player who'd come off second-best in a brawl.

I took the late afternoon plane to Toronto, where I had to wait for hours until the connecting flight to Ottawa arrived from out west. It was well after midnight by the time I reached 5 Blackburn

Avenue. The reception was icy. My father greeted me with "What the hell have you been up to?" Before I could explain, he added, "Well, we'll just have to make the best of it. But you're a stupid ass getting into this mess at a time like this." Cilla, at least, was spared the shock of seeing her future husband in a state of disrepair. She'd gotten tired of waiting for me and had gone home.

My mother, who was sympathetic to my cause, broke the news to Cilla, as delicately as she could, the next morning on the phone. After breakfast I screwed up my courage to face the music and took a taxi to her house. When she asked me what had happened, I told her and her mother that I had fallen down some basement stairs and cut my head on some pipes. They were both generous enough to accept the explanation—at least for the moment. (I learned later that my future mother-in-law didn't for one minute believe a word of it.)

Cilla's mother knew just the right doctor to take me to. He took off the bandage and pulled out the stitches. The cut had completely healed, and he remarked that it had been a very skillful job of stitching. We then went back to the house, where Cilla and her mother applied makeup. "I don't think anyone will be any the wiser," they both agreed. That was a relief, because we had a lunch date with one of the ushers and the head bridesmaid, and a reception to attend that evening.

Then, Friday evening, we had the dress rehearsal at St. Andrew's Presbyterian Church, followed by another reception at my family's. Through it all, my disguise held up nobly—or people were at least polite enough to ignore my predicament, so I was spared the embarrassment of being asked what had happened to my eye.

These polite people fortunately included Air Commodore Hugh Campbell (later chief of air staff), who signed a letter of permission for me to wear my RCAF uniform in the United States, where we would be spending our honeymoon. I was also married in my uniform, indulging in the fighter pilot's swank of leaving the top button undone. All the male members of the wedding party wore uniform as well.

One other problem needed sorting out. Trans-Canada Airlines (now Air Canada) had erroneously booked us on separate flights to Montreal, where we were to connect with a Colonial Air Lines flight to New York. Cilla had never flown before, and my father, switching his ire from my black eye, vented his fury on the errant airline. Eventually the situation was ironed out, but that wasn't to be our last vexation with TCA.

The wedding went off without a hitch that Saturday afternoon. Bob Hamilton, my old 401 Squadron buddy, stood up for me (stood *over* might be more apt—his six-foot-two to my five-foot-seven). Cilla, looking her loveliest in a white wedding gown and carrying a shower of gardenias and bouvardia, was escorted down the aisle by her distinguished-looking father. After exchanging vows, in what was one of the happiest moments of my life, we signed the registry. After that Lethbridge drove us across the Ottawa River to the country club for the wedding reception.

Once again my makeup stood up to the acid test—or so I like to think, anyway, as there were no remarks, not even curious stares. Ian Mackenzie, the Minister of Veterans' Welfare, proposed the toast to the bride, following which Hammy toasted the brides-maids. When my turn came, I prefaced my remarks by saying, "The next time I get married, I'm going to find a shorter best man!"

The reception continued while Cilla went to change into travel-ling clothes, then Lethbridge drove us to Uplands, where we finally enplaned for Montreal—on the same flight. But our flying prob-lems were far from over. The flight we boarded in Ottawa was an hour and a half behind schedule. Fortunately, Leth had the fore-sight to bring along a bottle of champagne and glasses, so we had a little wedding celebration all on our own in the car, killing time until we could board our plane.

Even though it took only half an hour to fly to Montreal, by the time we landed the connecting Colonial Air Lines flight had long left for New York, so we had to wait another two hours for the next flight. In those days there were no bars at Canada's commercial airports, so we had to while away the time in the coffee shop. It was nearly midnight when we finally reached the Ritz-Carlton Hotel, our week's accommodation there being a wedding gift from my mother and father.

We had just tipped the bellboy for bringing up our bags and I was pouring a drink when the telephone in our room rang. It was the wedding party from Cilla's family's house, hoping to catch us in the act. "Sorry to disappoint you, Hammy," I said, "but we just got here."

In New York we did the rounds, including taking in several shows, the most memorable of which was Rodgers and Hammerstein's *Carousel*, which had just opened on Broadway. Lunching at the Colony Restaurant one day, we had run into the Duke and Duchess of Sutherland, who had been guests at our wedding, and they invited us to their hotel, the St. Regis, for cocktails that evening. They had been to see *Carousel* the night before and were full of praise for it. The duchess insisted that we must see it and got her ticket broker on the phone, demanding the best seats in the house for us for the next day's matinee. Early next morning I got a call from the broker and taxied over to the ticket office to pick up the seats—front row centre. The Sutherlands had been right. It was a marvellous performance, particularly Billy Bigelow's classic 10-minute soliloquy, sung by John Raitt.

On our last night in New York we started off at the 21 Club and wound our way over to the Stork Club, where we got off to a bad start but finished with a happy ending. We were seated at a table next to a drunken, belligerent "Ugly American" army lieutenant with his leg in a cast. He kept nudging me and bellowing, "There'll always be an England as long as there's a U.S.A.," inviting me to step outside. For once I kept my cool. I pointed to my "CANADA" shoulder patches and told him that in the first place, I was not from England, but I was still a guest in his country. I added that I had no intention of becoming embroiled in a fight over nothing and that I was on my honeymoon. I then asked our waiter to move us to another table. With the help of two waiters and the people he was sitting with, the inebriated slob finally calmed down and we changed tables without further ado.

As it turned out, our new table was next to Johnny Bergen, a U.S. Navy Air Force air gunner whom I had met at the Surf Club in Miami, and with whom I had become good friends. He was dining with some others and invited us to join them, which we did. When he learned that we were on our honeymoon, he got word to Sherman Billingsley, the Stork Club's owner, who sent us over a bottle of champagne. Later we all repaired to the Copacabana, where Joe E. Lewis, whom I had first seen and met when he starred at the Copa in Miami, was performing. Johnny warned me, "His act isn't much good. He's not drinking any more!"

On and off, Cilla had been asking me where we were going to live once we got to Windsor. I was deliberately evasive, because it was certainly going to be a comedown after a week at the plush Ritz-Carlton. What could I say? I tried to break the news as gently as I could that she would find it rather small and unpretentious compared to what she had been used to. I was mindful that she had never lived away from home before. So I thought it would be helpful to ease into our situation by stages.

Instead of going directly to Windsor, we took the overnight train from New York to Toronto, where we spent a day in the company of some of my relatives, whom she knew. As well, we visited Hammy, who lived there, and another ex-401 mate, Tex Davenport, who was on a visit to the city. That evening we took the overnight train to Windsor, arriving at the station early the next morning. From there we took a taxi to the Pitt Street abode.

As Cilla remembers, "From the Ritz and the Stork Club to 30 Pitt Street, Apt. 301, was quite an experience, let me tell you. Arthur took me there, dumped me and our baggage, and took off for work at 8:00 a.m., leaving me to set up our first home.

"I cried my eyes out, first thing—everything looked so brown. 'We can't live here, I deserve better, I'll die!' I wept!

"But then something in me took over and set a precedent that is with me to this day. 'I'll make the best of this,' and I think I did. First thing, I went out and bought flowers. Then I bought cleaners and other supplies and scrubbed everything in sight, and decided to paint the place, the bathroom anyway (without a bath—only a shower that was like standing in a hailstorm, the drops were so big).

"Then I reverted to type and sat down and wrote my parents, describing the horrors of my new life.

"To make a long story short, I settled down to a bohemian life as the wife of a newspaper man, serving meals at all hours of the day and night, entertaining weird but wonderful *Star* reporters, sleeping erratic hours, and thoroughly enjoying myself."

Shortly after my return to work I was assigned to the night shift, which meant starting work at four o'clock in the afternoon and finishing up at midnight—or later if need be. When I got off work, Cilla and I would hold the normal evening cocktail hour well after midnight and carry it through into the wee hours of the morning. This schedule did not sit well with our next-door neighbour, a jewellery store owner who kept regular hours; we never met him, but nevertheless christened him "Mueller the Jeweller." Harold Larkin, the landlord's lawyer, summoned me to his office and said that "Mueller" had complained that he hadn't had a decent night's sleep in weeks. "He looked exhausted," Larkin said. We agreed to tone down our carousing. In any case, my tenure on the night shift did not have much longer to run. But during that time I wrote my first front-page story, the sort that every cub reporter dreams about covering.

At 9:30 one evening I had a phone call from Norm Hull, who was at home, telling me to get over to the police station right away. Six convicts had four days earlier successfully forced their way out of the Essex County Jail by overpowering the turnkey and a night watchman. Four of them had been captured by a mixed force of provincial and city police in a shack near Harrow, 20 miles due south of Windsor, and were being brought in. I called upstairs to enlist the photographer on duty, and we got in my car and drove lickety-split over to the police station.

We arrived just in time to photograph five prisoners being led to the cells, handcuffed to each other—the four convicts and a 59-year-old carpenter from nearby Colchester, who had been harbouring the fugitives in the shack. They all looked bedraggled, their clothes dirty and torn, and one of them shielded his face from the photographer with a soiled piece of rag he had in his hand.

I now needed to put the story together. Fortunately, on the return journey to Windsor, the four prisoners had talked freely to the police about their escape. After the breakout they had stayed hidden in the vicinity of Windsor, then walked and hitchhiked in a southerly direction. It was not immediately known how long they had been holed up in the shack.

The police had been tipped off by a phone call from someone—at this point unidentified—who had seen the prisoners' pictures in the paper. A squad of 14 armed policemen rounded up the fugitives: two Windsor police detectives, three city policemen, and nine provincial policemen, several of whom had been sent to Windsor to assist in an ongoing strike at the Ford plant. Three police cars carried the squad to near the shack and they surrounded it. Six of the policemen went to the door, where they were met by John Harris, the carpenter. They went inside and began a search, making their way into a makeshift bedroom, where the four convicts were grouped around a stove. At the sight of the police they threw their arms above their heads and surrendered peacefully.

None of the four men was armed, but they admitted they had possession of a rifle found on the premises, with which they had shot a rabbit and eaten it for supper. The other two escaped convicts were still at large.

Once we had photographed the arresting officers, we drove back to the paper, and I went to work on the story from the notes I had taken at the police station. This was a big opportunity for me and I really sweated it. I must have rewritten the lead—the head paragraph—a dozen times. By the time I got the story into the shape I wanted, one that I hoped Norm Hull would be happy with, it was 2:30 in the morning. In a jubilant mood I phoned Cilla, who was waiting up for me, and broke the news that I had just written a front-page story, giving her the bare details. She was just as upbeat—she had just finishing baking her first cake.

Early in the new year, 1946, we moved into an apartment in a house in Walkerville, the wealthy residential section of Windsor. It belonged to the King family, friends of Cilla's parents. With a living room and kitchen off the ground floor and two bedrooms (one guest room) and bathroom on the second floor, it was sheer luxury after Pitt Street. Because the Kings spent the summer at their cottage on Lake Erie, we had the mansion to ourselves during July and August.

One weekend, when we went to Ottawa to visit our parents, I asked my father if he could mention to George Drew, then premier of Ontario, that I would like to do some stories about the government. With a new party (the Conservatives) in power, the province was on a program of expansion, and there was lots to write about.

In April I received a call from Drew's office arranging for me to do a series of articles on the government's plans for reorganizing its northern Ontario departments and services. Cilla accompanied me on this assignment, and we flew on a Norseman float plane, courtesy of the Department of Lands and Forests Air Service Division (ASD), to the division's main base in Sault Ste. Marie ("the Soo").

There I met the lands and forests minister, Wesley Thompson, who announced to me that responsibility for the Ontario Game and Fisheries Act was being incorporated into his department. A new division was being formed that was to be called Fisheries and

Wildlife. After absorbing the details, I wired this exclusive announcement to the *Star*. This was a real breakthrough for me. When the article appeared, under my byline ran the words "Windsor Star Staff Reporter." I felt I'd really arrived.

That night I spent the evening drinking beer and swapping stories with the pilots of the ASD, many of whom I had known from air force days, in particular George "Pop" Phillips, a ferry pilot and instructor who had been with the provincial air service before the war.* This bull session provided me with ammunition to write a story on the Air Service Division.

Next morning, another story presented itself: the new Forest Insect Laboratory at the Soo, a joint project of the Ontario Lands and Forests department and the Dominion Department of Agriculture. Its purpose was to aid the fight against forest pests, which at the time accounted for three times as much timber destruction as forest fires. In this facility, insect behaviours were studied with a view to carrying out concentrated aerial insecticide spraying on budworm-infested forest areas. The Air Service Division would carry out the spraying.

Our next port of call was North Bay. There I gathered material for a story on the change of name of the Temiskaming and Northern Ontario Railway to the Ontario Northland Railway. This measure arose out of confusion caused by the use of the same initials by the Texas and New Orleans Railway. In many cases, the Ontario line was being billed for work done on the Texas and New Orleans railway cars. Although the Ontario T&NO had pioneered transportation to the northland from North Bay, no repercussions were reported from the diehard sentimentalists who liked the old name.

The assignment concluded with an interview with Minister Thompson in Toronto. One of the main things he stressed was the employment that the province's timber resources were creating. "I

---

* The story of Pop Phillips can be found in *Unsung Courage*, by Arthur Bishop.

would much rather give you statistics than dollars and cents," he said. And the statistics were impressive. In 1946, 26,000 people were employed in the woods, while another 40,000 worked in pulp and paper mills, and 40,000 more in other wood-based industries—altogether, a total of 106,000.

A week later, on May 14, I interviewed Major the Reverend John Weir Foote, who was Canada's fourteenth Victoria Cross winner in World War II. That night he was to be guest speaker at a dinner of the Windsor Lions Club at the Prince Edward Hotel. Known as "Padre X," he bore the distinction of being the only member of the Canadian Chaplain Service to win the Commonwealth's most coveted award.*

The purpose of his visit was to renew acquaintances with members of the Essex Scottish Regiment, with whom he had shared captivity as a prisoner of war following the Dieppe raid. When the order came to evacuate the beaches, Foote decided he would be more useful comforting the men in his regiment, the Royal Hamilton Light Infantry, as a fellow prisoner of war, than those who could get off the beaches and return to England. Foote surrendered to the enemy.

It was not hard to envision the inner depths of bravery in this man, although he preferred not to discuss his exploits. His face was strong and determined, but he was unassuming and friendly. During my interview with him, he turned the tables by inquiring how well I was adjusting from military to civilian life. It was one of his main concerns about veterans, particularly those with whom he had served.

Red Lockwood, of beer-bottle-fencing fame, congratulated me on the story I wrote about Foote. "Your writing is improving," he said. "It's much smoother." This was high praise from one of our best reporters, who often filled in a paragraph or two for the "Now" column

---

* John Foote's story is told in *Canada's Military Heritage*, volume 2, by Arthur Bishop.

at Dick Harrison's own request, and much to his satisfaction. Red was always at my elbow, urging me with such advice as "Tighten up your sentences. Where possible, use active verbs to give them more sweep" (for example, "It was raining" versus "Rain was falling"). He was a valuable ally.

Early in June, Cilla flew to Ottawa to see her family for a week. On the evening of June 17, when she was to return, I was getting ready to drive to the airport, a prospect I didn't relish. It was raining in buckets and there was a thunderish sound in the air, and the sky was turning alternately dark and pink. As I was about to step out the door, the phone rang. It was Norm Hull. He sounded harried, frantic. "Tornado!" he exclaimed. "Twenty killed. Many more injured. Get here as fast as you can." And hung up.

It was pouring when I went outside, and my first concern was to find out whether Cilla's plane had got down safely. I went back inside and tried to phone the airport, but it was hopeless; I got nothing but a busy signal. I decided I'd learn more by getting to the paper. Then, as I started out, I realized there were no street or traffic lights. The city was in darkness—the twister had knocked out the hydro plant. I worried all the way over, and when I inquired at the desk whether there was any news from TCA, everyone was too preoccupied to care. Norm Hull said, "It's down somewhere." Hardly reassuring, but I realized there was nothing I could do about it and there was a job to be done. The only illumination we had was candles at each desk.

One of my tasks was to visit the hospitals and get casualty counts. Doctors and nurses were frantically working under stress and duress, depending on emergency lighting. My most vivid recollection of that night was the sight at one hospital of a youngster, a boy of maybe 11 or 12 years old, with a piece of timber right through his thigh. He was weeping, but otherwise bravely bearing up. I could be criticized for my dereliction in not following that up as a story.

But I didn't have the heart to even ask him his name, for fear I might burst into tears myself.

Back at the paper, reports were coming in by phone of houses that had been damaged or demolished by the twister. Several car accidents. Police reported some house and store robberies. And finally, I learned with great relief that the plane in which Cilla was travelling had been diverted from Windsor Airport, where there was no lighting, and had landed safely at London Airport. The passengers had been transferred to a train. Late that night I drove home to find that Cilla had arrived, but she had to greet me with a candle in her hand.

It had been quite an ordeal for the city and for the paper in particular. Next morning when I arrived, Pappy Vaughan and Norm Hull and a couple of the other senior editors had been up all night. They looked exhausted—but happy. They had pulled off the impossible. Without power our presses were idle, but the *Detroit News* had come to the rescue and printed a special early edition of the *Star*. Our stories had not been in vain.

Pappy suggested that I drive around with one of the photographers and survey the damage. A lot of the houses that bore the brunt of the twister had been built under the Veterans' Land Act, and the families were shattered. Over the next few weeks they banded together to pitch in and help rebuild the battered structures—a case of cooperation in catastrophe.

At this stage in my brief journalistic career, I felt that the "Letters to the Editor" needed beefing up. In those days, in most newspapers, that feature was buried in the back pages, usually in the second section, and the letters themselves were banal and mundane, spouting off about pet causes, beefs, ideas, and views, most of them too polite for words. Contrast that with today's "Letters," right on the editorial page or facing it, inviting readers to take issue—or otherwise—with the paper's editorial viewpoints as well as the news stories.

I composed a masterpiece letter designed to annoy and insult just about everybody. I drew particular aim on returning veterans "strutting around in their uniforms." Who did they think they were, while I spent the war staying home with my mother and reading *Anthony Adverse*? And girls. Why were they always embarrassing me by winking and smiling and making me blush? Why couldn't they just leave me alone? And so it went. I signed my tour de force "Old Fashioned." Deacon Allen, the seasoned editor who supervised the section, said to me, "You're just too good to be true, Bishop, and you ought to be ashamed of yourself. But I'll run it."

At the same time I thought I'd do a little disturbing on the home front as well. Knowing my mother hated it when people called or referred to me as "Art" instead of "Arthur," I sent her the following clipping:

Population Estimate 139,196 in New City Directory
By ART BISHOP
"It's Here! It's Here!" they cried. When the commotion had died down, it was plain to see what they were talking about—the 1946 Windsor City Directory, hot off the Press.

A refreshing sight it was. No pages were torn, none had pencil marks, no pages were missing altogether.

Retribution was swift. In a letter by return mail, my mother wrote, "For God's sake get them to spell your name properly!" It quickly turned into a family joke—at least I thought so. Whenever I phoned or wrote to my mother, I would preface my message with "This is Art Bishop of the *Windsor Star*!"

Her reproof was mild compared to the general reaction to "Old Fashioned" and his deliberations. We did not keep secret from our friends who had authored the missive; some of them guessed anyway. One of our acquaintances reported that she had sat next to four youthful girls in the downtown Honey Dew who were practically apoplectic over what good old "Old Fashioned" had to say, and they were busy putting together a stinging rebuttal. They weren't the only ones. A week after the letter was published, 31 furious replies had been received, an all-time record. Reporting the tally, Deacon Allen wrote, ". . . and not one of them agreed with him." In fact, one respondent went so far as to state that he was shipping a bear trap to the paper under separate cover.

On Friday, June 28, the Governor General, Viscount Alexander of Tunis, paid a visit to the city, during which he decorated navy, army, and air force personnel from western Ontario and Windsor at an investiture held in Jackson Park. The *Windsor Daily Star's* own Don Grant received the Military Cross, which he had been awarded for two acts of valour as a photographer under fire. The first was on D-Day, when he landed with the Royal Winnipeg Rifles; the second was during the attack on Carpiquet airfield.

I was a busy young reporter that day, covering the Alexanders' visit in four different instances. The first of these was their arrival and reception at the Canadian National Railway station, and then an unscheduled tour, at Their Excellencies' own insistence, along the Huron Line, part of the area devastated by the tornado two weeks earlier.

Next a ceremony took place at the midway point of the Ambassador Bridge, which linked Canada to the United States. The Governor General, dressed in morning coat, complete with top hat, was greeted by the Governor of Michigan and the Mayor of Detroit. As he stepped across the international line, he saluted, then stepped back. In addition to our own reporters and photographers, press personnel from the Detroit papers were in attendance. When a female Detroit reporter asked Alexander if he had ever been in the United States before, he replied, "Just a moment ago, when out of habit I automatically saluted. I guess that's the soldier in me."

Astounded, the reporter then asked, "Oh, were you in the army too?"

That brought a roar of laughter from those assembled. But not from Michigan's governor, who turned to the reporter and angrily scolded, "Don't you read your own paper?"

That didn't shut her up either. She turned to me and several others and said, "Well, I knew he was a viss-count or something. But I didn't know he was a soldier. Was he someone important?"

A *Star* story was subsequently filed about the reporter who asked the former Allied Commander-in-Chief in the Middle East and Supreme Allied Commander in the Mediterranean during World War II if he'd been in the army. Reading it over was too much for the editor on duty at the city desk. He scribbled a heading: "Detroit Reporter a Bit Dumb."

Because one of my beats was the Windsor waterfront, I decided to write a feature on the two railway-car ferries operated by the CNR. From the Pitt Street side of the newsroom I had watched with some fascination as they cut back and forth through the Detroit River traffic, and I decided they would be worth a story. Only one of them was in service at the time, the *Huron*. Launched in 1875, it was the oldest vessel in general service anywhere in the Great Lakes system. Her sister ship, the *Lansdowne*, which was undergoing an overhaul, had been launched nine years later.

Because only one ship was used at a time, even when both were running, the two came under the same command. On the morning I went aboard the *Huron*, Captain Fred Tubbs, a hale and hearty, jocular man who had worked on the ferries since 1911, took great pride in the fact that he was the oldest crew member.

I began by learning all I could about how the vessel operated. The most noticeable feature of both vessels, compared to other car ferries on the river, was their relative smokelessness, because they burned oil and not coal. The *Huron* ran on two twin-screw wheel engines. Operating on a high steam pressure of 120 pounds, it made approximately 15 trips a day, each being of 10 minutes' duration.

I persuaded Captain Tubbs to let me try my hand at the wheel. I quickly learned it was no Spitfire—nor even a Lysander. I soon had the river traffic in a turmoil trying to get out of my way. I simply couldn't keep the damn thing on a straight course. Finally the skipper came to my rescue and sorted things out. Thankfully, being a cheery fellow, he got a big bang out of it all. Before I left, he said, "Today the river's running calm. Come back someday when the weather's rough, and I'll bet when you get back, the first thing you'll do is take a couple of bromos."

The morning after I filed my story, Lum Clark called me into his office. "You must have had a lot of fun out there," he said with a smile, pointing out the window. He'd witnessed the whole sorry performance, but he did congratulate me on my story.

One of my regular duties that I enjoyed was covering the monthly Riverside Town Council meetings. It gave me my first insight into political processes at the grassroots level. Those evening meetings were always spirited. At one of the first I attended, the deputy reeve, Ulysses Parent, took umbrage at a councillor who was absent on this occasion but who had earlier criticized him for his work in the community with the Veterans' Land Act for the community. "That man is a liar," he shouted. One of the others at the meeting agreed: "I say what is did, is did," he asserted, and praised Parent for his efforts.

I became very close friends with the mayor, Ronald Mott, an executive with the Ford Motor Company, who did a yeoman job keeping those lively meetings on an even keel. After each one we would retire to his house for drinks and go over my notes, outlining the story I would write for the next day. He was most helpful, and I learned a lot from him about the ins and outs and nuances of municipal politics.

I was also exposed to the political scene on the federal level. The Honourable Paul Martin (senior), the Liberal member for Essex County, was at the time secretary of state, and the *Star* strongly supported him. Whenever he visited Windsor, the paper would go all out, following him everywhere—almost to the bathroom—picturing him talking to people, visiting hospitals and schools, going to church—photographing almost his every step. After one such hectic weekend, several of us arrived early Monday morning, ahead of the editorial staff, to write cutlines for the mound of photographs piled on the news desk. But one reporter, named Robertson, said, "Enough's enough!" He reached into the pile, took out a handful of eight-by-ten glossies, and pitched them out the window onto Pitt Street.

Cilla and I got to know the Martins very well. The man had the most extraordinary memory I have ever encountered, which undoubtedly accounted for his success. It was really incredible. He remembered everyone he met, no matter how briefly. Many years after I had left the *Star*, I ran into him on Bay Street in Toronto. He stopped me and said, "Arthur Bishop, *Windsor Star*. And how is your wife, Cilla?"

In September, Cilla and I faced a domestic crisis. At the end of the month we would have to vacate our suite in Walkerville and find somewhere else to live. We weren't having much luck; rental accommodation was still pretty scarce. We were running out of time, and the only solution was for Cilla to go to Ottawa and live with her parents (My family had moved back to Montreal, where my father returned to his job as vice-president of McColl-Frontenac Oil.) and I moved into a hotel until something turned up. Then, suddenly, the picture changed.

One evening my father telephoned and told me that I had been offered a job with Ronalds Advertising Agency in Montreal, starting at the beginning of October. The salary was $275 a month with a $50 driving allowance. I knew nothing about advertising, but—all that money! I nearly jumped through the phone.

The offer had transpired in a roundabout way. The McColl-Frontenac advertising department was looking for a writer. Eddie

MacMillan, the ad manager, asked my father if he thought I might be interested. But when my father discussed it with Tom Twyman, the company's executive vice-president, he was cool to the idea. The president's son was already working for the company, and Twyman thought this would be stretching nepotism too far. Ronalds Advertising was McColl-Frontenac's agency and it was natural that Russell "R.C." Ronalds, the president, would hear about the idea. He approached my father.

I flew to Montreal several days later for a job interview. This was the first time I had met R.C., although I knew his son Leigh from BCS school days. His older son, Jay, who had distinguished himself as an RCAF transport pilot flying the Hump from Burma, and whom I had met when he was in training, was also working for the firm. Frank Walker, the vice-president, showed me around the office and introduced me to some of the staff. They seemed like a good gang—friendly—a happy ship.

I returned to Windsor to tender my resignation, with mixed feelings. I knew I'd miss the fun and excitement of being a reporter, not to mention my many good friends. But the ad agency did offer a fresh challenge and who-knew-what in the way of opportunity. And, as Norm Hull put it, "more money." During my interview with R.C., he had touched on new business development, which appealed to me. I wrote one last story for the paper before I left that was a fitting finale.

I covered the city's first postwar air show, sponsored by the Windsor Flying Club, which officially opened that Saturday, September 14, 1946. The highlight of the event was the Essex County race for the *Windsor Daily Star* trophy and $250, a handsome purse in those days. Hugh Graybiel, the *Star*'s publisher, presented the prizes to the winner, Sid Hutnick, a veteran flyer who had been a Lancaster bomber pilot overseas during the war.

On the following morning Cilla and I said our farewells to the paper. Mrs. Herman and Lum Clark invited us into the chairman's private office. They had some advice for me as I entered a whole new world. "As a reporter, you were always welcome. People had to see you, in fact," Lum told me. "But as an adman you'll have to convince them that you have a good reason why they should see you." Mrs. Herman added, "He knows from experience. That's where he started out—selling advertising."

We left them, waved goodbye to the others, busy at their desks, and drove home to pack. Leaving the *Star* building behind felt nostalgic and a little sad. But I knew then that I would never lose the desire to write—it had got into my veins during the past year and a half—nor would I ever want to.

Chapter 22

Life as a Huckster

Part One—Montreal, October 1946–December 1954

> Practically everybody dislikes advertising.
> . . . Nobody believes it, or at least admits
> to believing it. . . . But there it is, one of
> the dominant forces of the century.
> —Stephen Fox, *The Mirror Makers*

Ronalds Advertising Agency Limited was founded in 1923 by Charles Ronalds, a successful printer (he published the Bell telephone books) who wanted an agency to augment the services his printing business provided. He appointed his brother Russell (R.C.), who had been his star salesman, to run the company as president. By the time I went to work for RAA, if it wasn't the largest ad agency in Canada, it was certainly among those with the most class. That was immediately evident when you walked through the front door. The head office was on the seventh floor of the Keefer Building, on St. Catherine Street, two blocks east of its intersection with Côte des Neiges Road, in the heart of the uptown Montreal business district. The foyer reception area and the executive suite, which included the president's and vice-president's offices and boardroom, were panelled in brown mahogany. While not as elaborate, the account executive offices and departments were tastefully and comfortably arranged and furnished as well.

In the fall of 1946 the agency had gross commissionable billings of just over $4 million. These included such giant advertisers as McColl-Frontenac Oil, Bristol-Myers Canada, Canadian Industries Limited (CIL), Dominion Corset, and smaller but highly prestigious accounts such as Associated Screen News, Mussens Canada, and Clarke Steamship Lines. Among the accounts handled by the Toronto office was the Hudson Motor Company. *Crème de la crème.*

The agency gave integrity a high priority. Its philosophy was that its service to clients had to go beyond creating excellent advertising and placing it where it counted to produce results. Its policy was that the market was too competitive to ignore the fact that advertising had to be integrated with the other components of the marketing process: sales, distribution, display, and merchandising. Above all, the agency believed that market research was a necessary prerequisite. The agency's slogan—"Facts come first at RAA"— summed it up neatly.

Any organization owes it success to leadership, and RAA was no exception. R.C. Ronalds adhered to a doctrine once expressed by the British department store giant Gordon Selfridge: "The boss *knows* how; the leader *shows* how. The boss says '*Go*'; the leader says '*Let's go!*'" That was R.C.—the Skipper.

Applying those precepts, by his own example R.C. inspired confidence and loyalty and, in a way, a kind of worship. A dapper man who dressed in dark three-piece striped suits, wore spats, and carried a cane, he looked every inch the leader. He was kind, thoughtful, and friendly. By the same token, he was as shrewd as they come, knew how to turn a buck, and could be hard as nails. But his greatest attributes were salesmanship and his ability to size up people and pick the right person for the job.

When I joined the company, I was apprenticed to Mac Macpherson, the assistant account executive and copywriter on the McColl-Frontenac account (not to put too fine a point on it, my old man had now become my client). My relationship with Mac very rapidly ripened into a close friendship. He was responsible for preparing newspaper advertising and radio commercials. The latter were cut-ins for the weekly *Texaco Star Theatre* radio show, which originated in New York. Because McColl-Frontenac's products were sold under the Red Indian trademark, they differed from the Texaco gasoline and oil brands—thus the need to have the Canadian radio network cut the American message and run with Red Indian copy during the commercial breaks.

Other copy assignments for which Mac was responsible were outdoor posters; point-of-sale displays; a monthly dealer newsletter; *What's New*; and the quarterly company house organ, *The Pow Wow*. It was an entirely different type of writing from what I'd been accustomed to, but Mac diligently showed me the way, beginning with *The Pow Wow* and *What's New*.

The Pow Wow work was chiefly a matter of captioning photographs. I'd had plenty of practice as a newspaperman, so I found no difficulty with it. *What's New* was a sales piece for the dealers. I needed to study back issues and learn what was being advertised and promoted, with which Mac helped me. We also borrowed items from the Texaco counterpart. Mac encouraged me to try my hand at radio commercials. "Write like you talk," he counselled. I got the hang of that quicker than anything else.

In Montreal, Cilla and I moved into a second-floor apartment with a single bedroom, living room, and dinette in a brand-new apartment building, Shelbourne Towers, at the corner of Côte des Neiges Road and Pine Avenue. It was a 15-minute walk to the office and a 20-minute stroll to my family's mansion on Peel Street, halfway down the mountain. We furnished our abode with my air force gratuities allowance. It cost us only five percent of the purchase price; the Department of Veterans Affairs picked up the rest.

We made lifelong friends with two couples who moved into Shenky's Palace (nicknamed after Shenkman, the landlord) the same time we did. Sandy and Nancy Ellis were Americans. Sandy, whose family owned Fairfield Ellis and Grant, one of the largest insurance firms in the United States, had been sent to Montreal to gain experience with the company's branch office there. His wife's family were New Englanders whose eldest son, George Bush, would one day become U.S. president.

The other couple, Bob and Elizabeth "Binx" Mewburn, were from Edmonton, Alberta. Bob was going through McGill University for a doctorate in medicine. Binx's father, Ray Milner, head of the Alberta natural gas companies, was planning the building of the Trans-Canada Pipeline.

At the Peel Street mansion, my mother and father entertained lavishly. My father liked to show visitors around his large study at the back of the house, which looked onto the verandah and a small garden. The greats and celebrities were among the guests, including the Governor General, Viscount Alexander of Tunis, and his wife. That was a very formal occasion, calling for white tie and tails and evening gowns. Lethbridge wore his flight sergeant's white dress mess uniform with gold chevrons. (Protocol aside, Cilla, my sister, and I referred to His Excellency among ourselves as Al Toonis.) Among Alexander's entourage were his honorary aide-de-camp Frank McGill (ex–Air Vice-Marshal) and his wife, as well as an American general who had served on his staff in Italy during the war, with his wife.

Before dinner my father showed the Governor General and the other guests around his library. Behind the door hung a London newspaper poster, saved from the Edward VIII abdication days of 1937, that blazoned in large letters:

BISHOP
AND
MRS SIMPSON

The American general's wife, in a flat Midwestern accent, exclaimed rapturously, "I thought it was so-o-o-o romaantic!" Alexander could barely disguise his disgust, He turned to my father and said very quietly, "I haven't seen him [Edward] since he deserted my staff in Paris in 1940."

His reaction was much more cordial when I asked him if he remembered the Ambassador Bridge incident in Windsor when the Detroit reporter asked if he'd been in the army. "Yes," he chuckled, "I remember. Were you there?" Not knowing whether he would be pleased or annoyed, I replied that I had written the story for the Windsor paper. He said simply, "Good for you!"

By Christmas of 1946 I had absorbed a lot about the advertising agency business, McColl-Frontenac advertising in particular. I had become accepted by my fellow workers and had been appointed traffic manager of the M-F team. R.C.'s son, Jay Ronalds, in between hustling new business, helped out on a number of accounts in one way or another, including M-F. He, Cilla, and I had by this time become friends. He was a great troubleshooter and had his father's charm and a tremendous sense of humour.

As we headed into the new year, those of us directly concerned with the McColl-Frontenac account directed our efforts toward the "Changeover Campaign," a switch from the Red Indian logo to the Texaco red star/green T symbol, and from Red Indian gasoline and motor oils to Texaco Sky Chief and Fire Chief gasolines, as well as Havolin and Texaco motor oils.

The changeover campaign was a tremendous undertaking that would cost, all things included, some $2 million. Dealer meetings were planned for all the main centres across the country, to be conducted by two teams of McColl-Frontenac executives, one headed up by Tom Twyman, the company's executive vice-president, and the other by my father, each roughly following either the CNR or the

CPR railway route. An executive from the Texas Company would accompany each team, as well as representatives from our agency.

The dealer meetings were planned showbiz style, and at the agency we were charged with putting them together—writing speeches, preparing a slide presentation, and working with a design house to produce rotating stage props that dramatically transformed the old into the new: the red star/green T "banjo" sign, the Sky Chief and Fire Chief gasoline pumps, and giant-sized Havolin and Texaco motor oil cans. An immense canvas poster would unroll to form a backdrop announcing the changeover. It was a busy time around RAA in those days, and not without its share of crises.

The cross-country changeover dealer meetings took place during late June and early July. We travelled by private railway car; I was a member of the A team. John Pritchard Jr., the son of McColl-Frontenac's president, and I were responsible for the props, setting them up on stage then crating them directly after the meeting for shipment to the next city on the tour. During the meetings I was responsible for coordinating the slide show with a speaker's presentation, and also for operating the movie projector.

Our last meeting was held in Vancouver, after which I flew back to Montreal. Tom Twyman was kind enough to congratulate John Pritchard and me on handling the props during the meetings. He presented us each with a gold pen, and even went so far as to write me a letter:

Dear Bish:
    I have already told Mr. Ronalds how much I appreciate all that you and your confreres did in connection with our recent series of dealer meetings . . . Thank you very much for your splendid assistance.

Such testimony did me no harm! At Christmas time that year,

1947, I received a raise—and a bonus. Cilla was pregnant and the future boded well for the Bishops. Then misfortune struck.

In January 1948, I was hospitalized with an undefined back ailment. I was subjected to regular injections of penicillin, with needles stabbed into my behind every four hours. I began to wonder which was worse—the affliction or the cure. After three weeks of this torture, the doctor called a halt to the treatment, which had eased the pain somewhat, but not entirely. I was still confined to my hospital bed.

Early in February, on one of her regular afternoon visits, Cilla arrived with my mother. They broke the news to me that the baby, which was due in about two weeks, would be stillborn. When Cilla had gone to be examined by the obstetrician there was no heartbeat from the womb. He knew that I was in the hospital, so he felt obliged to break the news directly to her. Fortunately, she was staying with my family while I was in hospital, so they were nearby to console her. It must have been a stunning blow for her. I felt heartbroken not to have been there when she learned of that tragic turn of events, the time when she needed me most.

The saving grace was that Cilla was admitted to the same hospital—Montreal General—that I was in. Only one floor separated us, and I was allowed to visit her daily by wheelchair. At other times we kept in touch by telephone.

Typically for her, Cilla bore this adversity stoically and with great courage. We knew that we had to carry on, with the knowledge that time is a great healer. Following our discharges from the hospital we spent a delightful week recuperating at the Laurentide home of Gus (ex–Air Marshal) and Bea Edwards in St. Agathe, after which I returned to work. I was still a bit shaky, and R.C. said to me, "You've just got to take it easy until you get back into stride." It was an example of his considerate attitude toward his employees. I never forgot the fact that during the two months I was absent, the company paid my full salary.

•   •   •

1948 marked Ronalds Advertising Agency's twenty-fifth anniversary, an event celebrated with a dinner for employees and spouses on March 18, in the viceregal suite of the Ritz-Carlton Hotel. In November of that same year, against all odds, Harry Truman was elected president of the United States. The date, the third of the month, sticks in my memory for two reasons: It was our third wedding anniversary, and at lunch that day at the Peel Street house I met the American air ace Eddie Rickenbacker, who was in Montreal to attend a hospital fundraising function at which he and my father were guest speakers. Rickenbacker, a much taller man than I had expected—well over six feet—was one impressive guy. He had leadership and courage written all over him. On the American election result he said emphatically, "I never thought Dewey would come anywhere close, no matter what that damned *Life* magazine of Luce's said."*

Rickenbacker autographed two books for me. One was his biography, the other the story of how, during World War II, he and six others survived for 23 days on rubber rafts after ditching a Flying Fortress in the Pacific. The inscription in the first volume read, "May your life prove as interesting as mine." Though I can't complain—my life hasn't exactly been dull—Rickenbacker's would have been pretty hard to match.

Another aviation notable to cross the threshold of the Peel Street mansion was Alexander P. de Seversky, a close friend of my father's, who was affectionately known as "Sasha." He and my old man had a lot in common. During World War I, Seversky became the leading Russian ace of the Naval Air Force. He lost a leg during the conflict, and was a recipient of all the honours his country could bestow. He eventually became an American citizen and was appointed consulting engineer to the War Department. In 1931 he formed the Seversky Aircraft Corporation, designed the world's

* A month earlier *Life* had pictured Dewey with a caption that read, "The next president of the United States . . ."

first fully automatic bombsight, and developed and built the first turbo-supercharged air-cooled–engine fighter. His book *Victory Through Air Power* had won him international acclaim.

In 1948 Seversky was guest speaker at a Royal Canadian Air Force Association dinner at the Windsor Hotel. Next day my old squadron, 401, by this time an auxiliary unit, put on an air show at St. Hubert air station, to which we were all invited: Seversky, my mother and father, Cilla, and me. Seversky spoke with a slight Russian accent and Cilla couldn't resist correcting his pronunciation. For instance, when he said "haidge," she solicitously pointed out, "It's *hedge*." He took it good-naturedly. Cilla told me later, "For all his notoriety, Sasha had a great sense of humour. He was a real sweetheart."

At RAA, there was bad news. Erwin-Wasey, one of Texaco's advertising agencies in New York, was opening up an office in Montreal. It was going to take over the McColl-Frontenac account at the beginning of the new year, 1949. I was immediately assigned to the Dominion Corset account as an assistant account executive. At the same time, I was given a lot of smaller accounts to handle on my own, including the Mount Royal Hotel. This was a new experience for me, and an invaluable one that would stand me in good stead later on. I learned that the client had to be looked after on a day-to-day basis.

In the late spring and early summer of 1949 we turned our attention to the forthcoming federal election. Ronalds was a Liberal house—with good reason. We handled advertising for the Canadian Army, as well as the annual Canada Savings Bond campaign, and both of them had substantial budgets. The company pledged its election efforts behind the two chief Montreal candidates, Douglas Charles Abbott, Minister of Finance, who held the St. Antoine–Westmount seat, and the Minister of National Defence, Brooke Claxton, Member of Parliament for St. Lawrence–St. George.

Agency participation in an election was extensive. In addition to making up newspaper ads, preparing posters, and writing radio commercials, we were called upon for a myriad of supporting material: pamphlets, letters to the editor, window banners and stickers, building banners and flags, and other bits and pieces. We were also involved in the election process, arranging and participating in public political forum meetings, and liaising with the campaign managers. We needed plenty of help. Jay hit on the idea of hiring Billy Shaughnessy, a close friend of ours and an old schoolmate of mine (to give him his proper title, the Right Honourable Lord William Shaughnessy, whose grandfather was one of the builders of the Canadian Pacific Railway). He had wide connections, knew his way around politics, and had some news-wire experience at the editorial level. R.C. jumped at the idea and made "Shag" an offer he could hardly refuse. "Five hundred dollars to come and work with us. A thousand dollars if we win." Sold! Next day, Shag moved into the office next to mine. He fitted in perfectly with our crew, lordship or no lordship.

A week before the election I was entrusted with preparing a full-page newspaper ad in support of Brooke Claxton. When I was presented with the proof for checking, I went over every detail, dotting i's and crossing t's, correcting typos, scanning punctuation—carefully, so I thought. But not carefully enough. In the upper case banner headline I omitted to catch an error: the "E" had been left off Brooke Claxton's name. It stood out like a black eye. Next morning, the ad appeared in the Montreal *Gazette*. Before I left for the office, my mother phoned to say, "Some newspaperman you are. You didn't even get his name right!" That was a mild censure compared to what awaited me on the seventh floor of the Keefer Building. I decided to face the music, walked straight into Frank Walker's office, and admitted my mistake. He simply commented, "Yes, you have to be careful to get names right." I was excused, but far from exonerated.

I'd no sooner gotten in my office, taken my coat off, and hung it on the clothes rack when R.C. appeared, brandishing the ad in front of me. He glowered, "Didn't you check this out with the client?"

"I didn't have time," I replied weakly.

"Well, you should find it. Don't take that responsibility lightly. Face it like a man." And he stormed off.

Shag came in from the next office and said, "I congratulate you on keeping your temper. I couldn't have."

"Hey!" I told him. "I work here, remember? It was my fault. And I've long learned to live with authority."

On election day, June 27, 1949, I was given the job of overseeing distribution of box lunches to the polling stations in the St. Antoine–Westmount riding. I was stationed in the campaign manager's suite in the Windsor Hotel, where the couriers could report to me by telephone if any problems arose. It seemed straightforward enough, and all morning it was quiet—the lull before the storm. Around noon the trouble started, when every phone in the suite started ringing. "Where are the box lunches?" the polling station workers wanted to know, in irate tones. I felt helpless. There was no way to reach the couriers—there were no cellphones in those days. There was no point either in driving around the riding to try and find them.

I called Jay over at the office for help and then told Bruce Brown, the campaign manager, about our predicament. I then contacted the caterer and told him to make up a hundred box lunches and get them over to the hotel as quickly as possible. About 1:30 p.m., the lunches arrived while I was still being besieged by phone calls. I then started calling the polling stations in a pecking order beginning with the ones where the deliveries first should have been made. I checked off those that had received them—all of them late. Jay had arrived by this time, and by then I knew which stations were still wanting. We then started making deliveries to those still in need. By then it was getting past two o'clock, and we were not always greeted with open arms by the hungry, but relieved, workers.

I never did learn what really went wrong, though Bruce Brown later told me, "There's always a screw-up with that job." However, the election went well for both our candidates. Doug Abbott won handily over his Conservative rival, René de Lalanne, while Brooke Claxton swamped his opponent, George Ballantyne, by nearly three to one.

About this time, R.C. decided it was time to set the wheels in motion to try and recover the McColl-Frontenac account. John Pritchard, the M-F president, suggested that his best bet was to make an approach through the Texas Company. R.C. asked my father if he would introduce him to Star Rogers, Texaco's chairman of the board. My old man was only too happy to oblige, and he immediately contacted Rogers by telephone. That was to have some consequences, as we shall see.

In the fall of 1951, we were reassigned to the McColl-Frontenac account, starting in January of the following year. I knew that a heavy load was about to fall on me, as I was the only "other ranks" left of those who had worked on the account previously. But that was nothing to complain about; I looked forward to the challenge. But I'll deal with that later. Meanwhile—a digression.

One Saturday morning that summer, my father phoned to ask if I would like to join him and Gene Tunney, who was in town on business, for a round of golf at our club, Mount Bruno. Apparently the former world heavyweight boxing champion remembered me from my boyhood, when he had given me my first set of boxing gloves. Fred Beardmore, an old family friend, joined us too. Tunney was still a powerful man physically, and he made us all look like pikers off the tee. After we finished our game, we drove back to Peel Street for lunch.

The conversation naturally got around to boxing and Tunney's famous "long count" second bout with Jack Dempsey. Fred Beardmore piped up to ask him who he thought was the greatest boxer of them all. Without hesitation he answered, "Joe Louis. He had the longest reign of any other champion—12 years." He then related a story.

After Louis's first fight with the German Max Schmeling in 1936, in which the German prizefighter knocked him out in 12 rounds, President Franklin D. Roosevelt commissioned Tunney to take over coaching of the "Brown Bomber" for the return bout. He wanted to make sure that Hitler's prizefighting emissary was beaten by a black man—and soundly.

After studying films of the first encounter, Tunney discovered that when Schmeling led with his left, he turned in that direction, exposing his back just enough to make it a target. Tunney told Louis that he had the hardest right-hand punch he had ever seen, and that as soon as Schmeling turned, he should hit his back as hard and as often as he could, smack in the kidneys. "Schmeling wouldn't be able to stand up to that for very long," he said.

That's exactly what happened. In the first round of the return bout, in June 1938, Louis felled Schmeling with a single punch to the kidneys from that lethal right powerhouse jab. The German must have felt as if he'd been stabbed by a ramrod. As he collapsed, his shrill, agonized scream could be heard around the world—at least by those who owned radios (hopefully including *der Führer*)—while the ringside sports announcer, Don Dumfy, was shouting excitedly into the microphone, "Schmeling is down, down, down!"

On the business front, I was given responsibility for pulling together all the bits and pieces to make up the advertising plans for McColl-Frontenac. I worked with Frank Walker, who actually authored the plan, and Geoff Collier, who was responsible for copy. I handled the day-to-day contact with Jack King, McColl-Frontenac's advertising manager, but it was clear that a senior account executive would be needed full time to handle the contact at the top executive level, and the search was on for one.

Shortly afterwards Cilla again became pregnant, but this time she suffered a miscarriage. After she left the hospital she was instructed to stay off her feet as much as possible. Because friends and neighbours, as well as my father and mother, would visit her regularly, she left the door unlocked so she wouldn't have to get up from the sofa where she was reclining.

One afternoon my mother, Fred Beardmore, and a female neighbour from upstairs (whom I particularly disliked, and vice versa) dropped in, locking the door behind them. My father came by later and, to surprise Cilla, he took off all his clothes—except for his black fedora hat, shoes, and socks—before making his entrance. Finding the door locked, he pressed the bell.

Fortunately, the unlikable neighbour had left, and it was my mother who opened the door. Cane in hand, my old man breezily announced, "Just to show you I've got nothing to hide," and proudly marched in. My mother quickly steered him into the bedroom, retrieved his clothes from the hall, and threw them in after him, telling him to get dressed. Poor old Fred Beardmore was absolutely flabbergasted. "Imagine if anyone, particularly that woman you hate so much, had seen him," he said to me afterwards.

At RAA it was time to restaff. In 1953 Vic Hanna joined us as the account executive for the McColl-Frontenac account. Vic had considerable experience with petroleum advertising, having handled a major competitor, British American Oil (later renamed Gulf) at one of the other agencies. I was now officially his assistant and I found him a great guy to work—and drink—with.

Cilla had become pregnant again and late in April, the obstetrician phoned to say that, because her new pregnancy was proceeding so nicely, he recommended a Caesarean section as a precaution against anything going wrong at the last minute. A date was set: Tuesday, May 19. Instant childbirth! If I'd had my wits about me, I would have laid some bets and emerged a wealthy father.

On Sunday, May 17, Cilla was admitted to Montreal General Hospital. Next day she underwent a series of last-minute tests, and her mother arrived from Ottawa. She and I were on deck early that Tuesday morning. At around 8:00 a.m., Cilla was wheeled into the operating room and I began pacing the floor. My mother-in-law sat very quietly in the corner of the waiting room. I learned afterwards that she was just as nervous as I was. At 9:30 the nurse came in to announce that I was now the father of a baby girl. Cilla's mother and I trooped down the hall to the window of the room where newborn infants were assembled for parent viewing. There they held up our little bundle of joy where we could see her. "Isn't she beautiful?" my mother-in-law exclaimed. Indeed!

But we still had to give her a name. Cilla and I agreed it should end with an A, which would give it a graceful, becoming sound. Our choice was Diana, which we felt had a nice lilt to it and was a glamorous name as well. So, what's in a name? For what it's worth, her name probably means "bright one," because it has the root *di*, "to shine." In Roman myths Diana was goddess of the moon, of forests, of animals, of young maidens, and of women in childbirth. In Roman art she usually appears as a huntress, with bow and quiver.

These considerations aside, my mother nevertheless clung stubbornly to the notion that our daughter should be named Margaret. That was her own name, and her mother's before her, and her grandmother's before that. But it didn't cut any ice with us. When my father asked why we chose the name Diana, I told him bluntly, "Because we like it!"

"Fair enough," he agreed, putting an end to a petty family argument then and there.

On the advertising scene we were confronted with the advent of television, which in Canada was in its embryo stages. The only outlet was the Canadian Broadcasting Corporation (CBC), and in Montreal it aired a mixture of English and French on only one station. Our initial introduction was through *Texaco Star Theatre*, featuring Milton Berle—"Mr. Television." Employing the same arrangement we had used for its radio counterpart, we cut in with our own commercials that focused on Canada's Texaco products. Fortunately, we were able to monitor the shows at home; one of our clients was Emerson Electric, from whom we were able to buy television sets at a discount.

Vic Hanna and I were also involved with two other TV advertisers among our accounts: the Waterman Pen Company and Catelli Foods. Waterman's had introduced a new butane lighter under the brand name of Presto. It had a double-action friction wheel that maximized the spark—to ensure that it "always lights the very first time." Well, almost. In our first experiment with a live commercial, it took three tries before the gas ignited, compelling us to revert to film.

Catelli Foods had acquired the rights to market Bovril beef extract in Canada. In Toronto, viewers were exposed not only to the CBC-TV station but also to Buffalo stations, which carried all three American networks. The people in our office there made a study of the U.S. commercials, finding much emphasis on famous personalities—movie stars, singers, sports figures, and the like. Using that criterion, Frank Starr, RAA's director of radio and television, who was a radio sportscaster with close connections to the Montreal Canadiens hockey team, suggested we hire Maurice Richard to make a Bovril TV commercial. "The Rocket" was in his prime as a hockey player. He was particularly worshipped in the province of Quebec, but he had grudging admirers in Ontario as well. We hired him for the princely fee of $700 to make a 15-second commercial in both English and French.

The scenario opened on a pair of skates and a hockey stick propelling a puck forward, followed by a close-up of the skates coming to a sudden stop, sending a spray of ice right into the camera lens. The voice-over announced, "What a rush! What a stop!" Shift to a head-and-chest shot of Richard smiling as he lifted a steaming hot mug of Bovril to his mouth, saying, "I'll stop for Bovril every time."

The finished product may have run for just 15 seconds, but the commercial took all of one morning and the better part of an afternoon at the Montreal Forum to produce. The skating portion was somewhat tricky, requiring just the right lighting, and in particular the stopping scene, which Richard had to perform over and over until it was just right. But it was the part featuring the Rocket speaking that gave us the most trouble. The French version went fairly smoothly, no problem. However, when it came to shooting the same scene in English, Richard kept fluffing his line. In between takes the Bovril got cold, and the mug had to be refilled time and again with boiling water. Finally, we—he—got it right.

Two years earlier, the agency, under the direction of Ray Avery, our vice-president in charge of the Toronto office, had opened an office in Edmonton, a one-man show with just a manager and a secretary. A company presence there was logical. McColl-Frontenac had recently completed building a "cat cracker" there—a catalytic cracking refinery. The Canadian Army Western Command headquarters was located in the city. The community was flourishing as a result of the oil discovery at Leduc, 20 miles to the south. And, of course, it was the capital of the province of Alberta.

However, by 1954 the RAA office in the Petroleum Building, just off Jasper Avenue, in the heart of the rapidly expanding metropolis, had failed to live up to expectations. In fact, it was headed for trouble. Apart from the army account, which had been secured through our contacts in Ottawa (who were not happy with the way the advertising was being handled), the other clients were small, piddling firms, most of whom were well in arrears. In short, the office was going nowhere and the accounts receivable were piling up. R.C., who was getting fed up with the rising debt, instructed Ray Avery, under whose aegis the western office operated, to have the manager secure the payments personally. Therein lay the problem.

The manager was a deadbeat. Worse still, it was discovered that he was an alcoholic. Late in October, I accompanied R.C. to the regular monthly lunch meeting of the Advertising and Sales Executive Club of Montreal, at the Mount Royal Hotel. After we returned, he asked me to come into his office and told me to sit down. I had no idea what was up, but he came right to the point.

"Do you feel that you've gone as far as you can go here?" he asked.

I wondered, was this the pink slip? Hell no. That wasn't R.C.'s style. And his query was made in the friendliest fashion. But I didn't know quite what to say. I sort of nodded, as if in agreement, waiting to see what came next.

"You may know we've had a problem with the Edmonton office. [I didn't.] And we're going to make a change. How would you feel about taking it over as manager?"

I was dumbstruck, staggered. How many guys get this kind of opportunity at 31? Even before I could reply, he added quickly, "There's a salary increase of $1000 a year." The icing on the cake. I nearly jumped out of my skin—an offer I could hardly refuse! This was it, beyond my wildest dreams. But all I could do was mumble, "Thanks, skipper. I'll be delighted."

R.C. said, "You don't have to make up your mind right away. Talk it over with Cilla first." I didn't really need to; I knew what her answer would be. I went back to my office and phoned her, and, as I had foreseen, she was thrilled. I then called R.C. over the office intercom and said, "Can I see you?"

"No need," he said, "I take it the answer is yes. Congratulations. You've got the job."

Part Two—Edmonton, January 1955–December 1957

At the end of 1954, I made a familiarization visit to Edmonton to acquaint myself with the situation, during which I also found a house to rent. I returned to Montreal to pick up Cilla and Diana, then 18 months old, and at the turn of the year we took the train back. Cilla was tickled to death; she'd never been west before.

Our house was in Glenora, the old residential district of the city. It wasn't difficult to fit into our new community. Edmontonians are famously strong on hospitality, and we quickly made a host of new friends. We had letters of introduction from Jack Edgar (McColl–Frontenac's ad manager), and Binx and Bob Mewburn, though they no longer lived in Edmonton, had passed around word of our arrival. One of the neighbours—friends of the Edgars—even threw a welcoming party for us.

I quickly secured two new accounts for our office, both of them retail establishments, which augmented the billings we enjoyed from the army account (with which I had re-established friendly relations). As well, we were doled out token advertising from the Alberta government tourist bureau. The first new client was Hayward's Lumber, followed by the other Healy Motors, and the local Hudson dealer on Jasper Avenue, which Ray Avery had arranged for me to handle through Hudson's head office in Toronto.

Hayward's Lumber had just taken on an insulating wallboard line called Strammit. Made of compressed straw, it was economical, efficient, and—what intrigued me most from an advertising standpoint—absolutely fireproof. Although television in Edmonton was still in the embryo stage, CFRN-TV's audience was developing rapidly. I saw television as the ideal medium with which to promote Strammit. I also saw it as an opportunity to promote the fact that I was the only adman in Edmonton with any television commercial experience.

I proposed to Jim Jeager, Hayward's sales manager, that we demonstrate the fireproof quality of the product on television, with a live commercial. We would put a piece of board at right angles to the camera with a girl (my secretary) on one side and one of the Hayward's salesmen on the other with a blowtorch going full blast. With some misgivings, Jim bought the idea. I also talked him into letting me run a teaser ad in the *Edmonton Journal* (the city's only daily newspaper) that read "WATCH TONIGHT FOR THE MOST AMAZING TELEVISION DEMONSTRATION IN THE WORLD!"

The demonstration, enhanced by a voice-over message, was a huge success. When Hayward's opened for business next morning, the switchboard was besieged with phone calls, one anxious buyer ordering enough boards "to build a summer cottage." So successful was the commercial that we repeated it three more times over successive weeks. On the last performance, however, the salesman burned his hand with the blowtorch, and further demonstrations were put on hold.

One morning a month later, I received a phone call from one of the studio set men at CFRN-TV. "What do you want to do with the wallboard?" he asked. I told him to keep it. Silence, then: "Might as well throw it out." I waited for an explanation—and I certainly got one. "It's charred right through. It broke in two this morning when we moved it." One more demonstration and— I discreetly kept the news from my secretary. From then on we filmed the commercials with variations. One, to demonstrate Strammit's strength, had the board raised on stands at either end while a host of men walked across it. Another idea I had never came to fruition. Hayward's symbol was an elephant. I proposed to have the board propped up somehow with a model in a bathing suit underneath and a baby elephant walking across it. Jim Jeager said, "You're really asking for it, aren't you? You've burned a salesman. Now you're going to crush a girl."

That spring, Healy Motors was franchised as the Ford dealer for northern Alberta. It became a highly active account. I recommended that they plan regular special sales that could be supported with full-page newspaper ads, radio spots on all three stations—CJCA, (by then a client), CFRN, and CHED, one of the first rock and roll stations—as well as television, on which we were searching for a suitable vehicle. (I had already signed up Hayward's as sponsor of the weekly *Ellery Queen Show*.)

In June, when I received our monthly statement from the accounting department in Montreal, there was black ink in the profit-and-loss column for a change. The profit was small, but it was first time the western office had turned the corner in three years. This prompted a memo from Ray Avery saying, "Take a bow and have a Dow."* R.C. went one better. He told me to represent him at the forthcoming annual meeting of the Audit Bureau of Circulations (ABC), to be held at Jasper Lodge—and to take Cilla with me.

We spent a marvellous three days at that magnificent lodge, during which I attended the annual meeting and met Walter Lance, a vice-president of Bristol-Myers from New York who oversaw their Canadian operation. We managed two rounds of golf on Jasper's fabulously scenic course. I thought I played fairly well, but Cilla was too distracted by bears, particularly a mother bear chasing her two cubs out of a tree, to concentrate on her game.

•   •   •

In the fall R.C. told me that he and his wife, Irene, were planning a cross-country tour by train and would be stopping off in Edmonton on the way home from Vancouver in early November. He suggested that it would probably help me if I arranged for him to make a speech during his visit to our city.

I decided to make the most of their sojourn and laid out a schedule. I would hold a stag reception for R.C. at the Edmonton Club

* Dow was a brand of beer, but with an expense account, my tastes had graduated to Scotch whisky.

for about a hundred people—clients, associates, friends, and others. Cilla would organize a ladies' lunch for Irene at the house. I would escort R.C. to various clients, such as Inland Cement, the army, the McColl-Frontenac refinery. Gerry Gaetz, president of radio station CJCA and president of the Edmonton Chamber of Commerce, offered to host a small lunch with leading businessmen whom he thought would be of interest and might be prospective clients. John Ward, the advertising manager of the *Edmonton Journal*, arranged for R.C. to be guest speaker at the weekly luncheon of the Kiwanis Club (of which I was a member). This took a tremendous amount of organization, and my apprenticeship as my old man's aide-de-camp stood me in good stead. Healy Motors lent me one of their spanking new Ford Fairlanes and I hired a uniformed commissionaire to chauffeur us around. The royal treatment!

Everything went off like clockwork, and R.C. agreed to my request for a company car and permission to hire an assistant. He added that, as of the first of the year (1956), my salary would be increased by $1000 per annum, and that I would be receiving a hefty bonus at Christmas as well.

At the turn of the year I hired an assistant. Art Budnitsky, a local man, was as energetic a fellow as anyone could ask for. He had been working in the advertising department of a lumber company as a commercial artist. We were busy helping with a promotion of Ipana toothpaste for Bristol–Myers, which had relocated to Toronto from Montreal. The Toronto sales manager, Clem Nugent, was overseeing the radio campaign in both Calgary and Edmonton, and we made ourselves available to assist where we could.

Locally, our main concern was finding a TV vehicle for Healy Motors. We negotiated with CFRN-TV for co-sponsorship of the daily six o'clock newscast. The price was $25,000 a year. However, Dick Rice, owner of the station, successfully convinced our clients that the benefits of sole sponsorship (at double the price) would make the extra investment seem small. The car dealership would have the complete audience. Many discussions were required, as well as selection of a suitable newscaster. The final choice was Ab Douglas, a former broadcaster with Rice's radio station who adapted comfortably to the new medium in both appearance and personality. Finally an agreement was reached and a contract signed, the largest single local newscast sponsorship in Canada at that time.

It placed a heavy demand on us at the agency. We had to prepare fresh live commercials almost every day, although we did use some of Ford's canned film footage. In the spring our problem was getting the cars to the studio. Outside the studio doors, thick, bottomless gumbo mired the cars time after time, a situation that can be appreciated only by those who have lived out west. We had to run with copy improvised on the spot and read by Douglas with only a "limbo" background. Another problem was getting the commercials approved. Most times there was no one around at the dealership to vet them, so Art and I had to gamble that our copy was suitable. That account certainly kept us on our toes.

One morning in mid-April, Ray Avery telephoned to tell me that R.C. was retiring and selling the company to the employees. He, Frank Walker, and Jay were forming a holding company partnership known as Frayjay, which would control 51 percent of the stock. At the same time, Vic Hanna, Frank Starr, and Peter Gorlick from Montreal, Bob Loney* and Ted Bradley from Toronto, and I would become directors and be allotted blocks of stock. The first meeting of the new board would take place early in May. I was invited to attend and to bring Cilla east with me.

The following September my mother, who had recovered from a mastectomy the previous winter, visited us from Palm Beach,

* The uncle of my editor, Don Loney.

Florida, where she and my father were living. At the beginning of the second week of her stay, on September 11, we planned to drive to Banff for three days, where I had made reservations at the Timberline Hotel. The evening before we had dinner at the Mayfair Golf Club as a warm-up to our holiday.

I was awakened in the middle of the night by a phone call from Percy Lethbridge—my father had died in his sleep. I had to wake my mother to break the news to her and let her talk to Leth. I got back on the phone and told him to phone my sister. Then I called the TCA manager at home and asked him if he could reserve a seat for my mother on the earliest flight to Toronto; he assured me that under the circumstances it would not be a problem. I could not accompany her; I had too many loose ends to attend to.

I drove my mother to the airport, where I made a flight reservation for the following day. When I reached the office, I phoned Bob Loney in our Toronto office to ask him to make a hotel reservation for me. Next day I flew to Toronto, where my mother was staying with her brother, Hank Burden, and his wife, Gladys. My sister and her husband, "Hippo," had arrived from Ottawa.

Meanwhile, plans had been underway for the funeral service the next day at Timothy Eaton Memorial Church. There was to be a full-dress RCAF parade from there to St. James the Less Cemetery, where he was to be cremated. His ashes would be scattered in his home town of Owen Sound. My father's body lay in an open coffin at Miles Funeral Home on St. Clair Avenue. I took the liberty of undoing the top button of his uniform in the tradition of fighter pilots; I knew he would have liked that, and it had my mother's hearty approval.

The funeral was the largest military funeral ever held in Canada. A crowd of 25,000 waited outside the church. The casket was carried on a caisson preceded by three flights of 400 airmen, led by my old wing commander Buck McNair, marching to the throbbing notes of the "Death March" played by the 55-man training band. The procession took 70 minutes to pass. All traffic was stopped, and at intersections policemen wearing white gloves saluted, while along the route people bowed their heads as the coffin went by. Outside Deer Park and Rosedale public schools, students stood solemnly watching—as Richard Doyle of the *Globe and Mail* wrote—"the passing of a man their teachers had told them was one of Canada's most gallant sons." A brief service at the cemetery was followed by "Taps" and "Reveille," climaxed by a dozen RCAF CF-100 jets flying overhead in a final salute.

Though at the time I was awed and moved by it all—the sadness, the drama, the magnificence—its full significance did not fully penetrate until much later. That night, alone in my hotel room, it finally caught up with me, and I wept uncontrollably.

Healy Motors was still our most active account. I put out a bulletin to the National Advertising Agency Network asking the members to send us material relating to experiences they had had with car dealerships. I got the idea from Jay Keith, a NAAN member who operated an agency in Rhode Island. He was in town visiting his daughter, Muff Roberts, and her husband, Eddie, with whom we had become close friends. When he dropped into our office to say hello, he asked if there was anything he could help us with. I told him that we needed more hours in the day; the demands on us by Healy Motors were pretty heavy. He suggested we contact the Network. It worked—we were inundated with suggestions, material, and examples.

It was timely. Healy had become so successful—they were now the largest Ford dealer in western Canada—that the company opened a parts depot in Edmonton. Joe Healy introduced me to Rhys Sale, the Ford president who came out from Oakville to inspect the depot. Sale said, "An advertising agency is only as good as what you can squeeze out of it"—like a quote right out of *The Hucksters*. He wasn't fooling, either. It was symptomatic of Ford's attitude toward their agencies, which bordered on the sadistic.

A friend of mine had been a vice-president of one of the four agencies that handled the Ford account. He recalled an occasion one summer weekend when the satanic advertising director called a meeting for two o'clock on a Sunday afternoon. It meant that all four agency representatives had to shorten their weekend and drive down from their cottages to Oakville. Then they spent the afternoon waiting for the ad director, who failed to show up until seven o'clock that evening. Finally he announced that he had changed his mind about the topic he wanted to discuss—and called off the meeting.

Armed with our Network contributions, we put on a full-scale performance for our Healy friends in our new offices in the Tegler Building into which we had moved at the beginning of the year. They were highly impressed, and this gave way to planning two "spectaculars." The first of these was a sailboat sale. With the purchase of a new car, the buyer would receive a bonus in the form of a sailing dinghy, complete with trailer. The second event was an outdoor barbecue on the used-car lot, with music piped in over loudspeakers.

It was right after lunch on April 5, 1957, when we were discussing these programs at the dealership, that I received a frantic phone call from Bernice, my secretary. She told me that Cilla was hemorrhaging and had been taken by ambulance to the hospital. One of Healy's salesman drove me over. Bernice had already arrived by the time I got there. We had to go through the usual bureaucratic rigmarole with the receptionist before I was finally allowed to go upstairs and see Cilla. The doctor said that the hemorrhaging had been contained, but that to save the child he suggested a Caesarean section. Cilla agreed, and five hours later William Aylen Bishop, weighing in at a mere four pounds and a bit—two months premature—entered the world at 8:00 p.m. He spent most of his stay in the hospital in an incubator.

Graeme Shaw, who managed the Montreal Trust Company office in Edmonton, had taken me to dinner during the long wait.

Next day he sent his godson a gift with the note "To William the Conqueror." Diana, who was only four at the time, mispronounced her brother's title as "Willem Conker." I gave him that nickname—Willem—which I have affectionately called him to this day.

On June 10, 1957, the balloon went up for RAA. In the federal election held that day, the Progressive Conservatives under John Diefenbaker failed to win an outright majority, but they had more seats—112 out of 265—than any other party, enough to form a government. Thus ended an uninterrupted Liberal rule of 22 years, their 170 majority of 1953 having slipped to 105. For Ronalds Advertising, it spelled the loss of its two government accounts, the Canadian Army and Canada Savings Bonds. Where I sat, the Western Command account remained in place, but by year's end the agency had come up short by a million dollars in billings. That summer, management was looking for ways to trim costs and consolidate the two main accounts, McColl-Frontenac and Bristol-Myers. The former was solidly entrenched, but the latter was quite another matter.

Late that summer, Fred McBrien, president of Bristol-Myers of Canada, made his regular coast-to-coast tour, meeting with his sales representatives as well as key retailers and wholesalers. On this occasion, Mac Bristol, son of the chairman of the board of the American parent company, who was responsible for overseeing the Canadian operation, accompanied him. When they landed in Edmonton, they found time to visit our offices, meet our staff, and have dinner at my house. Fred told me that Mac was suitably impressed. That leg of their tour gave them a three-day holiday break; at the end of their visit, I drove them to Jasper Park Lodge, then to Banff, where we stayed at the Timberline Hotel.

In western Canada the national parks bristle with signs warning about the danger of feeding the bears. Nevertheless, this does not stop tourists from trying to cater to the wild animals. On our drive between Jasper and Banff, a car with a U.S. licence plate stopped right in front of us and the children playfully dropped food from open windows to a bear. It was a shaggy light brown beast—a grizzly—reputedly one of the most feral of the species. As the American car pulled away, the bear turned its attention toward us. Fortunately, because it was a brisk morning, we had all the windows closed. When the bear put its paws on the hood, I gave the accelerator a spurt, just as a huge paw with long, sharp claws scraped across the window on my side.

Mac Bristol was quite upset by the incident. He had a dread of bears arising from an experience in Yellowstone Park, when a bear climbed into the back seat of the convertible he was driving. And we weren't finished with bears yet on this junket—not by any means.

That evening we ate in the Timberline dining room, which opened on to a stone terrace with a waist-high wooden railing around the edge, a mostly psychological barrier to discourage bears from trespassing on the premises. A women at the table next to us suddenly got up, took what remained of her T-bone steak, and marched out onto the terrace. Beyond the railing a bear was roaming about on all fours. The woman reached across the barrier and offered the bone to the beast. The bear stood up on its haunches, and with a swipe of its front paw, knocked the bone out of her hand. There was a collective horrified gasp from the dining-room patrons, followed by shocked silence.

Next day Fred and Mac planned to take the afternoon train to Vancouver, while I would be heading in the opposite direction, to Calgary and then home. Before lunch we were sitting on the terrace in front of Fred's room having drinks, when a pair of bears started ambling along on a course that would take them directly past the railing in front of us. Mac took his drink and went inside. He'd had enough bears to last him for a while. Fred and I gathered up our drinks and joined him in the room.

To my surprise, Mac then raised the question of the handling of the B-M account. In no uncertain terms he said, "You can tell Jay and Frank Walker that they have until the end of the year to smarten up that Toronto operation, or else."

Fred couldn't refrain from a touch of sarcasm: "That rundown office of Avery's in the heart of the garment district hasn't even got any soap in the washroom. The last time before Mac and I visited, we brought several cakes of our own and presented them to him."

All this was something of a revelation to me. I had no idea the account was in trouble. Earlier when Ray Avery had visited Edmonton with his family on a western holiday, he had given no hint of it.

I learned later from Frank Walker, that following his visit, Ray had recommended moving me to the Toronto office. It was also later brought to my attention (by Fred's sales manager), that Mac Bristol had requested that Jay and Frank bring me east to handle the B-M account. In December this had all came to a head, resulting in my being transferred.

Part Three—Toronto, January 1958–December 1960

Bristol-Myers, one of RAA's oldest accounts. A leading Canadian drug manufacturer, producer of well-known brands, some of which can still be seen on the shelves today—Ban roll-on deodorant, Bufferin analgesic, Ipana toothpaste, Trushay hand lotion, Vitalis hair oil. Originally based in Montreal, in 1956 the plant and head offices moved to Etobicoke, a western suburb of Toronto.

B-M's annual advertising budget was a million dollars, a third of the company's yearly sales volume. Representing a quarter of the agency's annual billings, most of it was spent on television, in both spots and sponsorship. To a large extent, the creative end was guided by the American parent, though in most cases we laboured under entirely different government regulations and restrictions.

Our problem with Bristol-Myers was personal, a not uncommon occurrence in client to agency relationships. But this one cut deeper and had far more bitter over- and undertones than most. Ray Avery and Fred McBrien were totally at loggerheads. Purportedly this clash of personality stemmed from their youth, and the passing years had served only to aggravate it. If this had been simply a client's disenchantment with the account executive or with anyone else working on the account, while important enough, it would not be irremediable—the individual could easily be replaced.

But the Avery/McBrien contretemps was different. You don't replace your executive vice-president, senior partner, and major shareholder simply because one of your clients doesn't like him (detests him, in fact). You do the next best thing. You buttress the situation with a buffer. Enter "Buffer" Bishop, newly elected vice-president of the company. Superficially, the move made sense. I had curried Fred's favour during his many visits to Edmonton when I was quartered there. But I had no illusions that my charisma would last.

Traditionally such affairs have a short run, then the relationship comes down to basics—and my halcyon hiatus for the agency was no exception. Not that I hadn't been forewarned. With Avery *persona non grata* in Etobicoke, the mantle fell on Walker to maintain top management liaison with the B-M president, which he handled nobly, in spite of the inconvenience of making regular trips from Montreal.

After a six-month interim period of familiarization and induction on my part, Frank and I sat down with Fred and asked him for his assessment. It was favourable. However, when we were driving back to the office, Frank said to me, "Congratulations are in order."

"But," he warned, "watch it! It can change on you just like *that*." Jay Ronalds added his two cents, with this advice: "You can socialize with Fred, but remember—he's a mean bastard!"

These prescient alerts were not without foundation. McBrien had taken over the reins of the company in 1954 on Jay Ronalds' recommendation to New York, and had immediately established a reputation of eating agency account executives for breakfast. After myriad personnel changes, Jay had taken charge of the account himself, to everyone's satisfaction.

But when the account moved to Toronto, the agency decided that Jay should remain with the head office, and hired a young marketing hotshot to take over the account, moving with it to our Toronto office. This created a situation fraught with friction. McBrien resented what he deemed to be Jay's refusal to move with the account, and while he respected the ability of the marketing man, he considered him too young and cocky to be put in charge of a major account. Pour into that potpourri his difficult relationship with Avery. McBrien felt that the agency was not giving his account the service he deserved. He also thought that the Toronto manager was taking an easy way out, to profit from an extra million-dollar billing godsend without making a major commitment in personnel.

I had stepped into a minefield. However, the pay was good—the wheat was worth the chaff. But, being cognizant of Walker's and Ronalds' danger signals, I knew full well that peace could not reign forever, so I kept a sharp lookout over my shoulder.

The first explosion erupted with McBrien's accusation that the agency was not paying close enough attention to the Quebec market which represented a third of B-M's sales. He felt that our efforts were not sufficiently oriented to French-Canadians. (Unfairly—we had a highly experienced and knowledgeable French department, and many of our senior personnel were bilingual.) Specifically, the criticism was levelled at Bufferin's lagging market share in *la belle province* compared to the rest of Canada. McBrien pigheadedly refused to accept the fact that Anacin and Aspirin sales were suffering similarly. The reason was the Frosst 222 analgesics, which enjoyed the distinction of a codeine additive but which could be sold outside Quebec only by prescription. In its own province, the 222 ruled the roost. Even Don Frost, B-M's U.S. advertising director, quipped, "I wish I had two esses in my name."

McBrien and his two assistants made it clear that they expected me to carry out an agency survey of the province. Jay Ronalds put his finger on it when he said, "Fred's just trying to spend our money." Ray Avery underlined it by echoing with a sentiment of his own: "Arthur, we've been had." So it was that I set off on a drive-through survey of sales outlets in all the major centres— except Montreal, where the head office undertook store checks— Trois-Rivières, Shawinigan, Grand-Mère, Sherbrooke, and Quebec City.

From my findings we drew up a recommendation that B-M sponsor a French CBC Television network show. It seemed to us to be the only answer that made sense—blanket TV coverage of the entire province. But McBrien and his assistants, whom we nick-named the "Bobbsey Twins," weren't buying. In an uneven battle of one against three, I came in for a stiff share of nitpicking. I finally had to give in and settle for TV spots, which barely satisfied the clients. It also left those who had worked with me back at the agency highly disgruntled that all that work had come to virtually naught.

That was the turning point of Walker's warning "Watch it! It can turn on you just like that!" And McBrien certainly lived up to Jay's "mean bastard" characterization of him. From then on, things went from bad to worse. At the end of the year B-M hired a second agency, Vickers and Benson, which was handling products manu-factured by another drug firm that had recently been acquired by

Bristol-Myers. At the same time, several of our products were given to V&B. Some changes on our own part were indicated. I recommended that we bring in someone of the same calibre as Vic Hanna, who had met with such success handling the McColl-Frontenac account. And since our marketing man, who had been assisting me, had decided to leave the agency, I agreed to help the newcomer in any way I could. But it didn't quite work out that way.

In practice the reverse turned out to be the case. The plan called for me to acquaint our newcomer, Bill, with the account and introduce him to the client. Then, after a reasonable period of time, he would take over. It quickly became obvious, however, that Bill was not a take-charge guy. I was still saddled with the job of quarterbacking. For a while all went smoothly, with few complaints from McBrien and his Bobbseys. Too good to last.

That summer, while on a business trip to Vancouver, Fred McBrien had a heart attack and was hospitalized. Don Frost, the New York B-M ad manager, filled in for Fred. He was quite a contrast to work with—an absolutely delightful respite that ended all too soon.

That fall, Fred returned to the fold fully recovered and just as mean, cantankerous and ornery as ever with an even longer, sharper needle than before. *The Hucksters'* soap tycoon, American Tobacco's George Washington Hill; Ford's president, Rhys Sale; and his sadistic advertising director—all rolled into one. My relationship with him began to teeter on the edge of intolerable. It was not helped by Bill's inability to live up to expectations and his counting on me to bail him out whenever he got into trouble. Avery and Walker accused me of covering up for him, when in actual fact I was trying my best to rescue a difficult situation—which had been of their making, not mine. After all, they'd hired him.

By year's end it had become clear that I had no choice but to step aside. Another replacement was brought in, although in the end, he had no better luck than the rest of us. However, it helped fill the gap until we merged with Reynolds Advertising in the fall of 1961. Shortly afterwards—predictably—McBrien pulled the rug out and fired the agency.

By that time I'd had enough of the life of a huckster. I decided to strike out on my own, the words of my mentor, R.C. Ronalds, ringing in my ears: "When you've gone as far as you can go, get out!"

Chapter 23

PPS Publicity

Toronto—1964–1988

> Art Bishop is president of his own firm,
> PPS Publicity, Toronto, which specializes
> in "publicity" as opposed to what he calls
> "the haze of the public relations mystery."
> —*Sales/Promotion Magazine*,
> November 1967

When I decided to leave the advertising game, I made a personal survey of top executives in leading businesses with whom I was acquainted. They indicated to me that public relations was generally viewed with mistrust and skepticism. A lot of bullshit artists in the game were dragging it down. I wasn't about to try and change that—business is not built on crusades.

I certainly had no intention of wading into the field head-on, even though I'd had considerable PR experience during my brief run as aide-de-camp to my father, as well as 14 years' advertising agency experience. Instead, I opted for an end run. In my mind, what was missing—what was needed—was an acceptable, forthright, easily recognized and understandable approach. I decided to concentrate on what companies appeared to want most from any PR service—recognition—and that boiled down to coverage, pure and simple.

Once I'd established that basic concept, I began enlisting free-lance commission salesmen to solicit business for me. I also employed a freelance writer, Tommy Rimmer, who had retired from Ronalds-Reynolds, to prepare news releases. Cilla agreed to take over the chore of media selection, and we would share the job of media contact. In our early discussions while setting up the business, one of the potential sales representatives said, "Give me a package to sell." From this was derived the concept of a "packaged publicity service," eventually expressed in more memorable form as PPS Publicity.

We kept the concept simple, producing folders with such messages as

Let Us Make News For You
A complete
PACKAGED PUBLICITY SERVICE
At a Price You
Can Easily Afford

Why PPS? For one thing we can be objective and view your activities with a newsman's eye. Our business is finding the newsworthy elements in corporate activity; news in goods and services and the people who provide them.

We often see the forest where our clients are treed with detail. Conversely we count the trees and beat the underbrush for the hard facts that news media demand.

When we find news-making material in your activity we know how, when and where to tell it for maximum impact. That is what *publicity* is all about, isn't it?

Our literature also stressed the opportunities for publicity present in every form of organization, such as

Products—new and present
Product modifications
New appointments

Plant expansion
Case histories
Selling methods
Promotions
Installation of Employee benefits

One of my sales associates, who was with the Canadian Press Clipping Service, told me that on one of his calls to Dunlop Tire he had interested the advertising manager, Bill Booth, in PPS. Booth wanted to meet with us to discuss the possibility of hiring us. Bill arranged for me to meet George Plummer, Dunlop's president, at a dealer meeting in the Skyline Hotel a week hence. I had a long discussion with George, outlining my philosophy that any publicity effort should encompass objectives, message, methods, and media (OMMM). He said to me, "You're the first one I've been able to understand. Most of the other guys I've talked to tell me the cafeteria should be painted or some such nonsense, then they go into a diatribe that I can't even be bothered listening to."

He demonstrated an idea he had. Pulling a penny from his pocket, he inserted it into a tire tread. "When you can see two-thirds of the coin, it's time to get new tires," he said. I enthused over the idea and hired the resident photographer to take a picture of the demonstration. Then I ran with it. The press releases and photo appeared in daily papers across the country and the CBC-TV network also picked it up. We now had Dunlop as a client, a hefty shot in the arm for a brand-new business. Building on that success, I quickly picked up two local accounts, Mathers and Haldenby Architects and Wilson and Cousins, manufacturers of auxiliary firefighting equipment, plus several other firms, including two in Oakville.

To spread the word, I developed a single-page newsletter with a picture of myself at the top busily cranking out a news release on my typewriter (we had not yet graduated to computers in those days). These mailings, to both prospects and clients, featured various successes achieved for our clients. Conscious of the words of Harry

Bruno, a recognized public relations executive who numbered among his clients Amelia Earhart, and whose advice I regularly sought, to always "Think Big," I started to aim at elite prospects. One of them was Warner-Lambert Canada Limited, a cosmetic, drug, and confectionery manufacturer located in Scarborough. The company was an account of Ronalds-Reynolds advertising, but had been a Ronalds Advertising client long before the merger.

Even after I left the agency, Cilla and I had continued to visit Ray and Peg Avery in Scarborough on Grey Cup Day, along with a host of other old friends. These included Kay and Jim Hamilton, who was treasurer of Warner-Lambert. The Hamiltons had arranged for us to rent a cottage next door to them on Lake Simcoe one summer, and I now asked Jim for another favour. Would he introduce me to whoever was responsible for public relations at W-L? "It's Tony Pengelly," he replied. "I'll set it up for you."

I did not know Tony, although I had heard about him through friends in the Prisoner-of-War Association. He had joined the Royal Air Force before the war as a bomber pilot, and flew on the first RAF bombing raid on Berlin, on August 25, 1940. On a subsequent raid he was shot down and imprisoned in the notorious Stalag III, where 50 POWs were murdered by the German Gestapo as a reprisal for a mass breakout.

Tony, W-L's director of corporate marketing, greeted me warmly; he was wearing the air force tie. I'd had the presence of mind to wear my pilot's tie, which is the air force tie superimposed with pilot's wings. I didn't have to do much selling. After a cursory look at my sample book of news releases and clippings, he announced that he had set aside a seedling budget to test our services. Our focus was to be the Warner-Lambert Research Institute at Sheridan Park, in Mississauga, west of Toronto. This assignment was to have dramatic consequences for me.

The first publicity was built around the use of animals for product research. I had a rabbit photographed showing the lab technicians putting drops in its eye, illustrating the testing of eye makeup, hairspray, spray deodorants, shampoos, and spray cologne. The result was wide pickup by the daily newspapers and good trade coverage, as well as two mentions on the CBC-TV news.

That was only a warmup. I had become a close friend of Dr. George Lumb, a fellow air force veteran who headed up the research institute and who was also president of the Sheridan Park Community Association. When he learned that Prince Philip was scheduled to come to Toronto in January 1970, he arranged for him to visit the research park, steering him into the Warner-Lambert Institute. I took advantage of this by having myself photographed with HRH, George Lumb, and two technicians in the laboratory—in the nick of time, just before the Prince's bodyguard threw the photographer out by the scruff of his neck and the seat of his pants.

Using the picture as a focal point, I built a two-colour full-page advertisement that I ran on the back page of *Marketing* magazine, with the heading,

ARE YOU TAKING ADVANTAGE OF
OPPORTUNITIES LIKE THESE TO MAKE NEWS?
Visit of Prince Philip to Sheridan Park Research Community

followed by a list of 30 publicity opportunities: new products, expansion, plant openings, appointments, etc. Then I also listed

SOME OF THE 150 FIRMS
WHO HAVE SUCCESSFULLY USED PPS

A little salesmanship never hurt anyone!

Nor did being the author of a best-selling book with the prospect of a movie in the wind. In 1966 I had signed a contract with Howard Webster, publisher of the *Globe and Mail* and owner of the Lord Simcoe Hotel, giving him the rights to produce a film based on my biography of my father, *The Courage of the Early Morning*, with a three-year option. Wally Floody, chief tunneller of the Great Escape, and another ex–Spitfire jock, Larry Robillard, had been instrumental in bringing this about. Ex–heavyweight champion Gene Tunney, a partner of Webster, also contributed. Subsequently Floody put together a group to finance the project under the terms of the contract.

Coincidentally, and providentially, during the following year—Canada's Centennial—on June 19, my father was inducted into the International Aerospace Hall of Fame (IAHF) in San Diego, California, along with four other aviation notables. (The others were Louis Blériot of France, first to cross the English Channel in an aeroplane; Amelia Earhart, first woman to make a solo flight across the North Atlantic; Alberto Santos-Dumont of Brazil, first to achieve a manned, powered, and sustained flight in Europe; and Frank Whittle, designer of the aircraft gas turbine engine.) My father's induction into the IAHF generated wide publicity in the news media. This and the royal visit full-page *Marketing* ad began to pay off. Among the businesses they attracted to the fold was my alma mater, Ronalds-Reynolds Advertising. Working with that gang again was like old times, and even better, because I was now treated as a consultant instead of an employee.

At that time Tony Pengelly was serving a one-year tenure as chairman of the Association of Canadian Advertisers, and Warner-Lambert underwrote the cost of my services to ACA. This was the most important breakthrough of my career as a publicist. Tom Blakely was the full-time president of ACA, and when Tony stepped down, Tom hired us on a regular basis to cover the association's annual convention (in May) and annual meeting (in the fall).

I had met Tom some years earlier when he was vice-president and Montreal manager of the McConnell-Eastman Advertising Agency. He had offered me a job as account supervisor handling the Canadian National Railways account. I turned it down, partly because of Ronalds Advertising's experience with government accounts. The climate was moving toward a return of the Liberal government. That would mean the loss of the CNR account for McConnell-Eastman. Besides, I had no wish to return to Montreal. The action was in Toronto, which *Toronto Telegram* publisher John Bassett called "the most exciting city in North America."

For my money, Tom, who had distinguished himself during World War II as the gunnery officer of HMCS *Cobourg*,* represented the quintessential association manager. A brilliant advertising executive, he knew his stuff. He made it clear who was running the show and would brook no nonsense from his elected executive, who were changed annually anyway. It was a pleasure to work with this former newspaperman; he left the publicity end, which included operating the media newsroom, entirely up to us.

Quite apart from the compensation for handling the ACA publicity, the exposure—to every major Canadian advertiser—was enormous. It resulted in our acquiring such blue-chip accounts as Canadian Pittsburgh Industries, General Mills, Alberto-Culver, Boyle-Midway, and the Toronto Advertising and Sales Club, for which we handled publicity for every one of their monthly luncheon meetings. That in itself generated other new business.

York Steel was an icon of the Canadian steel industry, and for many years I enjoyed a warm and pleasant relationship with its president, Joe Tannenbaum, son of Max Tannenbaum, the founder. It was some years before I had the privilege of meeting Max, a legend in the business, to whom Joe introduced me one morning in his office. When Joe identified me with my father, Max, who had a gifted sense of humour, asked me, "What are you doing here? Why aren't you up there flying?"

His remarks were timely in a way. The musical play *Billy Bishop Goes to War* premiered at the Theatre Passe Muraille in Toronto on February 13, 1979. With the dollar sign firmly in mind, the produc-

* See *Corvette Cobourg*, by Tom Blakely.

ers pulled out all the stops to make this opening a spectacular one. An air force cadet band and honour guard were on hand. The event was well covered by the news media as I accompanied Lieutenant-Governor Pauline McGibbon to inspect the guard of honour. We then took our seats front row centre, Her Honour on my left, Cilla, Diana, and son Bill on my right.

Mere moments before the performance was scheduled to start, one of the touring company's major-domos, a large, overbearing female, leaned over to Cilla and told her—*told* her, not asked—that she and the children would have to move to a row further back, to make room for New York producer Mike Nichols and his entourage of two. Money before manners.

Cilla was humiliated, and I was no less furious. But, as I was seated beside the Lieutenant-Governor, I swallowed my rage in the interest of preserving proper behaviour and protocol and avoiding embarrassment (I'd get my innings later). Fortunately, I refused to let this outrageous display of discourtesy spoil the evening's entertainment for me.

John Gray, who wrote the book, directed the play, and supplied the music, and Eric Peterson, who played the starring role, provided an enduring parody of the Canadian folk hero, the small-town youth thrust into international acclaim and renown. They captured the true spirit of my father, who lived by the precept of always taking what he did seriously, but never himself. Billy Bishop would have loved *Billy Bishop Goes to War*. Peterson and Gray have given us something in which we can take a lasting national pride.

I have seen the show performed by others in many different venues. While their performances are commendable, they can never quite match the lofty standards set by the originators. Yet the production never loses its quality, its appeal, its depth, its glow and sense of fun. It is a masterpiece that will hopefully go on forever. I consider it one of the greatest and worthiest tributes to my father's memory—a salute I'll not forget.

•   •   •

On June 13, 1988, I celebrated my sixty-fifth birthday. Retirement age, ostensibly, but because I operated my own business, nobody could kick me out. And I had no reason to quit. Cilla and I were both in good health and enjoying our work. But, looking to the future, I could see underlying and overlaying factors that required careful, practical attention and consideration. As my old friend Dalt Waller used to say, "Nothing lasts forever." Agreed! Things do change.

We had successfully stayed in business for nearly a quarter of a century. But during that time, costs had climbed steadily; our over-head, office rent, parking, and so forth had increased tenfold. We were forced to move to less costly premises. That solved one prob-lem, but another remained that was insoluble. Our business was gradually drying up. PPS's clients, the people that we had been dealing with over the years, were retiring. A new generation was taking over in their place. Fresh out of business school, confident and gung-ho, with little understanding of or interest in the field of publicity, they had no time for this old fart. They had their own ideas, rightly or wrongly, about how things should be done. The writing was on the wall—I wouldn't last long in that milieu. I wasn't complaining; I'd had a good run at it. But obviously I needed to find something else to do.

Chapter 24

Author

Toronto—1988 to today

> Arthur Bishop has written six books
> on military history. He started when
> he was 68.
> —Jim Clemmer, *GROWING the Distance*
> ("Arthur!" he told me. "Keep growing!")

One spring evening in May 1989, I received a telephone call from Dave McIntosh in Ottawa. I didn't know him, but I'd heard plenty about him. I had read his thrilling book, *Terror in the Starboard Seat,* in which he related his experiences as a Mosquito night-intruder navigator with 418 Squadron (and in which he described his daredevil pilot, Sid Seid, as a "Jewish Billy Bishop"). After the war he had joined the Canadian Press, serving as foreign, defence, and political correspondent for 30 years.

His reason for phoning me was that he was finishing a war diary of 401 Squadron entitled *High Blue Battle,* which he wanted to conclude with personal comments from former squadron members. I gave him mine and suggested he contact some of my old buddies for others.

At the time I was working on several manuscripts of my own. My new chosen vocation was a logical one, given my background and the fact that I already had one book—my father's biography—under my belt. Besides, it had always been my lifelong ambition to become an author. All of my manuscripts were about military aviation and the history of aviation itself, but even with the help of an agent I was having no luck whatsoever in interesting a publisher. I asked Dave if he would put in a word for me with his publisher. However, he was most uncomplimentary about the house he had been dealing with, and hesitated to recommend them. Instead he suggested that I contact Don Loney of Collins Publishers, who had edited *Terror*, and whom he regarded as the most knowledgeable, enthusiastic editor of military history in the country. "He's got great ideas," Dave told me. That proved to be no exaggeration.

Loney—that name rang a bell. Of course! Bob Loney, a fellow director from my Ronalds Advertising Agency days, turned out to be Don's uncle. I wasted no time, setting up an appointment the following morning. Two days later, armed with manuscripts, I met with Don in his office on Avenue Road, near the Park Plaza Hotel. After scanning my stuff, we repaired to the hotel's rooftop bar for a discussion. Don said that he thought we could work something out together. He then told me that he was changing jobs; soon he would be moving to McGraw-Hill Ryerson, and once there he would circulate my work to his executive and staff.

We met again two weeks later and he advised me that his people considered my work—the key manuscript being *Brimstone and Fire, the History of Air Power*—too general for home consumption. However, he said that McGraw-Hill was open to other suggestions. In the meantime, he wanted to republish two books my father had written, *Winged Warfare* and *Winged Peace*.

Because I had acquired the copyrights to both books before my mother died—through an arrangement with the Willis Wing Agency in New York—I gave him the go-ahead. They were duly published as a boxed set (but also could be purchased individually) in paperback form. It wasn't a big deal, but it got things off the deck with McGraw-Hill. At our next get-together, I proposed the idea of a who's who of all the world's air aces, from both world wars and the Korean War.

Don recommended that I backtrack a little and think in terms of the Canadian market—a who's who of outstanding Canadian airmen. As our discussion progressed, we agreed to extend this to include the army and navy as well. In the end we decided on a trilogy called "Canada's Military Heritage": *Courage in the Air, Courage on the Battlefield,* and *Courage at Sea.*

That decided, I began preparing a plan of action. The centre of my attention had to be Ottawa, where, fortunately, my daughter was working as parliamentary correspondent with CTV, which solved my accommodation problem. My first objective was to seek the help and support of National Defence Headquarters. Paul Manson had recently retired as Chief of the Defence Staff (CDS) of the Canadian Armed Forces (the first airman to hold that office). I had met him on several occasions when I was a director of the Canadian International Air Show. He introduced me to the new CDS, General John de Chastelain. John provided me with entree to the Directorate of History (D-Hist), where Carl Christie, senior research officer, pledged his full cooperation.

I also made contact with Vic Suthren, director of the Canadian War Museum, whom I had known for many years, and the museum's former curator, Dick Malott. Dick had contacts everywhere: the National Archives, the Conference of Defence Associations Institute, and the Organization of Military Museums of Canada, of which he is executive director, to name just a few. My daughter, Diana, introduced me to another important source— Chris Terry, director of the Canadian Aviation Museum. Don Pearsons, assistant to the director of Air Command, was another useful contact. I had met him when the new Air Command Headquarters in Winnipeg was named the Bishop Building. Through Don I was introduced to the learned researcher John Grodzinski, who at the time was working with the Royal Military College in Kingston. Closer to home, I sought out and received the enthusiastic offer of cooperation and assistance from Anne Melvin, librarian of the

Royal Canadian Military Institute, and Lesley Bell, team leader of the main reference centre of the Toronto Reference Library. This was the network I set up at the outset of my new career.

The income derived from writing books is essentially paid in advances and through royalties earned from sales. To cover costs ranging from travelling to printing, photocopying, computer supplies, telephone and fax charges, postage and courier services, and sundry other expenses, it is often necessary to supplement that revenue by seeking funding from other sources. Over the years, five such sources have came to my aid: Hartland Molson, the Air Force Heritage Fund (through Don Pearsons), the Conference of Defence Associations Institute (through Ben Shapiro, Bill Yost, and Ian Cameron), Willis McLeese, and the Henry N.R. Jackman Foundation (through Hal Jackman).

At the end of the summer of 1992, *Courage in the Air*, the first of my military heritage trilogy, had begun to hit the bookstore shelves. I was invited to attend Aerodrome 92 over the Labour Day weekend, an air show in Guntersville, northern Alabama, featuring a hundred World War I warplane replicas from all over the United States and Canada. Other Canadian guests so honoured were Otto Roosen, the oldest living Great War combat pilot—a German whom my father had shot down in 1918; Anna von Stryk, niece of the Red Baron, Manfred von Richthofen, a charming woman who was accompanied by her husband, Hans, a former Werhmacht officer; Earl Hewitson, director of the RCAF Museum in Trenton, Ontario; and Bill Cole, holder of the Canadian high-altitude parachute fall record, among other feats.

This unique event was the inspiration of our hosts, Frank Ryder and his wife, whose company, Ryder International, manufactured equipment for NASA as well as a line of proprietary products. They were also in the process of building a World War I aircraft museum. They treated us royally.

The airfield was a few miles from our hotel. There, for the next three days, we were dazzled by a flying display of SE5a's, de Havillands, Curtis Jennys, Nieuports, Fokker triplanes, and Sopwith Camels, some alone, some in tandem, others in formation. In addition, there were displays of model aircraft and actors dressed as German, French, British, and American troops who simulated battles. Aircraft strafed them while the gunners fired back, all realistic fun without a single casualty.

Another re-enactment struck close to home. Fred Jungelaus, a 50-year-old artist/designer from Martinsville, Indiana, decided that Aerodrome 92 provided the ideal venue to marry his fellow artist Martha Powell, since both of them were World War I airplane buffs. At 3:00 p.m. on Sunday, the wedding was performed right on the airfield. The bride, dressed in a period-style gown of white lace over a peach underlayer, arrived in a vintage vehicle. The groom wore a U.S. Army Air Service uniform.

Following the ceremony, the newlyweds passed under the crossed swords of actors playing flying comrades. Immediately afterwards, Fred, as if answering the call to duty, left his bride stranded on the airstrip; then he climbed into his SE5a British scout plane (which he had taken 12^1/$_2$ years to build) and took off into the wild blue yonder. Martha accepted it all philosophically. "After all, Billy Bishop got married in 1918 and returned to battle," she remarked to me.

That afternoon at a press conference in the operations hut, Otto Roosen described his encounter with my father. A painting that hung on the wall depicted that short, sharp clash, showing my father's SE5a hot on the tail of Otto's two-seater Rumpler observation machine. The one-sided attack had taken place at 10:25 on the morning of June 17, 1918, between Staden and Hooglede, 2000 feet over Belgium on the Western Front.

All ears pricked up as Otto told the assembled news media, "Billy Bishop shot me in the back."

"Otto," I interrupted, "I'd prefer it if you said 'he got on my tail.'"

"He came from above, out of the sun," Otto continued. "All of a sudden, *zip-bang!* Bullets all around me. My engine stopped. He made one pass and was gone. He saw that he got me. I managed to force-land in a field. I had no engine power."

That night we dined at the magnificent Guntersville Golf and Country Club, situated at the top of a hill overlooking a lake. After Otto Roosen had been introduced, I told the dinner guests, "I'm sure that if my father had ever met Otto he'd have been the last person he would have wanted to shoot at—he's such a great guy.

"But not to take any chances, when I checked in at the American Air Lines ticket counter in Toronto, I told the girl at the desk, 'To play it safe, make sure Otto is sitting in front of me and not behind me.'"

That evening I played host to the Canadian contingent in my suite. I learned from Anna von Stryk that her mother was in some way related to the Kaiser's family. Because she was Richthofen's niece, toward the end of the war Goering had sent his limousine to drive her to safety.

It had been a memorable weekend in every way. But, alas, this episode had a tragically sad ending. Two years later, Frank Ryder, his wife, and two of their children were killed in a flying accident.

By 1994 I had two more books published: *Courage on the Battlefield* and *The Splendid Hundred*, the story of Canadians who fought in the Battle of Britain. Another, *Courage at Sea*, was in the works when I received a phone call from Rita Mullins of Time-Life Books in Alexandria, Virginia. They were in the process of putting together a "Wings of War" series and wanted to include my father's book *Winged Warfare*. I explained that the book was now under contract to McGraw-Hill Ryerson and that she should contact them to make the necessary arrangements. This presented no problem, and the deal went ahead. However, when I received my royalty statements after a reasonable passage of time, there was no mention of the Time-Life deal. I called Rita and asked her what was happening. She couldn't understand it because she had sent McGraw-Hill a cheque six months earlier.

Rita advised me to get a literary agent to look after my interests (the agent I had earlier was only a temporary arrangement that had long since lapsed). She recommended Frances Hanna in Toronto, whose husband, Bill, was a vice-president of Stoddart Publishing. The Hannas lived quite near to where Cilla and I lived, and we found that we had many friends and other things in common. We struck up a partnership, and a close friendship, right off the bat.

Frances offers these observations: "Occasionally you meet people with whom you're so comfortable that you feel you've known them all your life. So it was for Bill and me with Arthur and Cilla Bishop. To me they're like a favourite uncle and aunt—only much more fun! And working with Arthur on his books is a new and different experience each time. Arthur is an original, as his dad must have been. Here's to the next book—and all the ones after that!"

In addition, with Frances I enjoy a "two for the price of one" benefit. As well as being the top literary agent anywhere, in my opinion, she is also an experienced editor who started in the publishing business in London, England, in 1969.

Our association was timely. McGraw-Hill Ryerson was going through a senior personnel change at practically every level, from vice-president to publisher. I proposed to Frances that for starters we embark on a book about Canada's Victoria Cross winners. I submitted my outline to Julia Woods, the new vice-president, and Frances took it from there. *Our Bravest and Our Best* proved to be a real winner. However, it was the last of my books to be edited by Don Loney for some years. He left McGraw-Hill Ryerson to become business editor of HarperCollins Publishers, and later, fortunately for me, military books editor. I wrote three more books that McGraw-Hill Ryerson published: *Canada's Glory, Salute,* and *Destruction at Dawn.*

During the millennium we (Frances and I) changed publishers.

On September 21, 2000, I signed a contract with HarperCollins to publish a new book, *Unsung Courage*, which McGraw-Hill Ryerson had turned down. This was like coming home—Don Loney was once again my editor!

From Don: "I have known Arthur for many years. His books have brought the stories of Canadian veterans and Canadian military history to a wide range of readers. What kind of value can you place on a contribution like that? I value our relationship of author and editor most highly, and we have grown to be firm friends over the years, and I hope for many years to come."

I have found the occupation of an author to be an interesting, rewarding, and at times exciting experience. The people I have worked with at the Directorate of History (now closed down), the Canadian War Museum, the Royal Canadian Military Institute (RCMI), and the Toronto Reference Library have always been helpful, interested, and willing, and, at times, a lot of fun. Writing books has its moments of anxiety and stress. But as one virtually weaned on deadlines and pressure during my career as a reporter, adman, and publicist, by comparison I have nothing to get all that upset about.

Fortunately, this career has kept me in touch with the subject closest to my heart—the Canadian military. Aside from my affiliations in Ottawa and through the RCMI, a good example is the Canadian Fighter Pilots Association (CFPA), of which I am proud to be one of the founders, along with Gib Coons, De Bub Hayward, Bob Hamilton, and others. The organization existed from 1960 to 1998, with regular reunions until it was disbanded into regional wings. Cilla and I always attended the annual Ormston barbecue—held every fall at Ormy's fabulous 100-acre estate outside Kitchener—to renew acquaintance with old buddies and their wives. None of us ex–fighter jocks have ever lost touch with those valiant years we shared together.

It has been my hope that what we accomplished in our flying days is not lost on the generations that have followed, despite the indifference of boards of education toward teaching Canadian military history. I am not alone among veterans who are concerned about the lack of Canadian history being taught in our schools. To illustrate what I mean, I recommend Jack Granatstein's excellent book *Who Killed Canadian History?* In it he writes, "Canada must be one of the few nations in the world, certainly one of the few Western industrialized states, that does not make an effort to teach history positively and thoroughly to its young."

There are some exceptions, though, and I am glad to be associated with them. At Lawrence Park Collegiate in Toronto, under the direction of Mike Laidlaw, assistant principal, a slide presentation every Remembrance Day commemorates the students of Lawrence Park who gave their lives in World War II. On these occasions, I, along with other veterans such as Bernard Danson, former minister of national defence, have been called upon to make a short address.

I was also privileged to serve on the Jackman Foundation Statue Committee, which inaugurated the Air Force Memorial located on University Avenue at Dundas Street in Toronto, adjacent to the Royal Canadian Military Institute. The memorial was unveiled by Queen Elizabeth II on September 29, 1984, to the accompaniment of a flypast of fighters from the Canadian Forces and vintage aircraft from the Canadian Warplane Heritage Museum.

I am glad that the Billy Bishop Museum, the house in which my father was born and lived as a youngster in Owen Sound, has been designated a historic site. Open to visitors in the summer, it has helped to perpetuate his name and legend.

The question continues to be asked of me: What is it like to be Billy Bishop's son? It is difficult to give a straight answer, because my response would have been different at different points in my life. Let me generalize by saying that no one ever held it against me, it never did me any harm, and it did have certain advantages.

As a schoolboy, I think it impressed me because it impressed others. In the air force, while it surprised many that I got no special treatment, I was certainly given every consideration. As fighter pilots, we were all brothers. But as the son of an air marshal, during my tour of operations, I certainly found that the Germans didn't treat me with undue respect.

When I was a reporter, the editors didn't give a damn who you were—the prime minister's nephew or a crown prince. Everything rested on one thing and one thing only—the story! A reporter is a reporter, first and last.

I do not deny that referring to me as the son of Billy Bishop on the jackets of my books is anything but an asset in marketing the product—up to a point. But here again, it is performance that counts. The success or failure of a book hinges not necessarily on who you are, but on what you write—and how.

To summarize from quite another direction, I can answer the question by stating simply that it was a lot of fun. He was a great father and father-in-law, and had he lived long enough, I am sure he would have been a great grandfather to my daughter and son. He was full of mischief. The obituary that appeared in the September 24, 1956, issue of *Time* magazine corroborated it in a way: "Through it all Billy Bishop somehow retained much of the spirit of the boyish rambunctious aviator. At his yellow stone mansion on Peel Street in Montreal, he liked to clink glasses with his friends and spin tales about fighting days."

That was part of my father's legacy to me—the mischief. I also inherited that fabulous Bishop luck that saw both of us through our respective wars. The list of priorities that he passed on to me was in this order: health, wealth, family. His advice was always sound. One of his maxims, as I have mentioned earlier, was to "take what you do seriously, but never yourself." The other that he impressed upon me from an early age was "No one, no matter who or whatever the circumstances, deserves a free ride. Do your best. That's all anyone can ask of you."

In *Winged Combat*, for better or for worse I have done my best to adhere to those principles, which, for the most part, have served me well. I hope I have succeeded.

But I'll let Cilla have the last word: "We've had our ups and downs, some rough spots and smooth sailing, some good times and bad. But all in all, it was worth it in the end.

"But not quite the end. I'm sure you'll be hearing from Arthur again."

Roger. Over and out.

My Message

Ups and downs, risk and journeys, but always the sense of motion, and the illusion of hope . . . Come on now, all you young men, all over the world . . . You have not an hour to lose. You must take your place in life's fighting line . . . Don't be content with things the way they are . . . Don't take no for an answer. Never submit to failure.

WINSTON CHURCHILL

Acknowledgments

Cilla and I wrote this book together. Each weekday evening we sat down to cocktails and reviewed my day's output. Cilla was a splendid critic and never let personal feelings or prejudices colour her judgment in offering her astute comments, crticisms, and suggestions, a formidable task given this was a very personal work deeply affecting both of us. Sadly, her untimely passing robbed her from enjoying the fruit of her endeavours. The book did not see publication until a year after her death.

It is a tribute to her memory.

I would like to thank the following for their assistance in helping me write this autobiography.

My literary agents, Frances and Bill Hanna, who, by any measurement, are in a class by themselves in their field.

My editor, Don Loney, for navigating this flight on the right course. Gillian Watts for a knowledgeable and masterful job of close editing. And the following for their input into the story.

Alfred Dobell, my lifelong friend and former schoolmate.

Bob Hyndman, my flying instructor.

Gib Coons, my fellow squadron buddy.

My printer, Wes Douglas.
My daughter, Diana, for writing the foreword to this book.

To all a hearty thank-you. Cheers.

ARTHUR BISHOP

Toronto

Index